CHINA'S LEAP INTO
THE INFORMATION AGE

China's Leap into the Information Age

Innovation and Organization in the Computer Industry

QIWEN LU

OXFORD

UNIVERSITY PRESS

OXFORD
UNIVERSITY PRESS

Great Clarendon Street, Oxford OX2 6DP
Oxford University Press is a department of the University of Oxford.
It furthers the University's objective of excellence in research, scholarship,
and education by publishing worldwide in

Oxford New York

Athens Auckland Bangkok Bogotá Buenos Aires Calcutta
Cape Town Chennai Dar es Salaam Delhi Florence Hong Kong Istanbul
Karachi Kuala Lumpur Madrid Melbourne Mexico City Mumbai
Nairobi Paris São Paulo Singapore Taipei Tokyo Toronto Warsaw

and associated companies in Berlin Ibadan

Oxford is a registered trade mark of Oxford University Press
in the UK and certain other countries

Published in the United States
by Oxford University Press Inc., New York

British Library Cataloguing in Publication Data
Data available

Library of Congress Cataloging in Publication Data
Lu, Qiwen.
China's leap into the information age : innovation and organization in the computer
industry / Qiwen Lu.
p.   cm.
Includes bibliographical references.
1. Computer industry—China. 2. Computer software industry—China.
3. Computers—China. I. Title.
HD9696.2.C62 L82 2000   338.4′7004′0951—dc21   99-086804

ISBN 0–19–829537–5

1 3 5 7 9 10 8 6 4 2

Typeset in Garamond 3
by Best-set Typesetter Ltd., Hong Kong
Printed in Great Britain
on acid-free paper by
T.J. International Ltd, Padstow, Cornwall

To Lily, Mindy, and Jessie

Foreword

Qiwen Lu (1958–1999)

IN September 1990, just after his arrival from China to enter the Ph.D. programme in sociology at Harvard, Qiwen Lu answered an advertisement that I had posted for a research assistant. His English was faltering—and my Chinese non-existent—but within ten minutes I knew that here was an unusually insightful and motivated person with whom it would be interesting to work. I offered Qiwen the job. From that time to his death on 11 August 1999, I came to know Qiwen as a researcher, a student, a colleague, and a friend.

When we met, Qiwen was 32 years old. In 1977 he had been among the first cohort of students to attend college in the aftermath of the Cultural Revolution, as China embarked on its economic reforms. He received an undergraduate degree in engineering from Zhejiang University in 1982, and then went to work for Xinxing Group Co., an oil and chemical processing enterprise located in Beijing, as a research scientist in the company's industrial lab. In 1986 he won a national science and technology progress award for developing a pollution-free chemical processing technology for metal surface polishing.

In 1984 Xinxing sent Qiwen to a patent law training programme sponsored by the National Patent Bureau. Stimulated by this experience, he enrolled in courses at Beijing University to study Chinese business and patent law in his free time, and received an associate degree in law in 1986. But, with the economic and political reforms in progress, Qiwen was not satisfied with confining his learning to technology and its business applications. He wanted to understand the transformations that were taking place in Chinese society and the possibilities for economic and political change. More than that, like so many other young people in China who were inspired by the prospects for change that the reform process promised, Qiwen wanted to help China become a better society. He therefore decided to study sociology.

From the late 1950s until the early 1980s, it had not been possible to study sociology in Chinese universities. In 1986 Qiwen was among the first students to enter Beijing University's newly established Master's programme in sociology. He was attracted in particular by the prospect of studying with Fei Xiaotong, the author of many books on Chinese social structure and process, who was not only a professor at Beijing University but also Vice-Chairman of the Standing Committee of the National People's Congress.

While studying sociology at Beijing University, Qiwen held a part-time job as legal counsel for Sanyou Patent Law Firm. At Sanyou, Qiwen provided advice to

I am grateful to Lily Lu for providing me with details of Qiwen Lu's life as well as insights into his motivations, aspirations, and hopes that have helped me to write this tribute to her husband. I also received very helpful comments on Qiwen's decision to become a sociologist from Wenjun Du, who is married to Jie Yang, Qiwen's best friend while studying sociology at Beijing University. Jun Jing also provided me with information.

leading non-governmental high-technology enterprises in the areas of intellectual property rights and patenting strategies. One of his clients was Stone, the pioneer among China's non-governmental high-technology companies in the 1980s.

Following the completion of his Master's degree in sociology in 1988, Qiwen became assistant professor of sociology at Beijing University, teaching courses on statistical methods in sociobiology and social demography. Through the University's Centre for Social and Economic Development, he began doing research on industrial wholesale markets in rural areas in northern China. But, soon after accepting this academic position, he came to the conclusion that to get a broad, deep, and independent perspective on the economic and social changes that were transforming China, he would need to study abroad. He felt that within China at the time there were strict limits on the abilities of social researchers to address the problems and possibilities of the reform process in a critical manner. In his decision to pursue his education in the United States, he was encouraged by Jun Jing, a colleague at the Centre for Social and Economic Development, who in 1989 went to do a Ph.D. in anthropology at Harvard University. During the momentous spring of 1989, Qiwen was busy doing his TOEFLs and GREs[1] so that he could apply to do graduate study in the United States.

The research on which Qiwen worked with me in the United States focused on 'indigenous innovation'—the process of developing technology within a less advanced national economy, based in part on knowledge imported from a more advanced economy, to generate capabilities that enable economic development to occur. At the time, William Mass and I were studying the indigenous innovation process as it had occurred historically in Japan, with a focus on the development of the cotton textile and textile machinery industries, and ultimately on the transition from textile machinery to automobiles as exemplified by the Toyota Motor Company's origins in the Toyoda Automatic Loom Works. This project included a collaborative effort with Takeshi Abe of Osaka University and Kazuo Wada of Tokyo University. In collaboration with Bill Mass, Qiwen became engaged in research on the transfer of textile machinery technology from Japan to China and the implications for indigenous innovation in textile technology in China in the decades prior to the Communist revolution. Qiwen wrote a Harvard Master's thesis and a working paper on the development of the Chinese cotton textile industry.[2] More recently, when he was in China doing the research on computer electronics that is the subject of this book, Qiwen continued to mine the historical archives in Shanghai on the development of the Chinese textile machinery industry. Shortly before his death, Qiwen and Bill Mass completed a publication on technology transfer in textile machinery from Japan to, and subsequent indigenous innovation in, pre-revolutionary China.[3]

---

[1] Test of English as a Foreign Language examination and Graduate Record Examination.

[2] See Qiwen Lu, 'Industrial Organization and Underdevelopment: The Case of the Chinese Textile Industry, 1890–1936', Master's thesis, Department of Sociology, Harvard University, 1993; Qiwen Lu, 'Organizational Structure and Market Competitiveness: A Comparative Study of the Managerial Structures of Chinese Textile Companies and Japanese Textile Companies in China in the Pre-World War Two Period', Working paper, Center for Industrial Competitiveness, University of Massachusetts Lowell, 1995.

[3] Qiwen Lu and William Mass, 'Technology Transfer and Indigenous Innovation in Pre-Revolution

In gaining this historical perspective on the interaction of organization and technology in the development of China's economy, Qiwen's goal was to understand the dynamics of industrial development as it is occurring in the present. In particular, he was interested in analysing the evolving relation between the Chinese economic reform process and indigenous innovation in a leading sector in the 1990s and beyond. Hence his decision to do his Ph.D. dissertation on the Chinese computer electronics industry, which is the subject of this book.[4] Here, his background in engineering and patent law came in handy, as did some connections that he had made with people in key companies such as Stone during the period that he worked for Sanyou. Not surprisingly, Qiwen's research for his dissertation and this book emphasized the relation between the science and technology infrastructure (or national innovation system) and the strategies for learning within high-technology enterprises.

In 1994 the Harvard Business School awarded Qiwen an Alfred D. Chandler, Jr., Traveling Fellowship that enabled him to launch his research on what he eventually would characterize as 'China's leap into the information age'. Funding for the remainder of Qiwen's dissertation research came through the University of Massachusetts Lowell Center for Industrial Competitiveness, where Qiwen was working with Bill Mass and me. Over the next two years Qiwen did most of the research on Founder, Legend, and Stone—the three company case studies included in his dissertation—and some of the research on Great Wall, a fourth case study that was later to be completed for inclusion in this book. I had the pleasure of serving with Ezra Vogel on Qiwen's dissertation committee, and, in June 1997, saw him defend his thesis with great enthusiasm, insight, knowledge, and skill.

At that time, as still remains the case, I was dividing my time between the University of Massachusetts Lowell and INSEAD, the international business school, in Fontainebleau, France. With generous support from Arnoud De Meyer, then director-general of the INSEAD Euro-Asia Centre, Qiwen was able to join me in France during the spring and summer of 1997 to continue his research as a post-doctoral fellow. Philippe Lasserre, co-ordinator of INSEAD's newly created Asian Business area, recognized that Qiwen would be an important addition to the faculty. Starting in January 1998, a decade after he had been appointed assistant professor of sociology at Beijing University, and after much hard work and often very lean times, Qiwen became assistant professor of Asian business at a leading international business school. At INSEAD Qiwen taught courses on innovation systems and human resource development in Asia. He also began to supervise some of his MBA students in the writing of cases on business in China.[5] During his time at INSEAD, Qiwen went to

China: Mechanical Engineering Capabilities and Textile Machinery Enterprises', *Journal of Industrial History*, 2/1 (1999).

[4] See the Preface to this book, which Qiwen wrote in May 1999, and which I have edited for English, leaving the content unchanged.

[5] In June 1999 INSEAD published a number of cases on the life insurance industry in China that were written under Qiwen Lu's supervision, of which the major case is 'Back to the Roots: American International Group in China' (written by Guido Meyerhans), INSEAD-EAC Case 06/1999-4839.

China to teach executives and to do further research. In transforming his Ph.D. dissertation into this book, Qiwen used these trips to gather material on the case of Great Wall—thus completing the studies of China's four leading computer electronics companies that are featured in this book—and to bring the whole manuscript as up to date as possible. In June 1999 he submitted the final manuscript version of *China's Leap into the Information Age* to David Musson, his editor at Oxford University Press.

Off and on during the two years that we were together at INSEAD, Qiwen and I collaborated in turning one of the cases, that of Founder, into a journal article that could draw out the larger implications of the case study for the transformation of China's national innovation system.[6] Toward the end of July 1999, with no premonition that some two weeks later Qiwen would no longer be with us, we submitted what turned out to be the final version of the article to *Research Policy*. One week after Qiwen's death, I received a letter back from the journal, stating that the article would be published in its current form. With great sadness, I added a note to the article that would appear in print, informing the readership that Qiwen Lu had passed away.

The following week, I got word from Oxford University Press that the copy-edited manuscript of his book was ready for corrections and clarifications, a task that is most easily done by a book's author. Fortunately, at INSEAD, Patricia Reese, who had already worked with Qiwen in editing the manuscript prior to submission, told me that she would be honoured to help ensure that Qiwen's book would get into print as soon as possible. By the beginning of October the work was completed.

Of course, for Qiwen Lu, *China's Leap into the Information Age* was supposed to be the beginning of a long, illustrious, and influential career. In mid-June 1999 I had a long discussion with Qiwen about his many plans for future research. Toward the end of June he had lunch with me and Mary O'Sullivan, an assistant professor at INSEAD who had come to know Qiwen well when they were both graduate students at Harvard. As was usually the case when the three of us got together, as we often did at INSEAD, Qiwen was the determined optimist, ready and eager to live his dreams. During his two years at INSEAD, our relationship with Qiwen had deepened, as we witnessed his abundant enthusiasm and optimism amidst the stresses that are normal to anyone in a high-pressure junior faculty position and exacerbated in Qiwen's case by the fact that his family was unable to join him in France. We both remember saying a fond goodbye to Qiwen before he took off for the summer to do research and spend time with his wife, Lily, and two children, Mindy and Jessie, who had continued to live in the Boston area. That was the last time that we saw him. On 2 August he called us from the United States to tell us that he would be going into hospital two days later to have a tumor removed from his liver. Forever the optimist, Qiwen expected a successful, even if slow, recovery.

---

[6] Qiwen Lu and William Lazonick, 'The Organization of Innovation in a Transitional Economy: Business and Government in Chinese Electronic Publishing', *Research Policy*, forthcoming. See also Qiwen Lu and William Lazonick, 'China: A National System of Innovation in the Process of Formation', in J. C. Ciscar and J. Lievonen (eds.), *Techno-Economic Analysis Report 1998* (European Science and Technology Observatory, 1999).

Such was not to be. *China's Leap into the Information Age* was one of Qiwen Lu's dreams. He was justly proud of his own accomplishments, and even prouder of China's achievements as an industrial innovator in the 1990s. But Qiwen Lu's legacy is not just what he himself learned, produced, and communicated in a life that was all too short. His legacy was also the way he went about his business—with integrity, compassion, enthusiasm, and determination. That I take to be his real legacy for the people, and perhaps also for the nation, that he loved.

William Lazonick

Preface

THIS book is based on my Ph.D. thesis, 'Innovation and Organization: The Rise of New Science and Technology Enterprises in China', submitted to the Department of Sociology at Harvard University in 1997. When, in 1994, I first proposed a study of Chinese high-tech enterprises in the Beijing High-Tech Developmental Zone as the topic for my Ph.D. dissertation, my adviser at the time, a leading China scholar, expressed strong doubts about the importance of the topic. After all, high-tech firms only accounted for a minute percentage of Chinese GDP, and even the success of these enterprises was likely to be based more on the advantages of cheap labour than on technological development.

I viewed China's problem differently (and I ultimately resolved my own particular academic problem by changing advisers). Sustainable economic growth depends on technological development somewhere in the economy, although it may take a long time for the development and diffusion of technology throughout the economy to make their impacts on productivity and wages felt. By exploring the technological transformations taking place in the Beijing Experimental Zone for the Development of High-Tech Industries, I wanted to gain some insights into China's potential for overcoming the technological backwardness that has characterized its economy during this century.

Five years have passed since I began this research, and, over that time, even to my own surprise, China has been successful in one high-tech sector, the PC industry. In 1993, in a Chinese PC market of less than 875,000 units, domestic producers had less than a 30 per cent share. By 1997 the domestic market had grown to 3,500,000 units, and the domestic share to over 70 per cent. In 1998, in a market of 4,000,000 units, the share of the top four foreign brands was 20 per cent, while the share of the top four Chinese brands was over 24 per cent. Some might downplay the significance of the rise of the indigenous producers on the grounds that the PC has already become a commodity, the assembly of which does not require high-technology capabilities. But the success of China in the PC industry reflects the indigenous development of a much wider range of technological capabilities, including electronic components and semiconductors, as well as systems integration. The acquired capabilities of the four leading high-tech enterprises in China's computer industry that are featured in this book have industrial applications that go well beyond PC assembly. For example, Stone manufactures semiconductors and is also the leading internet service provider in China. Legend is now among the top five suppliers of PC motherboards and add-on cards in the world. Founder is the technological leader in the pictographic-language publishing systems market. Great Wall is the world's third largest manufacturer of advanced magnetic resonance heads, the key component for high-capacity computer storage devices.

The importance of these developments for the Chinese economy, moreover, may go far beyond the successes of these particular companies. The more fundamental phenomenon that I analyse in this book is the emergence of an institutional and orga-nizational infrastructure for technological development—what many would now call a 'national innovation system'. Such a system, once in place and operating effectively in one sector, can provide the foundation for the development and diffusion of tech-nology in many sectors of the economy on a sustained basis.

My own personal experiences in China in the 1980s played an important role in my choice of research topic. In the mid-1980s, when I was a graduate student in Beijing University, the Zhongguancun area surrounding the campus witnessed, in 'Silicon Valley' fashion, the emergence of new high-tech firms, mostly in com-puter electronics. The most notable example was the Stone Group. Started as a rural township enterprise, Stone soon became what foreign media called (for lack of proper terminology because there is no corresponding category of enterprise called non-state or non-governmental enterprises in the Western market economies) the largest 'private' high-tech enterprise in China. With a background in patent law and engi-neering, I was personally involved in advising the company's product development team on patenting strategy. But as a sociology student, I was more interested in the organizational innovations that Stone and other new high-tech enterprises were bringing to China and the implications of these changes for the long-term develop-ment of the Chinese economy.

It was with the goal of studying the transformation of Chinese society that I left China to pursue a Ph.D. degree at Harvard University in 1990. At that time, the Chinese economy was still in the post-1989 depression. Most people, including myself, remained optimistic about the prospects for the Chinese economy and society, and indeed before long the Chinese economy was booming again, this time on a larger scale and at a higher speed than previously. In 1994, supported by an Alfred D. Chandler, Jr., Traveling Fellowship from Harvard Business School, I returned to China for the first time in four years to witness the changes taking place and to begin my dissertation research. At the time, Stone became the first non-state Chinese enter-prise to be listed on the Hong Kong Stock Exchange, and other non-state high-tech companies such as Legend and Founder were making rapid progress.

A two-year doctoral fellowship from the Center for Industrial Competitiveness (CIC) at the University of Massachusetts Lowell made it possible for me to return to China for an extended period of time in 1996 to conduct the fieldwork and write up the dissertation. I would like to thank the co-directors of the CIC, Bill Lazonick, Bill Mass, and Michael Best for their support. Special thanks go to Bill Lazonick. The dissertation as well as this book would not have been finished without his unfailing support throughout. I have drawn inspiration from his theoretical as well as histor-ical studies. His insistence on the integration of theory and history has provided me with the methodological approach that I have taken in my research. I have also ben-efited from reading the work of Mary O'Sullivan, a fellow graduate student in eco-nomics at Harvard and my colleague at INSEAD, and from my many discussions with her while doing my dissertation and writing this book.

After returning in 1996 to the Harvard Sociology Department after a two-year stint in Washington, Ezra Vogel became the chair of my thesis committee. He gave each chapter a careful reading, followed by detailed comments and suggestions. A six-month post-doctoral fellowship from the INSEAD Euro-Asia Centre in 1997 made it possible for me to test some conclusions from my company case studies, using firm-level data for over 500 Chinese companies in the Beijing Experimental Zone for the Development of High-Tech Industries.[1] I would like to thank the Euro-Asia Centre's director-general, Arnoud De Meyer, for providing support. In addition, funding from INSEAD R&D, after I became a faculty member there, made it possible for me to do field work in China on Great Wall, a case that was not included in my dissertation, and to update the industrial and market data more generally. Philippe Lasserre, Jonathan Story, Helmut Schütte, all colleagues at INSEAD, provided me with valuable comments on various chapters. I also benefited from discussions with long-term friends and fellow graduate students at Harvard, Jing Jun, Fu Jun, Huang Yasheng, and Edward Steinfeld, all of whom are now pursuing their careers as China specialists in major US and Chinese universities.

Anyone who conducts research on China knows how difficult it is to get access to data. Thanks are due to all the people who agreed to be interviewed. I would particularly like to express my gratitude to Ms Ye Yanhong, Head of Human Resource at Stone; Mr Guo Wei, Vice-President of Legend; Professor Liu Qiuyun, Vice-President of Founder; and Ms Zeng Yanming, Senior Manager of Great Wall. Without their assistance, it would have been impossible for me to gather the data that is the substance of this book.

My good friend Rita Towsner provided me with editing assistance when I was finishing my dissertation. I would also thank Patricia Reese at INSEAD for editing the whole manuscript of the book, with great professional skill. My secretary, Joan Lewis, deserves special thanks for taking care of a multitude of matters that made it possible for me to complete this book in the midst of my teaching responsibilities at INSEAD.

My wife Li Li tolerated my ups and downs during the long journey, one that at times seemed never-ending, to the completion of my dissertation and then this book. Our two lovely daughters, Mindy and Jessie, have always been sources of joy and hope, making life more colourful. To the three of them this book is dedicated.

---

[1] See Qiwen Lu, 'Organizational Arrangements and Innovative Performance of High-Tech Ventures in a Transitional Economy: A Resource-Collective Action View of the Firm', paper presented at the 10th Annual Conference on Socio-Economics, Vienna, July 1998.

Contents

List of Figures

List of Tables

Abbreviations

ASIC	application specific integrated circuit
CAS	Chinese Academy of Sciences
CCDC	China Computer Development Corporation
CCID	Centre for Computer and Microelectronics Industry Development Research
CCP	Chinese Communist Party
CGC	China Great Wall Computer Company
CITIC	China International Trust and Investment Corporation
CKD	completely knocked down
IC	integrated circuit
ICST	Institute of Computer Science and Technology
ICT	Institute of Computing Technology
IIPC	International Information Process Corporation
I/O	input and output
IPO	initial public offering
LSIC	large-scale integrated circuit
MEI	Ministry of Electronics Industry
NIE	newly industrialized economy
OBM	original brand manufacturing
ODM	original design manufacturing
OEM	original equipment manufacturing
PCB	printed circuit board
RIP	raster image processor
RMB	Renminbi—Chinese currency
S&T	science and technology
SKD	semi-knocked down
SMT	surface mounting technology
SOE	state-owned enterprise
UPS	uninterruptible power supply
VAT	value-added tax
VGA	video graphic adapter

Abbreviations of Chinese Sources

BDFZ   Beida Fangzheng (Beijing University Founder Group's Newsletter)

CJB   Changcheng Jishuanji Bao (Great Wall Computer's Newsletter)

JNWJ   Jinian Wenji (Recollections at the 20th Anniversary of Project 748), MEI (1994)

LXB   Lianxiangbao (Legend's Newsletter)

LXZGBD   Lianxiang Zhigong Bidu (Required Reading for Legend Employees)

LXZR   Lianxiangzhiru (The Legend Way), Renmin Ribao Chubanshe (*People's Daily Press*), 1992

STR   Sitongren (Stone's Newsletter)

SYQB   Shiyan Qubao (The Beijing High and New Tech Industry Experimental Zone News)

ZDYD   Zhongguancun Dianzhi Yitiaojie Dashiji (Chronicle of the Zhongguancun Electronic Valley, 1980–1988, 1993)

1

Learning and Innovation in
a Transitional Economy

In 1997 a *Business Week* article entitled 'Going Toe to Toe with Big Blue and Compaq' reported:

After years of getting outclassed and outmuscled in their own market, Chinese companies are starting to bridge the once enormous gap with the likes of Compaq, IBM, and AST. Legend Group, Beijing Founder Electronics, China Great Wall Computer Group, and other producers . . . are snapping out models that are *often cheaper, and just as up-to-date*, as foreign ones.[1]

The rapid catch-up of Chinese companies in computer industrial technologies came as a surprise to *Business Week* reporters, as shown in the subtitle, 'Suddenly, Chinese computer makers are holding their own'.

A detailed analysis of the growth of the Chinese computer market and changing patterns of market dominance substantiates the journalistic description above. The Chinese computer market was small and almost negligible throughout the 1980s, as was the domestic computer industry. However, at the start of the 1990s, accompanying the opening up of the market to foreign competition, the Chinese computer market was growing at an extraordinary pace. Market size has grown from almost negligible to the second largest in Asia (second to Japan), with more than four million units shipped at the end of 1998. In the early 1990s, when the market was just opened up, foreign competition had effectively wiped out domestic producers. However, in a period of merely six years, indigenous firms had staged a comeback. The share of indigenous producers in the largest segment, the personal computer market, increased from less than 30 per cent in 1991 to 67 per cent in 1997 (Fig. 1.1). It is widely predicted that the Chinese market will continue to experience rapid growth and will become one of the world's largest in the early years of the new millennium. The share of domestic makers will continue to rise (New Century Group, 1997*a*). This has to be viewed in the context that the computer market is one of the most open and competitive markets in China, and the competitiveness of Chinese domestic PC makers is based mostly on price and performance.[2]

---

[1] *Business Week*, 14 Apr. 1997.
[2] The competitiveness of indigenous Chinese PC makers should not be attributed to high tariffs, because almost all major international PC-makers had set up manufacturing operations in China and have been competing directly with the Chinese firms from within China. More specifically, since 1993, AST, Compaq, IBM, HP, and most recently Dell, had all set up PC manufacturing operations in China, which

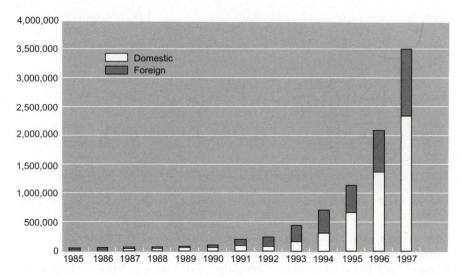

Fig. 1.1. Growth of the Chinese PC market (in units)
Source: Centre for Computer and Microelectronics Industry Development Research (CCID).

Another indication that China is catching up in the computer industry is that it has become a net exporter of computer electronics goods since 1991. While exporting computer electronics products increased almost twentyfold between 1991 and 1997—from US $450 million to US $8.7 billion—trade surplus in these products has widened from less than US $40 million to US $4 billion (see Fig. 1.2). Although foreign-invested firms played important roles in this respect, indigenous Chinese firms such as Legend and China Great Wall Computer are among the largest exporters. In fact, Legend is now one of the world's largest suppliers of computer motherboards and add-on cards.

China's catching up in the computer industry is not limited to computer hardware either. It also includes sophisticated computer information systems integration technologies. This is best demonstrated by China's technology leadership in markets for pictographic electronic publishing systems. China's Founder has dominated markets in professional Chinese-language publishing systems not only in China, but also in Hong Kong, Macao, Taiwan, Singapore, and other overseas Chinese communities. It is also making inroads into the large market for Japanese-language publishing systems.[3]

Why were indigenous Chinese companies able to catch up in a high-tech industrial sector such as computers? This book tries to answer this question through

---

coincided with the explosive growth of the market (New Century Group 1997*b*). See also *Business Week*'s report, 'Foreign Rivals vs. Chinese: If You Can't Beat 'Em . . .', 28 Feb. 1999.

[3] In Nomura's June 1997 report entitled 'China's Computer Industry: The World's Fastest Growing Market for Personal Computers', it was stated that 'printing systems in Japan are generally 10 years behind those of Founder'.

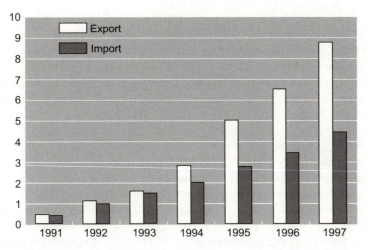

Fig. 1.2. China's trade surplus in computer electronic goods, 1991–7 (in billions US $)
Source: Centre for Computer and Microelectronics Industry Development Research (CCID).

detailed case studies of four leading Chinese computer enterprises: Stone, Legend, Founder, and China Great Wall Computer. The book will focus on how these enterprises acquired the technological competencies that enabled them to compete head-to-head with foreign multinational companies. It will be seen that the rise of these indigenous Chinese computer enterprises was neither sudden nor surprising. It was the result of a long-term process of capability building or technological learning, which could be traced back to government initiatives in reforming the nation's science and technology (S&T) system in the early 1980s. My central argument is that the Chinese computer enterprises followed a unique mode of technology learning, which is coupled with unique organizational and institutional arrangements.

In order to gain technological competencies for indigenous enterprises in a developing country such as China, it is necessary to acquire technologies through a learning process. Here, learning is defined broadly as a process of capability acquisition—the capability of developing technological resources and turning them into commercial successes. Traditional theories emphasize the importance of technology transfer from abroad. I would call the dominant theory the bottom-up linear model of technology transfer, starting with the assembly of imported kits, then the localization of parts and components, the third step being product redesign, and the fourth, product design (Leonard-Barton 1995: 220–58). It is bottom-up because it starts at the lowest level of the technology ladder. In this model, which has dominated the study of technological learning in developing countries, the technology receiver or the learner is passive and dependent. Although it was originally used to characterize technology learning in the context of import substitution, similar models were also developed to describe the export-led technology learning in the

East Asian newly industrialized economies (NIEs). For example, the model, described by Hobday (1995), of export-led technology learning in the East Asian NIEs, starting with cheap labour assembly, progressing from OEM (original equipment manufacturing), through ODM (original design manufacturing), to OBM (original brand manufacturing),[4] had a similar bottom-up linear sequence.[5] Research on technology development in China, including the most recent research, has implicitly followed these models (Feinstein and Howe (eds.), 1997; Naughton (ed.), 1997). This made it difficult to explain China's rapid catch-up in certain high-tech industrial sectors, most notably computers, and more recently, in telecommunications equipment.[6]

There are no a priori reasons why technology transfer, or technology learning for that matter, has to follow a strictly linear sequence.[7] Learning could start at any stage of the technology ladder, and traverse through it in any manner. This could lead to radically different trajectories or modes of technology learning. One such a trajectory is to start at product design or redesign, and then go forward or backward to transfer or learn technologies at other levels. This could be categorized as a top-down mode of technology learning. Since product design or redesign is innovation by definition, the mode of technology learning could also be seen as an innovative mode of technology learning.

The reason most developing countries followed the bottom-up mode of technology learning is due to their poor indigenous technological capabilities. East Asian export-led NIEs have followed a similar bottom-up trajectory of technology development because of, as Hobday points out, their dislocation from the main international sources of technology and mainstream international markets (Hobday 1995: 32–49). China was different in both respects. Unlike most developing countries, China had developed an S&T infrastructure during its central planning era, so a relatively advanced S&T resource base existed already. Thus, Chinese firms were able to tap technologies from two sources—domestic and foreign—in their journey to acquire technological capabilities. Unlike the East Asian NIEs, which had to rely almost exclusively on export markets, China had access to a domestic market with enormous potential. Local specific user-needs, in this case a need to process Chinese characters in computer systems that were created for processing alphabetic language information, provided a stimulus for indigenous technological innovations. The indigenous innovations, in turn, allowed local firms to establish their own brand image in the market early on and were able, thus, to develop independently. In short, a combination of indigenous technology capabilities and specific conditions of local demand created the technology-push and the demand-pull for indigenous product innovations, hence leading to the possibility of the unique top-down mode of technology learning.

What stood in the way for turning this possibility into reality in China in the earlier years, however, were the organizational or institutional barriers to innovation

---

[4] For the origins the terms OEM and ODM, see Hobday 1995: 49 n. 8; Johnstone 1989: 50–1.
[5] Also see Wortzel and Wortzel 1981; Lall 1982; Dahlman et al. 1985; Westphal et al. 1985.
[6] See 'Silicon Valley, PRC', The Economist, 27 June 1998.
[7] For a critique of the linear-sequence models of innovation in general, see Forrest 1991.

inherent in central planning. It was well known that centrally planned economies lacked the organizational mechanisms to translate S&T resources into industrial or commercial products, or innovation in the Schumpeterian sense (Schumpeter 1934). They lacked incentive structure for promoting innovation as well as organizational channels between S&T research units and production enterprises (Berliner 1976; Levine 1983; Goldman 1983; Simon and Rehn 1988; Simon and Goldman 1989; Rosenberg 1994: 87–108).[8] The key, therefore, was to create novel institutional and organizational arrangements conducive to translating the accumulated S&T resources into the commercial capabilities of enterprises.

To put this in context, let me give a brief review of the Chinese S&T system developed under central planning, the accumulation of indigenous computer research and production capabilities within that system, and the reform initiatives that created conditions for the emergence of new institutional and organizational arrangements.

1.1. Organizational Barriers to Technological Innovation under Central Planning

Research and development (R&D) activities in China's traditional centrally planned economy, like all of its economic activities, followed the Soviet model. They were organized into an extensive hierarchy, independent of industrial enterprises.[9] The first tier was the Chinese Academy of Sciences (CAS), which oversaw several dozen research institutes (each containing from several to dozens of research labs) and dozens of research universities. They were specialized in basic as well as applied scientific research. The second tier consisted of dozens of military-industrial research labs and industrial research labs under the authority of various industrial ministries. Most of them focused on applied scientific R&D. The third tier comprised research institutes under various industrial bureaux of regional governments.

This hierarchical structure had the merit of being able to concentrate scarce resources into strategic sectors as well as assembling an elite corps of highly talented scientists and engineers with a clear mission. Indeed, it was relatively effective in building a comprehensive infrastructure for basic research, as well as in developing sophisticated military-related technologies at a relatively low stage of economic development. Typical cases reflecting this were China's successes in developing the atomic and hydrogen bombs, and satellites (the projects later were called 'two bullets, one star—*liang dan yi xing*').[10] Each project involved a whole industrial ministry respectively—the atomic energy ministry for the bombs and the aerospace ministry for rockets and satellites—including dozens of their industrial research labs. Top scientists from the research institutes under CAS were also heavily involved. All resources necessary for carrying out the projects, including financing, manpower,

---

[8] For a detailed discussion of the problems of structural separation of research activities from industries in the Soviet centrally planned economy, see Berliner 1976.

[9] For an illustration of the organization of the Chinese S&T system, see Simon and Goldman 1989: 74.

[10] For the case of how China built the atomic bomb, see Lewis and Xu 1988.

materials, and scientific instruments, were guaranteed from state budgets. In fact, the projects were so typical that 'two bullets, one star' became a buzzword and a token of the successful organization of large-scale R&D under the old system. However, resources were allocated by priority under central planning, which meant that under budgetary constraints, very few resources would reach the bottom of the hierarchy, where they were most likely to serve the needs of civilian industries. More significantly, the organizational structure put in place segregated the S&T system from industries.

Berliner (1976) has characterized military-related research as mission-oriented activity as opposed to economic activity. The distinguishing feature of mission-oriented activity is cost-insensitivity. According to him, there should not be any important differences between modern industrial nations in mission-oriented activities when it comes to matters of national priority. In other words, the organization of China's nuclear weapons project should not differ fundamentally from the United States' Manhattan Project. However, industrial R&D plays an integral part in capitalist market economies, where there are strong in-house R&D capabilities within companies. Whereas in the Soviet-style centrally planned economy, all R&D activities seemed to have been organized outside industrial enterprises, resulting in the segregation of the S&T system from the rest of the economy. This was the case in the Chinese S&T system in its pre-reform state.

Many problems appeared. First, the S&T's most talented scientists were concentrated in CAS's labs, military research labs and research universities, constituting self-contained ivory towers that were inaccessible for the most part to industrial enterprises. Second, even though the industrial research institutes under various industrial ministries and bureaux were designated to serve industrial needs, they were entrapped within the vertical authority of their respective ministries or industrial bureaux. There existed almost no direct horizontal channels among research institutions and enterprises across authoritative boundaries of various industrial ministries or bureaux. Third, within the same administrative authority, communication between research labs and enterprises was more or less along vertical channels via administrative organs at the top. Direct horizontal links between labs and enterprises were often secondary.

The organizational barriers were further reinforced by the system's incentive structure. There were no direct financial rewards for transferring technology to industry. S&T products were not proprietary. Research funds were allocated directly from the central planning authority, not derived from revenues of technology transfer. As a result, instead of serving industrial enterprises, research institutes within industrial ministries or bureaux tended to be self-contained and independent from enterprises. Very few scientists and technologists took industrial needs into consideration when choosing research projects. The majority of the scientific researchers followed a routine: choosing a project, conducting the lab experiment, achieving a result (usually a lab prototype), undergoing peer evaluation, then receiving an achievement record in his or her personal dossier as a basis for promotion. The routine was so prevalent that the whole process became a vicious circle. To use Chinese expressions, most of the final products stemming from applied S&T research projects ended at the prototype stage, in one of the forms of three '*pins*': *yang-pin*, *zhan-pin*, *li-pin* (samples, exhibits, and/or gifts), never reaching the stage of *sang-pin* (commodity).

The problem was as much on the demand side as it was on the supply side. Industrial enterprises that were supposed to be using the technologies lacked the initiative and the resources to introduce them. Of course, a typical industrial enterprise under the Chinese central planning system was first and foremost a production unit. It was not an enterprise in the Western sense but more like a plant within a large corporation. It was not management within the enterprise that was concerned with co-ordinating production such as strategic planning, marketing, purchasing, financing, etc., but rather government bureaucrats. Furthermore, unlike plants in Western market economies that deal with only one corporate headquarters, Chinese enterprises had to deal with multiple government agencies. The system was designed to ensure the execution of state economic plans at each and every level. It enabled the state to set economic priorities by means of direct resource allocation. To an extent, the system worked well for an industrialization strategy that was biased towards the military and heavy industry.[11]

The biggest problem, however, was the lack of innovation initiatives at the enterprise level. The priority of enterprise managers was to fulfil planned targets. They had neither the incentives nor the resources to engage in innovation, particularly product innovation, given the high uncertainties associated with it.

With no incentive for enterprise managers to innovate, any significant innovation within the centrally planned system had to come from the central planning apparatus. Yet due to information and resource constraints, the central planning authorities could only initiate a limited number of innovative projects. Meanwhile, the system's structural segmentation meant that even this limited number of innovation projects would not be effectively executed. The development of computer technologies and the IT industry in China was such a case.

1.2. The Development of Computer Technology and the IT Industry in China prior to the Reform

Due to its strategic importance, the development of computer technology had been a priority of the Chinese government ever since the start of the planning system. It

---

[11] It could be argued that the system was relatively effective in mobilizing resources to build a heavy industrial base and a military power under the real or imagined threats from outside during China's decades of half-forced and half-self-imposed isolation. Nixon's visit to China in 1972 marked a turning point. It ended the era of China's international isolation. Soon after, China launched the 'Four-modernization Plan' (i.e. modernization of industry, agriculture, science and technology, and defence) in 1974, indicating a shift of economic priorities from single-minded military and heavy industrial build-up to raising the living standards of ordinary citizens. After that the old system started to lose its rationality. However, serious economic reform was only possible after Mao's death in 1976, and it actually started after the Third Plenum of the Eleventh Central Committee of the Chinese Communist Party (CCP) in 1978.

TABLE 1.1. *Computer models developed at ICT*

Model	Year of completion	Speed (million instructions per second)	Equivalent foreign models
111	1971	0.18	
655	1973	1	IBM 360 Series
013	1976	2	IBM 360 Series
757	1983	10	Gray-1

Source: Chinese Academy of Sciences, iii (Modern China Press 1994), 174.

was on the agenda of the very first long-term S&T development plan initiated in 1955, identified as one of the six key technology development areas.[12]

The initial team, led by a prominent Chinese mathematician, set up the first national computer research institution—the Institute of Computing Technology (ICT) within CAS. ICT built the first computer in China, Model 103, a copy of the Soviet Mark-3, in 1958, with blueprints provided by the Soviets.[13] The institute started independent development of computer models after the breakdown of Sino-Soviet relations in the early 1960s. It was responsible for developing several generations of computers in China afterwards, mostly large-scale mainframe computers (Table 1.1). ICT became China's top research institute in computer technologies, with more than 1,500 research and support staff by the early 1980s.

Other research institutions under various ministries and research universities also jointly or independently developed several models of computers for use in developing the atomic bomb, satellites, and mathematical weather-forecasting models. At that time, computers were considered as being mostly for military and scientific applications, and development was focused on raising their computing speed.

Not until 1973 was the large-scale production of computers for industrial and commercial uses conceived. The Ministry of Electronics organized a strategic planning meeting on the computer industry's development, whereby it shifted emphasis from pursuing computing speed towards developing a product series that would build up an industry with large-scale production. It was decided to develop a minicomputer series, compatible with international standards. In August 1974 the first model of the DJS-100 series computer, modelled after Digital's Minicomputer Series, was developed. Almost 1,000 units were produced, marking the start-up of large-scale computer production in China.

---

[12] The materials for this section, except otherwise indicated, are based mainly on 'Zhongguo Jishuanji Gongye Sishi Nian' (40 Years of the Chinese Computer Industry), *Changcheng Jishuanji Bao* (*Great Wall Computer News*), 8 Aug. 1996; and *Zhongguo Kexueyun* (Chinese Academy of Sciences), vol. iii (*Dangdai Zhongguo Chubanshe* (Modern China Press), 1994); as well as personal interviews with the former deputy bureau chief of the Computer Industry Administration under MEI in Apr. 1998.

[13] For a general description of the importance of technology transfer from the USSR to China in the 1950s, see Howe 1997: 2–4. For a detailed account of the roles of Soviet scientists in China, see Klochko 1963.

As computers were geared to be used in information processing to accelerate the application of computers to Chinese-language processing, five ministries initiated a large-scale project, the Chinese-language Processing Technology Development Project, in August 1978. Code-named Project 748, it would later lead to Founder's market dominance in Chinese-language publishing systems.[14]

By this time, the advent of microcomputers had accelerated the pace of the development of computer technologies outside China. The Chinese saw a microcomputer for the first time at a French industrial exhibition held in Beijing in 1974—a mere three years after Intel had developed the world's first microprocessor. The technocrats at the Computer Industry Administration Bureau (Computer Bureau thereafter) under MEI retained the model. They quickly assembled a group of elite research institutes and state-run enterprises to develop microcomputers based on the French model. Three years later, in 1977, China had come up with its first microcomputer prototype, using Intel's first-generation microprocessor 8008 as the CPU. In the ensuing years, China went on to develop several generations of microcomputer prototypes, closely following new developments abroad. As these prototypes were rolled out even before IBM had decided to get into the PC market in 1981, it seemed that China would develop an indigenous PC industry either in step with the world trend—or at least not too far behind it.

In reality, the pace of its development of its nascent domestic computer industry turned out to be rather slow. This was certainly owing to the organizational rigidity of central planning, compounded by the autarkic nature of development. Due to China's international isolation up until the early 1970s, the development of computer technology, as well as the industry in China, was almost completely self-reliant. It had not taken advantage of the international division of labour, nor was there any direct technology transfer from abroad. There were no scale economies. The semiconductor industry, the backbone of the parts-and-components industry, was generations behind in technological terms. All of these, however, were not such a big problem for developing mainframe computers because demand was very low, for several hundreds at the most. Though mainframe development could take place in a few research institutes with help from industrial enterprises under the co-ordination of government bureaucrats in a mission-oriented way, this was not enough to launch a viable computer industry. By 1981, China had only produced a total of 2,000 or so microcomputers, far from meaningful scale production.

Nevertheless, the advent of microcomputers and the shift of computer applications from mere scientific calculation to general information processing created a demand for computers in China. It was the first real opportunity to develop a computer industry geared to mass production. Foreseeing this potential, the technocrats at MEI's Computer Bureau shifted their strategy to one of import substitution in 1980. Starting with the importation of production lines and assembly of imported kits of parts and components in semi-knocked-down (SKD) or completely knocked-down (CKD) conditions, China could move gradually to localize its production of

---

parts and components, particularly for less technically sophisticated peripherals such as monitors, hard drives, and floppy drives. It was a typical bottom-up approach to technology learning.

The organization was centred on manufacturing enterprises. Dozens of state-owned electronic enterprises under MEI were assigned as manufacturing sites. Each enterprise would import production lines and was given foreign currency quotas to import SKD or CKD kits. The plant would then assemble the kits into the final products and sell them in the domestic market. The government spent hundreds of millions of hard currency on this: in 1984, at its peak, it spent US $50 million, and the industry produced RMB 500 millions' worth of microcomputers.

Given the large differences in import duties between kits and final products intended to protect the development of the domestic industry, the business was artificially profitable in the beginning. Eventually, enterprises outside the planning channel were lured into the assembly of computers, often from smuggled kits, because of very limited requirements on production skills. Meanwhile, imported PCs were technically poor in handling Chinese fonts, and very little application software in Chinese existed. Limited by a shortage of applications, the market was soon saturated. Finally, expectations that the designated state-owned enterprises would move up the technology ladder did not happen either.

The industrial policy of import substitution had bypassed the research institutions that had accumulated capabilities in computer technologies. This was due again to the organizational separation between research institutions and production enterprises. Though the research institutions were following the newest developments of computer technologies abroad, were trying to come up with new generations of faster computers, and were also working on developing the technology for Chinese-language processing, their activities had nothing to do with the enterprises' production activities, which were simply assembling PC models using imported kits with little value-added and virtually no indigenous technological input. This situation was not sustainable, simply from the need to balance hard currency.

A new strategy was needed. The objective was to develop an organizational structure that eliminated the organizational gap between S&T institutions and manufacturing enterprises. This finally happened as a result of the initiative of reforming China's national S&T system.

1.3. Reform of China's National Science and Technology System and the Rise of New Science and Technology Enterprises

The Chinese S&T system developed under central planning fell into disarray during the Cultural Revolution. After the Cultural Revolution, the Chinese government initially tried to restore the S&T system to its pre-Cultural Revolution state; that is, the original Soviet model. As economic reform unfolded during the early 1980s, Chinese leaders recognized the deficiencies of the old system, especially its linkages to the economy (Simon and Rehn 1988: 14–19). In 1980 the Central Committee of the Chinese Communist Party (CCP) and the State Council created a policy initiative, calling for close links between S&T research and economic construction. The following motto captured the crux of the new S&T policy: 'Economic development should rely on science and technology; science and technology should serve the needs of economic development' (Yu 1988: 32).[15]

After extensive discussion, consensus building, and experimentation, the CCP's Central Committee announced in March 1985 a programme for reforming China's S&T system.[16] The goal was clear—to forge horizontal links between research labs and enterprises so as to facilitate the flow of technologies from the state S&T system into industry. It was believed that the way to reach this goal was to create a market for technologies, and several measures were proposed. They included: turning the majority of the previously 100 per cent state-funded research units to for-profit units by gradually reducing direct grants from the state; creating incentives for enterprises to adopt new technologies; and reforming S&T's human resource management system to allow scientists and technicians to move into newly created markets for science and technology personnel.

It was soon realized, however, that transforming scientific breakthroughs into commercial successes was a very complicated organizational process, which could not be accomplished just by creating a market for technologies. Two things stood out. First, substantial effort had to be made in the development stage before research breakthroughs could eventually yield commercial successes (Yu 1988: 12, 124–6).[17] This often entailed substantial investment. Second, a new product's market acceptability was unclear: uncertainties in market demand led to difficulties in evaluating the value of laboratory results. The few enterprises that did introduce new technologies tended to underprice them, given that they bore the uncertainties of development and marketing.[18] Research institutions had few incentives while the resources required were often prohibitive for translating laboratory results into commercial products.

It was against this background that a new breed of enterprise called 'Science and Technology (S&T) Enterprise' (*keji qiye*), came onto the scene. These enterprises, embodied a new type of organization and even had a special legal status.[19] They were

---

[15] The policy motto was declared by the then Prime Minister Zhao Zhiyang during the National Science and Technology Reward Conference on 24 Oct. 1982 as the guiding principle of a new national science and technology policy (see ZDYD 1993: 8). It was the result of several years of consensus building. The new policy initiative could be traced back to the National Science and Technology Convention in Dec. 1980. The policy issue of serving industrial needs was, for the first time, systematically discussed in the document issued by the State Science and Technology Committee after that convention (CCP Document Research Office 1982: 759–76).

[16] For details on the process of drafting the programme, see Saich 1989a: ch. 5.

[17] Nathan Rosenberg has distinguished economically feasible products from technologically feasible products. In this categorization, the lab results only indicate technological feasibility, not commercial feasibility. The process of technology commercialization, or more narrowly, the process of technology development, could therefore be defined as a process of turning technological feasibility into economic feasibility Rosenberg 1994: 130.

[18] For a general discussion of the market for technologies and the corresponding pricing problem in China, see Simon and Rehn 1988: 34–5.

[19] This special legal status was within the framework of government industry policy for promoting high-tech industry in the context of the creation of high-tech industrial zones. I will discuss this issue in the case studies.

akin to the high-tech ventures in Western market economies and acted as organizational vehicles for turning technology potential accumulated in the state S&T sector into commercial realities.

It was by no means coincidental that the four leading enterprise groups in the Chinese IT industry, Stone, Legend, Founder, and China Great Wall Computer, were among these new S&T enterprises. Stone was the first S&T enterprise that succeeded in commercializing a Chinese word processor, revolutionizing Chinese word-processing in the office, thereby imparting a degree of legitimacy and popularity to the new S&T enterprises. Legend was a spin-off of the Institute of Computing Technology under CAS. It later became the largest PC maker in China and one of the world's top suppliers of PC motherboards and add-on cards. Founder took over Project 748 and became the technological leader in markets for pictographic-language electronic publishing systems. Great Wall was a spin-off of the Computer Industry Administration Bureau under MEI. It developed one of the top indigenous PC brands and became the largest OEM supplier of computer parts, components, and peripherals in China. They all succeeded in acquiring the organizational and technological capabilities that made them competitive in their respective product markets. More specifically, the four enterprises have the following characteristics in common:

1. They are non-governmental enterprises (*minying keji qiye*) except for Great Wall Computer. 'Non-governmental' means that they are established outside either central or local government budgetary channels. Stone was originally registered as a township enterprise in a nearby rural town with a RMB 20,000 loan. Legend 'borrowed' its initial capital of RMB 200,000 (equivalent to the value of four personal computers at the time) from CAS's Institute of Computing Technology. Founder's initial capital, RMB 300,000, came from a budget surplus from Beijing University. Only Great Wall received its seed money from a state budget. Yet as will be seen, Great Wall was also fundamentally different from traditional state-owned enterprises.

2. They are very young and have grown exceedingly fast. Stone and Legend were founded in 1984, and Founder and Great Wall in 1986. By 1995 the enterprises' revenues all had reached billions of RMB.[20] Although they are still small compared with large multinational companies in the West, they are among China's 500 largest enterprises.

3. They are very competitive and are leaders in their respective product markets. Stone has warded off competition from similar products later designed and manufactured by major Japanese electronic companies and marketed by other Chinese firms, including a subsidiary of one of the largest Chinese state-owned investment trusts, CITIC. It has occupied 80 per cent of the integrated Chinese word processor market in China. Legend has been competing with IBM, Compaq, and AST in China's domestic PC market with its own brand-name PC that became the Chinese market's number one PC brand by 1996. At the same time, it has been supplying a

---

[20] See *Computer World* (Chinese version), no. 592, 20 May 1996.

significant amount of PC motherboards and add-on cards to the world market through its Hong Kong subsidiaries, putting it among the world's top five suppliers of computer motherboards and add-on cards. Founder has defeated all major international makers of electronic publishing systems from the United Kingdom, United States, Germany, and Japan in the market for high-resolution Chinese electronic publishing systems. It has also dominated this market in Taiwan, Hong Kong, Macao, Europe, and the United States. Great Wall invented the first IBM compatible PC that had integrated capabilities for handling Chinese characters. It became one of the most successful domestic PC manufacturers and the largest supplier of PC components and peripherals in China.

4. They are among the first Chinese enterprises that were restructured into joint-stock companies and went public either on the Hong Kong Stock Exchange (Stone, Founder, and Legend), or the domestic stock exchange (Great Wall). Yet they are still controlled by holding companies that are in turn 'owned' by government institutions or collectively owned. Stone is legally a 'collectively owned enterprise' (*jiti suoyouzhi qiye*); Legend, Founder, and Great Wall are still categorized as state-owned enterprises (*guoyou qiye*).

As the driving forces behind China's rapid catch-up in IT, these four enterprises represent the four largest enterprise groups in the Chinese computer industry in terms of revenue.[21]

1.4. Enterprise Governance and the Mode of Technology Learning: An Analytical Framework

Coming back to the beginning of this chapter, my argument is that indigenous S&T capabilities accumulated during the central planning era provided the necessary conditions for Chinese enterprises to follow a unique top-down mode of technology learning. Given the problems of central planning with regard to innovation, the key was the organizational breakthroughs that made it possible for the new S&T enterprises to use the accumulated S&T resources and turn them into commercial successes. What organizational arrangements would most likely underpin such an innovative mode of technology learning in the context of economic transition? Such is the question the case studies will try to answer. Embarking on an empirical inquiry necessitates an analytical framework.

For many years, discussions of economic transition have been limited to privatization issues at the enterprise level and price liberalization at the macroeconomic level within a neoclassic economic framework (Blanchard *et al.* 1991, 1993; Sachs 1994). That is based on the conviction that the problem with central planning is resource misallocation; therefore, the remedy for the ills of central planning is to create private enterprises that could respond to price signals to improve the

---

[21] Notice the definition of the computer information technology industry here is broader than PC manufacturing. It contains enterprises that produce hardware and software for information processing. In the Chinese context, it includes Chinese-language processing. PC manufacturing is nevertheless the backbone of the industry.

allocative efficiency of *given* economic resources. The default organizational arrangement is privately owned enterprises within an extremely decentralized market structure (Debreu 1959; Demsetz 1991). However, by treating technology as exogenous, the theory precludes the analysis of the *development* of economic resources which results from technological learning and innovation. By treating the firm as a black box and technology as given, the mainstream neoclassic economic theory is not suitable to answer the question of what kind of organizational arrangements at the business enterprise level are conducive to technology learning and innovation in a transitional economy (Nelson and Winter 1982; Murrel 1991; Stiglitz 1994).

An analytical framework that deals with the issue of what are the proper organizational arrangements for technological learning or innovation in the context of economic transition has to, first, employ a basic understanding of the nature of innovation, and second, take into account the specific circumstances of the transition from a centrally planned economy to a market-oriented one.

Innovation as a process of turning technological invention into commercial success requires resources, both financial and human. Hence, an innovation decision is also an investment decision. Yet both technological and market uncertainties are inherent to innovation. For example, innovative products might not be technologically feasible and even if they were, the market might reject the quality/cost mix. Return on investment cannot be determined *ex ante*. Therefore, the necessary condition for an innovation's success is the commitment of resources, especially financial resources. Innovation is also a learning process to acquire knowledge to reduce the uncertainties and to increase the likelihood of success. Given the complexity of modern technology, innovation involves a large number of individuals working in an intricate web of division of labour, making this kind of learning a collective endeavour. These two basic features of innovation—innovation as an investment decision and a collective learning process—point to the importance of institutional and organizational arrangements within which investment decisions are made, and the learning process takes place.

Lazonick and O'Sullivan have identified enterprise governance as a central unit of analysis in this regard. In their theory of the innovative enterprise, enterprise governance is defined as a set of social institutions that influences the strategic allocation of resources and returns in business enterprises.[22] The importance of enterprise governance lies in its impact on the innovation process, influencing who makes investment decisions, what types of investments they make, and how investment returns are distributed (Lazonick 1990, 1991; Lazonick and O'Sullivan 1996; O'Sullivan 1996).

Who makes investment decisions is important, because the position of the strategic decision-makers relative to the learning collective will determine their cognitive capabilities in making innovative decisions.

---

[22] Notice this definition is different from the conventional definition of corporate governance. The focus of the latter is the principle–agency relation between shareholders and management. The research concern is how to ally the interests between the two. See Jensen and Meckling 1976; Fama and Jensen 1983; Jensen 1989; for criticism of this perspective, see Lazonick 1992.

What type of investment is important because not all investment decisions are innovative. Lazonick has made important distinctions between adaptive and innovative strategies with regard to resource allocation or investment (Lazonick 1991). The adaptive strategy subjects itself to the constraints of *given* economic resources and tries to maximize the returns under those constraints. However, the return will be competed away in a competitive market. The innovative strategy tries to transcend resources constraints by investing in the *development* of new resources, that is, embarking on innovation. The latter often incurs high fixed costs, and the return from the fixed investment is uncertain.

How returns are distributed is important because it determines the incentives and abilities of strategic decision-makers to pursue innovative strategies.

Such an analytical framework that links enterprise governance with innovation is suitable for the analysis of the rise of innovative enterprises in China's transition from a planned economy towards a market-oriented one. One of the biggest puzzles of the Chinese case was that most of the innovative enterprises, including the enterprises in the computer industry, were and still are state-owned or collectively owned. On the surface, the persistence of state or collective ownership might reflect the gradual nature of China's economic reform. The puzzle was how state-owned or collectively owned enterprises could ever be innovative. The issue could not be dismissed on the ground that these enterprises were merely exceptions, a point difficult to support as they are responsible for the rise of a whole indigenous industry. What this fact reveals is the limit of the dichotomy of state or collective versus private ownership as an analytical framework for the issue in question.

There were at least two profound reasons for a state-owned or collectively owned enterprise to be innovative in the context of economic transition. The first has to do with a specific set of conditions: Chinese enterprises could use S&T resources in the state S&T sector accumulated in the central planning era and turn them into commercial products without having to start from scratch. Theoretically, it was possible to internalize S&T resources in the public domain through a market mechanism, that is for the enterprises to pay the government for these resources. In reality, most S&T resources were intangible, which meant that their value was indeterminable before being actually turned into marketable products. Hence, these resources were not tradable in factor markets.[23] In other words, property rights could not be well defined over these resources *ex ante*. To use these resources, some kind of vague ownership arrangements are necessary. The second reason follows from the nature of innovation: the process of technology commercialization, or innovation defined as such, is a prolonged organizational learning process that is fraught with uncertainties. It requires long-term sustained financial commitment. Private enterprises would not necessarily be willing to commit sufficient financial resources due to the risk-averse nature of private capital (Arrow 1962). State- or collectively owned enterprises might provide the needed financial commitment. The key was to provide an organizational structure that would provide sufficient incentives for the people in the learning

---

[23] For a comprehensive discussion of the non-tradability of asset stocks, see Dierickx and Cool 1989.

collectivity. Taking enterprise governance as a unit of analysis, the puzzle of how state-owned enterprises could still be innovative can be resolved. What had really changed was the structure of enterprise governance, even though the ownership structures remained public or collective in nature. Under this framework, the problems of central planning with regard to innovation were clearer. Under the central planning system, bureaucrats at different levels made the investment decisions. These bureaucrats were not integrated into the production process and knew little about the actual production process. Consequently, although central planning was investment driven, the types of investment were mostly routine and adaptive. The distribution of the returns on investment was to ensure the bureaucrats' full control over financial resources to be allocated later in accordance with the central plan. As a result, very few innovative activities occurred at the enterprise level, and therefore on the level of the economy as a whole.

It follows that the new S&T enterprises must have differed fundamentally in their governance structures from enterprises under central planning. Hypotheses could be drawn with regard to the governance structures of these enterprises in terms of who makes investment decisions, what kind of investments they make, and how returns are distributed.

Hypothesis 1. We should expect that it was the enterprise managers rather than the government bureaucrats who made strategic investment decisions. In the context of economic transition, it is a matter of managerial autonomy from direct government intervention. In the case of the Chinese computer enterprises, an important question is how managerial autonomy was attained under public ownership arrangements.

One of the most important aspects of managerial autonomy is control over financial resources. In the absence of private venture-capital markets, as was the case in China, financial resources other than the ones from the government budget were limited. It is, therefore, interesting to learn how these enterprises acquired the financial resources that fuelled their explosive growth without giving up control over their allocation.

The S&T resources accumulated in the state sector must be important, for they were intangible resources resulting from the government's past investments. It will be interesting to learn how enterprise governance was structured, allowing them to take advantage of these essentially public resources, while maintaining their independence from the state. It is, therefore, necessary to look at various organizational arrangements between public research institutions that were the reservoirs of the intangible technological resources and the enterprises that set forth to commercialize these resources.

Hypothesis 2. The enterprises in question must have adopted innovative investment strategies to confront the uncertainties inherent in the innovation process. The focus here is on how these enterprises developed capabilities that enabled them to overcome both technological and market uncertainties. What is important is not making innovative investment decisions per se, but how to make innovative investments in order to reduce the uncertainties of innovation. For the computer enterprises in question, the product design capabilities accumulated during the central planning era were particularly important: they would reduce both technological uncertainties and market uncertainties. First of all, starting at product design or redesign would bring the enterprises directly to the user/producer interface in the market. The literature of innovation studies has long indicated this as one of the important factors behind the development of new products acceptable to the market (Lundvall 1988; Fagerberg 1998). It would ensure market acceptance before committing resources in building up in-house manufacturing capabilities, which often incurs high fixed-cost investment. This would reduce the risk of investment. Second, the tight coupling between product design and market requirements would allow these enterprises to establish their own brand images and grow independently. Third, possessing independent product design and marketing capabilities, these enterprises would be more independent and flexible in negotiating technology transfers from abroad.

Hypothesis 3. The institutional arrangements that govern the distribution of returns should strike a balance between providing incentives to learn and innovate, and having sufficient resources to sustain the innovative strategies. This was essentially a balance between individual remuneration in the learning collectivity and the regime of accumulation, that is, reinvestment out of retained earnings. Therefore, it is interesting to know the rules that govern the wage-and-benefit policy and the allocations of the retained earnings.

Since all four enterprises had their core businesses listed in stock exchanges through corporate restructuring, looking at the realignments of the governance structure after the listing is interesting. It is of particular interest to find out who ultimately controlled the listed enterprises and how the financial resources raised on the stock market were allocated.

The subsequent case studies are organized around the above propositions and the corresponding research questions. The interaction between enterprise governance and the trajectory of technological learning is the analytical focus. The premise is that the mode of technology learning among the Chinese computer enterprises should be no more than a manifestation of an underlying organizational mechanism of learning and innovation that operated in the specific context of China's transition from a centrally planned economy to a market-oriented one. As such, the cases of the Chinese enterprises have a 'dual character of situational groundedness and theoretical generality' (Harper 1992: 139).[24]

Data for the case studies were gathered mainly through fieldwork in China. It consists of four field trips between 1994 and 1999, including two months in 1994, six months in 1996, one month in 1998, and one month in 1999. Two major data-gathering methods were used:

---

[24] Social scientists have not yet developed a universally accepted methodology for case studies. It is not my intention to go into the details with regard to the methodology of case study here. For a comprehensive discussion of the various methodological underpinnings of case studies, see Ragin and Becker (eds.) 1992. For the methodological stance adopted here see the articles by Walton, Harper, and Wieviorka respectively in that book. In my view, most social science inquiries fall into the category of what the mathematician Polya called 'Plausible Reasoning' (1968). In other words, our studies help to improve our understanding of the social world but do not exhaust it.

1. *Intensive interviews*. The small number of cases permits in-depth studies. I used semi-structured interviews with managers and staff in R&D, financing, marketing, and manufacturing in each of the enterprise groups as well as officials in the corresponding supervisory institutions, local governments, and ministries. In total, I interviewed more than seventy people, with most interviews lasting one hour and some several hours. Some key figures were interviewed several times. Because most of the interviews were arranged through personal connections using snowball methods, almost all of the interviewees, except one senior manager, were open to my questions.

2. *Documentary data*. In addition to the semi-structured interviews, I collected a large amount of documentary data, including: (1) company archives; (2) press reports about the four enterprise groups; (3) internal company newsletters; (4) special collections on each enterprise group—several books in this regard have been published by major Chinese publishers; (5) collections of government policies and regulations regarding economic reform in general and new S&T enterprises in particular; and (6) reports on companies' general and financial information by these enterprises' major underwriters. These reports are considered to be some of the most accurate sources of data on the companies' capital structures, internal organizations, major investment decisions, corporate control, and financial situations due to the stringent disclosure requirements the Hong Kong and Shenzhen Stock Exchanges.

2

The Stone Group Corporation: Turning Technological Potential into Commercial Success under a New Organizational Framework

> Stone is often mistaken for a private company since it operates with such a high degree of autonomy. The company is considered a 'people-owned people-run science and technology enterprise' (*minyou minban keji qiye*), a designation that has no bearing on its ownership but confers a higher degree of autonomy than usual for collectives. As a collective, however, the Stone Group as a whole is not permitted to liquidate its assets or conduct a share offering that would result in the transfer of majority control to private hands.
>
> Scott Kennedy, Brookings Institution, 1995.[1]

In China the name 'Stone' is synonymous with both a product—a Chinese electronic typewriter (integrated Chinese word processor)—and a company—a new type of enterprise in China that is called 'people-owned people-run science and technology enterprise' or non-governmental S&T enterprise.[2]

Stone is the company that first brought to the market an integrated Chinese word processor, a product that revolutionized Chinese word-processing, and it has dominated that market ever since. Stone is also well known for being the largest non-governmental enterprise in China. The company's market success in new high-tech products is considered to be closely related to the organizational framework that evolved at Stone. In fact, it is recognized in China that Stone has created a new

---

[1] Kennedy 1995.

[2] Because there is no equivalent ownership structure in the Western market economy, and because of the difficulty of explaining the peculiarity of the company's ownership structure, Stone is often mistaken for China's largest private enterprise in the Western media (e.g. *Washington Post*, 19 June 1987). The term 'Non-Governmental S&T Enterprises' was coined upon the establishment of the government-sponsored national association of 'people-run enterprises', as a result of consultation with the Official Xinhua News Agency for disseminating news in English regarding the activities of those enterprises. From personal interviews with the former secretary-general of the National Association of Non-Governmental S&T Enterprises. One of the earliest discussions of the Non-Governmental S&T Enterprises in English journals can be seen in Suttmeier 1988.

organizational form that can effectively translate the technological potentials accumulated in the state sector during the central planning era into commercial successes within a new market environment.

This chapter is intended to document the characteristics of Stone's new organizational structure, and the strengths and limitations of that structure for allocating the resources and creating the incentives required for organizational learning. I define organizational learning as the process of capability acquisition in R&D, marketing, and manufacturing, revolving around the task of technology commercialization.

2.1. The Founding and Early History of Stone

Stone was founded on 11 May 1984 by a group of alumni of Qinghua University. Since Qinghua is the best engineering school in China, Stone's founders represented some of China's top engineering talent. Previously, they had been scattered among the top research labs of the Chinese Academy of Sciences (CAS) and the research institutes of major industrial ministries, as well as state-owned computer manufacturing enterprises. Their motivation to set up a company of their own was to bridge the gulf between the nation's science and technology system and the needs of the economy. To a large extent, the act was a response to the government's policy initiatives designed to integrate science and technology activities into the industrial development process.[3] These policies were intended to encourage experimentation with new organizational forms, but they did not provide any appropriate legal framework within which this experimentation could take place. As a result, the process of founding Stone was a chain reaction of ad hoc personal connections centring around the network of Qinghua alumni.

The process started with one Qinghua alumnus, Liu Haipin. Liu was an engineer in the Beijing Number Three Computer Manufacturing Plant, a state-owned enterprise under the Ministry of Electronics Industry (MEI). In early 1984 he felt compelled to start a high-tech company. He discussed this idea with one of his closest friends and college classmates, who suggested that he seek advice from a senior alumnus, Yin Pusheng. Yin was very much interested in the idea; however, he was not able to participate personally because he was an army officer then. But he recommended his college room-mate, Wan Runnan, saying that this person would be indispensable to running the type of high-technology company that Liu had in mind. Besides, Yin said, he knew that Wan was also interested in starting a company.

Wan had majored in civil engineering at Qinghua University and was a self-made computer engineer at CAS's newly established computing centre. He was transferred to the computing centre at CAS—China's top research institution—through a personal connection (*guanxi*) in the early 1980s. Three months after his arrival, he had mastered the principles of the then new Z80 series of central processing units (CPUs), thereby proving his qualifications as a computer engineer. At the time of starting

---

[3] See Introduction.

the company, Wan was on leave from his research position at the centre, studying English in preparation for a visiting scholarship at the University of Florida's Department of Computer Science. Wan, in turn, invited Shen Guojun, a senior staff member in CAS's Office of Science and Technology, to join the group of high-tech entrepreneurs.

No one in the group had any prior knowledge about how to start a company. So they went to visit a handful of new science and technology enterprises in the region. Meanwhile, Yin went to talk to the party secretary of the Haidian District Committee, Jia Chunwang, who was also a Qinghua alumnus and a personal friend. Jia suggested that they should try to collaborate with the Evergreen Township, one of several rural townships within Haidian District's jurisdiction. Evergreen Township was already an impressive economic concern with an annual income of more than RMB 170 million from agricultural, industrial, and commercial activities.[4] Jia took it upon himself to make the connection. He called up the head of the township, Li Wenyuan,[5] who turned out to be a very open-minded person. At the time the township had a dozen or so factories, producing goods ranging from clothes and beer to construction materials, industrial boilers, and electronics, but no high-tech products.

On 20 March 1984, the two sides held their first meeting in a conference room of the Haidian District's Party Committee. The township was represented by the head of the township, Li Wenyuan; the director of the township's printed circuit board factory, Li Wenjun; and the party secretary of the township's chemical and light industry company, Liu Zhiming. Representing the scientists were Yin Pusheng, Wan Runnan, Wan Dabang (Wan Runnan's father, a retired accountant), and Shen Guojun. The district's party secretary, Jia Chunwang, presided over the meeting.

During the meeting, Wan set out what the scientists intended to do. He said:

We live in the Haidian District. We would like to contribute to the industrialization of the region. Haidian is full of intellectuals.[6] Our intention is to use the energies of the intellectuals and to translate science and technology into direct forces of production. . . . Nowadays, rural township and village enterprises are very competitive. If we could update their technology, they could definitely compete with the state-owned enterprises. The township has the capital and the land, we possess the technologies and human resources. If we co-operate, we will succeed.

Shen added:

The government urges CAS to contribute decisively to the nation's economic development over the next twenty years. The government grants RMB 800 million per year to the CAS for research and development. This amount of money could buy many technologies directly from abroad. A serious problem is that fruits of science and technology research have not been

---

[4] See *China Daily*, 26 June 1985.

[5] The head of the district party committee has a rank equivalent to the district governor. Evergreen Township is within the jurisdiction of the Haidian District government. So Jia was literally Li's supervisor in the Chinese hierarchical system.

[6] Habitually, the Chinese tend to refer to all learned people as intellectuals. Scientists and technologists are naturally in this category. This has to do with the Confucian tradition, on one hand, and the communist political structure, on the other. For the latter, see Konrad and Szelenyi 1979.

translated into forces of production. There are lots of opportunities now. Computerization is a grand trend. Although the market for large computers is small, we could concentrate on small microcomputers. Now there are several electronics factories in the Guangdong Province assembling computers on the SKD basis.[7] They are very profitable. We could do more than that. We could develop software, adding new functions to computers, for example, the Chinese word-processing function. In short, we shall establish knowledge- and technology-intensive enterprises.

Li Wenyuan agreed that the township should co-operate. He hoped the scientists and technologists could help to upgrade the township's industrial structure, adding high-tech content to their products.

In subsequent meetings, the two sides worked out the actual form of co-operation. To have maximum freedom of action, Wan and his colleagues decided to give up their job tenure (the 'iron rice bowl') in the state sector—an action that signalled their strong commitment to the new enterprise. Li helped with the legal procedures for the company's registration.

On 16 May the company was formally established as a rural township enterprise under the jurisdiction of the Evergreen Township. According to the company charter:

The company's name is the Sitong New Industry Development Corporation. It is a collectively owned enterprise with an initial capital, office space, and other necessary facilities provided by Evergreen People's Commune (Evergreen Township),[8] inviting scientists and technologists from state research institutes, universities, and industries to provide technological and managerial skills. The corporation's organizational principles are independent management and financial self-reliance. The company will develop technology-intensive products by adopting a new organizational mode of integrating R&D, manufacturing, and trade. It is intended to contribute to the upgrade of the industrial structure in the areas around Beijing.

The township loaned RMB 20,000 as start-up capital to the company (with the company agreeing to return this money within one year), and provided free office space and a telephone for interim use. The head of the township became the company chairman. Wan Runnan was appointed general manager.

The company's Chinese name 'Sitong' took the first Chinese character of the name of the Evergreen Township, 'Si-ji-qing', and its pronunciation is close to the English word 'Stone'. Wan and his colleagues coined this name with several connotations in mind. First, it recognized the connection with the Evergreen Township. Second, the word 'Si-tong' in Chinese means multiple avenues, implying smoothness and success. Its English homonym 'Stone' implies exploration, that is, exploring new avenues in the process of Chinese economic reform, as in an old Chinese saying: 'When you go

---

[7] SKD is a special commercial term. It stands for parts and components in 'semi-knocked down conditions'.

[8] Under the Chinese socialist system, a rural town was organized into a people's commune, which is a social entity that integrated government and production functions. Around 1982 the people's commune system was abolished after the successful implementation of the rural household responsibility system. Since then, the governmental function of the people's commune has been handed over to the rural township government. Production was assigned to various agricultural, industrial, and commercial business enterprises. However, because of the collective nature of most of the rural township enterprises, the town government is still heavily involved in economic activities. There was de facto integration of the political and economical organizations at the township as well as village levels.

out into the dark night, the first thing you must do is throw out a stone to see where the road is' (*toushi wenlu*).[9] Obviously, Wan and his associates were cautious about their mission. They knew they were creating something new, something unknown in the existing system. They were fully aware of the risks, including the political risks.

However, with the risks came opportunities. For Wan and associates, the opportunity was the rising demand for Chinese information-processing technologies in the aftermath of massive imports of personal computers in the early 1980s.[10] Most of the installed computers in China at the time were either underused or sat idle, due to the lack of complementary Chinese information-processing and input-output technologies. While such technologies were being developed within various national research labs, lack of initiative and organizational channels resulted in the slowness of state research institutions or state-owned enterprises actually commercializing these technologies. The opportunity was left to foreign companies until the new S&T enterprises came onto the scene. For example, there was only one Toshiba-made printer capable of handling Chinese characters. The state-run Electronics Import and Export Company imported it into China, selling it at a very high price.

Soon after the company was set up, one of the co-founders, Liu Haiping, received word of a low-priced imported printer from the Bureau of Electronics Industry of Beijing Municipal Government, where he had very good personal connections. Mitsui & Co., Ltd., was planning to sell the Chinese a new generation of printer developed by the Japanese company Brother. This printer was more compact, lighter, and less expensive than Toshiba's model. The only problem was that it was not capable of handling Chinese characters. So Mitsui signed a contract with the Bureau of Electronics Industry to add a function for handling Chinese characters in the printer. The task was assigned to a team at the computing centre of the Beijing Municipal Government. However, the team was not able to solve the problem at the time when Liu received the information. Stone's management quickly made a decision to take over the job. Through Wan's personal connections, Stone had access to two very bright, young computer engineers at CAS's Computing Centre, who developed the technology in a very short period of time. Stone then went to negotiate with Mitsui, and secured the sole distributorship for the printer in China.

The re-engineered printer could be sold at a fraction of the price of the Toshiba model, and it soon drove the Toshiba printer out of the market. The company made a fortune and accumulated a sizeable capital in its first two years, laying the foundation for its future development. Soon after, Stone successfully developed an integrated Chinese word processor with the help of a Japanese company. Applauded for

---

[9] Traditionally, Chinese are superstitious about choosing a name for their business—or even choosing its location, which is why they often hire a geomancer for the business's geographical location. Wan actually stayed up an entire night at Yin Pusheng's home, trying to find the right name.

[10] The massive import of computers (mostly in the form of component kits to avoid paying high tariffs) was the result of an extensive national discussion of the so-called 'new technology revolution' happening around the world. Several books, for example, Tofler's *The Third Wave*, Netsbit's *Megatrends*, and Bell's *Post-Industrial Society*, became instant best-sellers in China around this time. The information technology revolution was seen as the basis of the new revolution, creating a computer frenzy. For a discussion of Chinese reaction to the 'new technology revolution', see van Woerkom-Chong 1986.

having revolutionized Chinese word-processing, the product became an instant market hit. It became the company's cash cow for quite a long time.

Stone's speed in developing commercially viable technologies was impressive. From 1984 to 1988 the company released at least one new product model per year (Table 2.1). Backed by this technological capability, the company's sales grew at an annual rate of 300 per cent in its first four years of operations (Table 2.2).

The unusual business performance, and particularly the unique organizational approach underpinning Stone's success, attracted much attention at both local and national levels. At the time when most enterprises were used to responding to commands from various state agencies, the company's autonomous practices and its resulting market successes were truly distinctive. Additionally, the nation as a whole

TABLE 2.1. *List of Stone's new technology products, 1984–1988*

Year	Product	R&D strategies
1984	M2024 Printer	Re-engineered, added Chinese font driver (software)
1985	M1570 Printer	Re-engineered, added Chinese font card (hardware) and driver (software)
1986	MS2400 Chinese Word Processor	System Design, ODM by Japanese firm
1987	MS2401 Chinese Word Processor MS2402 Chinese Word Processor OKI8324 Printer	System Design, manufactured in Stone–Mitsui joint venture
1988	MS2406 Chinese Word Processor	System Design, manufactured in Stone–Mitsui joint venture

Source: Yu 1988: 161.

TABLE 2.2. *Stone: The first four years*

	1984	1985	1986	1987
No. of employees (at year's end)	67	113	246	417
Sales	9,760	32,200	123,580	317,130
After-tax profits	1,430	4,250	9,340	25,000
Taxes	730	1,570	2,920	6,380
Wages and salaries	136	302	558	661

Note: Currency figures in 1,000s RMB. Taxes include circulation taxes as well as income taxes. The number of employees are for year-end figures. The large increase in 1987 is partly due to the setting up of the Stone–Mitsui joint venture in Beijing in the latter part of the year. Hence, the corresponding increases in wages and salaries are not proportional to the increase of the number of employees.

Source: Yu 1988: 159.

was earnestly seeking new organizational breakthroughs in the process of economic reform, and this company's experience was invaluable. Stone soon became one of the most high-profile enterprises in China. The president of the company became an instant economic hero. The media regularly gushed with news and reports about Stone in national and local newspapers and magazines. From 11 August to 10 September 1988 the major national economic newspaper, the *Economic Daily*, even ran a month-long column on 'the Stone phenomenon'.

2.1.1. *Relations with Evergreen Township*

As a rural township enterprise, Stone was under the jurisdiction of the Evergreen Township. The township played an important role in the early days of Stone's development. First and foremost, the township provided an institutional framework for Stone to start as a new venture. The rural township enterprise was one of the most flexible organizational forms at the time,[11] making it possible for Stone to experiment with new organizational rules and practices, which laid the foundation for the company's success. Financially, the township provided initial capital (albeit in the form of loans), free office space, and other facilities.

Stone's governance body also included cadres from the township. According to the company charter:

The company's governance body is the board of directors. The duties of the board of directors are: (1) drawing up and revising the company charter; (2) making long-term plans for the company, and approving major business decisions; (3) determining the organizational structure and appointing general managers, associate general managers, and department heads; (4) reviewing and approving the company's business plan, financial plan, and annual reports; (5) other important matters (Provision 10).

The board of directors appoints one general manager and several associate general managers. The general manager is directly responsible to the board of directors. Associate general managers assist the general manager. The general manager makes business and financial plans under the guidance of the board of directors; organizes the company's daily business activities; appoints staff with the authorization of the board of directors; reports to the board of directors regularly (Provision 12).

Management posts were allocated to the following:

Chairman: Li Wenyuan, the head of the township government.
Vice-Chairmen: Shen Guojun, a former staff member from CAS; Liu Jufeng, a senior staff member at the State Science and Technology Committee; Zhang Yanzhong, the associate general manager of the township's Agriculture, Industry and Trade General Company; Liu Zhiming, the party secretary for the township's Chemical and Light Industry Company.

---

[11] In the early 1980s no private enterprises were allowed, at least in urban areas, for ideological reasons. The maximum limit of employees for a rural household-run business (*geti jingji*) was eight. Private enterprises were formally legalized in 1988 as indicated by the State Council's issuance of the 'Temporary Statute for Private Enterprises'.

Directors: Wan Runnan, an engineer from the Computing Centre of CAS; Liu Haipin, an engineer from the Beijing Number Three Computer Manufacturing Plant under the Ministry of Electronics Industry; Ren Shude, the head of the township's Enterprise Management Office.
General Manager: Wan Runnan.
Associate General Managers: Shen Guojun and Ren Shude.

The governance body was carefully organized to balance power between the scientists and the township, with each side roughly taking half the posts. However, the people from the township held mostly full-time positions with the township and were involved in company affairs only on a part-time basis. More specifically, they only attended the meetings of the board of directors, held twice a month. In contrast, most of the scientists had quit their respective state research or work units and had become full-time employees of the company.

During the first year of operations, the company basically followed the rules set out in the company charter. Regular meetings of the board of directors played an important role in business decision-making.

According to an initial agreement, Stone had to turn over 60 per cent of its profits to the township, and the township would reinvest 40 per cent of it in the company as a development fund. It appeared that the township had ownership rights equivalent to 60 per cent of the company's equity. The distribution of the first year's profit was basically in accordance with this assumption.[12] However, new developments soon changed the situation.

On one hand, although rural township enterprises enjoyed favourable tax treatment (only 33 per cent of net income) as compared to other collectives and state-owned enterprises (up to 55 per cent), it was nevertheless obliged to pay a certain amount of income tax. Yet other S&T enterprises in the region were mostly registered as labour-service enterprises, that is, enterprises that hired a certain number of unemployed urban youths in exchange for a three-year tax break. This prompted Stone's board of the directors to change the company's legal status. On the other hand, the company's surprising business performance brought a momentum of growth. The company expanded by setting up new subsidiaries with an independent legal status. New subsidiaries were set up as labour-service enterprises for taxation purposes, which necessitated the revision of the initial agreement between the company and the township.

Under the new agreement, the profit-base for calculating turnover to the township was limited to the profit of one of the subsidiaries—Stone Computer Technology Co. To prevent the company from purposely lowering the profit level of the subsidiary, the township asked for a fixed amount of RMB 526,000 in 1988, a figure that was derived from the previous year's profit.[13]

---

[12] According to a company record, the first year (1984) financial performance of the company was (in RMB): revenue: 9,762,000; sales tax: 299,000; expenses: 8,037,000; pre-tax profit: 1,426,000; income tax: 471,000; net profit: 955,000; turnover to Evergreen Township: 191,000 (20% of net profit); retained earnings: 764,000 (company archives).

[13] This figure is from a company employee's private archive.

A more crucial event that set the tone for the changed relation between Stone and the township in the long run was a political campaign initiated by the government. In the middle of 1985 the CCP's Central Committee and the State Council jointly issued an administrative order, demanding the separation of government and party officials from direct involvement in commercial activities. The order's purpose was to eliminate the institutional seeds of corruption. As a result, the officials from the township all resigned from their various posts in the company, except for two officials from the township who resigned from their posts in the township and formally joined the company as full-time employees (one associate general manager and one accountant). As a result, they were no longer representing the township. These changes decisively diminished the influence of the township over the company. Thereafter, the general manager, Wan Runnan, became chairman of the board of directors. As a result, the two-tiered governance body was combined into one.

Stone was later reorganized into a general holding company in December 1984, and then into a group company in May 1986, with a multi-subsidiary structure to accommodate all the newly founded subsidiaries. The group company was nominally put under the direct jurisdiction of the Haidian District government. However, the latter had little influence over the company's business. Thus, the company operated with the greatest autonomy that a collective could have at the time. Fig. 2.1 shows the early evolution of the company's corporate structure.[14]

The subtle relationship between Stone and the Evergreen Township illustrated the resolution of the issue of property rights over the assets of a large number of collectives formed in similar ways during the reform period. Some people on the Evergreen Township side thought that Stone's accumulated assets, worth some hundreds of millions of RMB, were the products of the original RMB 20,000-loan from the township. People in the company, however, thought Stone's assets had little to do with the seed money given by the township. In fact, the money was only symbolic. The working capital needed for the first few business transactions came from loans from the local branch of the State Agricultural Bank. As the head of Stone's financial department explained:

Fortunately, the RMB 20,000 was a loan. It is a debt, not an equity in accounting terms. Besides, the township asked us to return the RMB 20,000 as soon as we made money. We returned it within a year; otherwise, according to a recent government decree based on the principle of 'who invests, who owns', the township would have held equity rights over Stone.[15]

If the Evergreen Township was not the company owner, who was? The issue is confusing, particularly for observers from Western market economies. The confusion could be best illustrated by the fact that Stone was often cited by media in Hong Kong and the West as China's largest private enterprise. However, the participants and relevant government officials in China are much less confused. As Wan, the

---

[14] A note on titles: in the beginning, the head of the company's executive body was called the 'general manager'. After the company formed subsidiaries and became a group company, the head of the company was called the 'president'. The title of general manager was given to the heads of the various subsidiaries.

[15] Personal interview in May 1996.

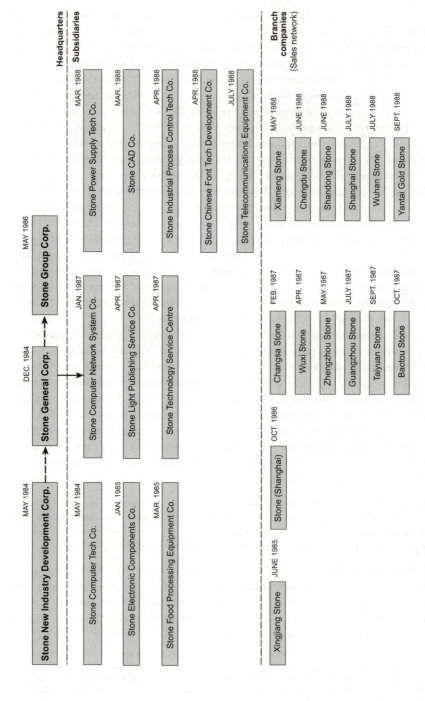

Fig. 2.1. Evolution of Stone's corporate structure

former president of Stone, said at the company's second anniversary celebration: 'The assets of Stone do not belong to one or several people. They belong to Stone or all of its members as a collective. No one has the right to partition them' (see also STR 75: 9). Wan's claim sounds rhetorical, but it was not without cause. Under Chinese law,[16] the company was collectively owned by its employees. Yet the equity could not be divided among individual employees. This meant that employees owned the company in so far as they constituted a collective; individual employees who left the company could not take equity shares with them. It was also prohibited by law for the company to sell its assets and distribute the proceeds among its members. The ultimate owner of the enterprise is only meaningful upon liquidation. Pursuant to the laws governing collectively owned enterprises, the surplus assets upon liquidation shall be applied towards providing subsidies to unemployed and retired employees and paying the expenses for the re-employment training of employees. Thus, in normal times, the company itself as a legal entity became the de facto owner of the company.

2.1.2. Technology sources

The major technologies that Stone developed into commercial products all had their roots in the state sector. As an extreme case, the two technologists who re-engineered the first printer were young computer experts in the CAS's Computing Centre. They were colleagues of Wan Runnan and were very capable. As Wan recalled:

The Computing Centre was developing the management information system for CAS. Cui, Tong, and I were on the same project team. CAS sent us to Hitachi in Japan to learn the newest computer technologies for several months. We started with the core computer technologies. I knew intimately the abilities of these two men. So when the need to re-engineer the M2024 printer came up, I told Shen Guojun, my associate general manager, to contact them. Our feeling at the time was that if they could not do it in one month, we would abandon the project. They actually solved the problem in eight days.[17]

The two young engineers moonlighted for Stone for extra income. The cost Stone had paid for developing the technology was a consulting fee, equivalent to several months' salaries of the two young technologists. Compared with the million-plus profit that Stone collected from selling the product, the development fee of several hundred RMB was negligible. Similarly, the technological capabilities for developing the integrated Chinese word processor also had their roots in the state sector.

According to one of the team members that developed the integrated word processor, Chinese word-processing technology was ripe for a breakthrough. If Stone had not developed it, some other company would have. But the state research institutions and state-owned enterprises were not in a position to bring about the breakthrough, as best illustrated by the personal experience of Wang Jizhi, the company's

---

[16] The relevant laws governing the collectively owned enterprises are Article 8 of the Constitution of the PRC (1982) and the Law Applicable to the Urban (Cities and Towns) Collectively Owned Enterprises of the PRC (1991). [17] Personal interview in Mar. 1997.

former chief engineer and the system designer of the integrated Chinese word processor, prior to joining Stone.

Wang had worked in the Metallurgy Automation Research Institute under the state's Metallurgy Ministry, where he had been exploring Chinese word-processing technology for years. He recalls:

The task of my institute is developing metallurgy-process automation technology. My research team was working on the automation of the steel-rolling process. My computer knowledge was greatly advanced at the time from working on the computer controlling system of the large-scale imported steel production line at Wuhan Steel Co.

From 1979 there was a climate of openness. Following that time, there was a nationwide computer frenzy. My institute also imported several personal computers from Australia. They came with the English-language word-processing software WordStar as well as DBASE II. These software programs had just been released, and few people in China were aware of them. I found they were very powerful. I thought that if I could make them process Chinese information, it would be a real contribution. So I started developing Chinese word-processing technology and achieved a certain degree of success. In the process, one of my sister's classmates loaned me an imported printer. I was surprised by the fact that each dot of the printing head is programmable. I, therefore, wrote a program to print out Chinese characters. It worked. I then wrote a Chinese character input program. By doing all these, I basically developed a complete Chinese information-processing system. Although it was primitive, it was a significant achievement at the time. I then developed an accounting software program for the institute's accounting department and a Chinese-language database system for housing exchanges. That was in 1982.

In September 1983 the First International Conference on Chinese Information-Processing Technology was held in Beijing. I submitted a paper reporting my results, and it was accepted.[18] It caused a shock within my research institute. Notice, the first research paper I wrote was about Chinese information-processing technology, not metallurgy. This was very important for me. However, my supervisors thought I was doing irrelevant things. They did not let me continue, instead asking me to work on another metallurgy project.

I was starting to think about the organizational problems in the old system and planning to set up a company. There were already dozens of new computer companies in the Zhongguancun area. The first thing I needed to start a company was, of course, money. I talked to the heads of my institute to see if the institute could invest some money to start a company. They let me write a plan. However, it was not approved, and no explanation was given. I felt that it was impossible to do these kind of things within the research institute. I then went on to talk to the head of the R&D department of CITIC.[19] This guy spoke very good English (very Westernized), but he told me that my idea was very capitalistic; it would definitely fail in the socialist system. It was really disappointing. That was basically my experience before I joined Stone.[20]

Wang Jizhi came to Stone by coincidence. He met one of Stone's managers, Wang Anshi, in central Beijing in the summer of 1984. At that time, he was frustrated by

[18] Wang's paper was later published in the Symposium of the First International Conference on Chinese Information Processing Technology, where there were more than 50 research papers. The symposium's content clearly showed that the basic technologies behind Chinese word processing were already taking shape in various state research institutions.

[19] CITIC is one of the largest state-run investment trusts in China.

[20] Personal interview.

not being able to persuade people to put his idea into a working agenda. Wang Anshi, an associate general manager at the time, invited him to join the company. They had met one another in a cadre camp during the Cultural Revolution. There, Wang Anshi had witnessed Wang Jizhi's potential: he had seen Wang Jizhi transcribe the music of an entire concert while listening to the radio, and then conduct it afterwards during one of the camp's social events. Wang Jizhi accepted the invitation, and left the state institute. Stone paid him a starting salary of RMB 500 per month, which was about four times higher than his salary from the state research institute.[21] He was soon appointed head of the development team for the integrated Chinese word processor. The company provided him with all the necessary resources. The project allowed him to fulfil his potential. Within a year, the integrated Chinese word processor was out on the market. Wang's case is often cited by Stone's management as an example of its capability in translating technology resources, previously under-utilized in the state sector, into commercial realities.

In fact, all three members of the development team for the integrated Chinese word processor were from state research institutes or state-owned enterprises. One of them, another self-taught expert in Chinese word-processing technology, had an experience very similar to Wang Jizhi's. Having met him at a conference, Wang invited him to join the team developing the word processor. The third person was a senior computer scientist from CAS's Institute of Computing Technology. With his strong computer technology background, he provided valuable suggestions to Wang on key technological issues. Interestingly enough, he formally joined Stone only after the product was developed. In other words, he provided his technology service to Stone when he was still an employee at the Institute.

When asked how much Stone had benefited from drawing resources freely from the state sector and using them to develop their products, one of the former members of the development team, currently a senior vice-president, said frankly:

Incalculable. All of us received our training in computer science and technology when we were working for various state work units. There were tons of technological deposits in the state sectors. Under the old system, no one cared about commercializing them. The researchers finished one lab project and went on to another. Just look at CAS, thirty years of government investment helped to accumulate huge amount of technology resources. To use Wan's [the first president of Stone] words, you could pick them up everywhere freely. What Stone did is to commercialize them. Again, to cite Wan, if you spend one unit of energy to develop the technology, you need to add two more units of energy to develop it into a product, then you need seven units of energy to market it (STR 75: 6).[22]

The fact that it was Stone, and not an existing state-owned enterprise or research institution, that had first brought the product to market indicates its effectiveness in developing new technology products. This stands in sharp contrast to the

---

[21] Money did not seem to be the major reason for him to join the company, for he had to give up all the benefits as a state employee such as job tenure, virtually free housing, health insurance, guaranteed pensions, etc., which were not exactly comparable to what he received. The major motivation for him, according to his own account, was to be able to translate his idea into reality.

[22] Personal interview in May 1996.

traditional mode of technology development under central planning. In fact, the Ministry of Electronics Industry had actually planned to develop the products; it never happened. To cite a former member of the development team again:

At the time, the Ministry of Electronics Industry actually assembled a five-person investigative team, including people from two research institutes and two computer manufacturing plants under the Ministry of Electronics Industry. The five-man team went to the US, Japan, and Europe. They came back with a proposal to develop the product. I remember that the chief engineer of the state-owned Beijing Number One Computer Manufacturing Factory once told me: 'we thought of the product earlier than you, but when your product was already on the market, our proposal was still pending approval'.

The reason for state sector's slow action was the cumbersome bureaucratic procedures that were institutionalized during the central planning era. Only after a project was approved and put into the state's budgetary plan, could the money for developing a new product come forth. This process usually took years.[23] Without substantial reform, the state-owned enterprises or institutions were certainly not in a position to develop products with rapidly changing technologies.

2.2. The New Institutional Structure of Enterprise Governance

The key to Stone's rapid success was that it created a new organizational framework that could effectively use the technological potential accumulated in the state sector and translate that potential into commercial successes. The system designer of the integrated Chinese word processor concluded after the product's huge success: 'to be honest, without the skills in Chinese information-processing technologies that I and my colleagues had accumulated in the state sector, the product would never have been developed so rapidly. Conversely, had we not come to Stone, the technology would perhaps still be a dream. Stone provides a good organizational environment for technology development' (STR 87: 4).

In fact, company management portrayed Stone through the media as a pioneer in China's economic reform. The company's English name 'Stone' was interpreted more specifically as exploring new directions in China's intricate economic reform. The company logo was designed as a stone hitting a hard wall with sparks coming out. It implies that 'Stone is exploring a new avenue for Chinese economic reform. It is a small stone paving the way for economic reform. If it succeeds, however, it could be a milestone' (STR: 17).

Of course, Stone was not the first non-governmental S&T enterprise in China. However, its huge success in the market place placed its organizational rules and practices in the spotlight. In fact, most of these rules and practices were later institutionalized as organizing principles for all new S&T enterprises in Beijing's Haidian

---

[23] This implies that state enterprises either had no incentives to invest their own financial resources in new product development, or they simply had no autonomy in making investment decisions. It seems both were the case at the time.

District (where Stone was located) when part of the district was officially designated as an experimental zone for new and high-tech industries in 1988.[24]

Stone's management summarized its organizational principle as the 'four autonomies'—autonomy in financing, in recruiting, in managing, and in balancing the budget. The four autonomies were meant to contrast with the organizing principles of the traditional enterprises under central planning. They later became the defining features of China's non-governmental S&T enterprises.

The organizational principle that Stone had pioneered represented a new institutional structure of enterprise governance—if we define enterprise governance as an institutional structure that determines who makes investment decisions, what types of investments they make, and how returns generated by these investments are distributed (O'Sullivan 1996). In this section I will discuss the issues of who makes the investment decisions and how returns are distributed. I will document what type of investment was made in the next section.

2.2.1. The 'four autonomies'

To a large extent, the new organizational principle that Stone embodied represented a breakthrough in the direction of separating the regulatory function of the state from that of the management of enterprises. The four autonomies formed a coherent organizational principle.

To start with, unlike the start-up of a new enterprise under central planning whereby a large chunk of start-up capital was granted by various levels of governments via state budgetary channels, Stone started with a small loan from a rural township. Its operational capital was almost exclusively from bank loans in the beginning, and from bank loans and retained earnings later on.[25] In this way Stone was responsible for its own gains and losses. In other words, it was financially independent from the state. The ramification was that the boundary between the government and Stone was clarified; the government no longer had the right to take away profits from Stone other than legally defined taxes. Correspondingly, the government would no longer assume the obligation to subsidize the enterprise should it incur losses.

Furthermore, unlike the fact that the recruitment for a new enterprise under central planning was an integral part of the state's capital budgetary plan, Stone recruited its employees independently. All of Stone's founders had left their state work units, and given up the privileges associated with their state-employee status. It meant that their wages or salaries were no longer under the state personnel budgetary plan (*renshi bianzhi*). The subsequent recruitment of new employees was conducted through personal references in the beginning and, from 1987, open-market

---

[24] Stone was praised by a high-level government official as a birthplace of new ideas for economic reform (STR 72: 2).

[25] As an experiment, Stone had also issued some stocks to its employees in 1985 and 1986, but it was small compared with the total capital needs. This is because the stockholding company as an institutional framework did not surface until the early 1990s in China.

operations (STR 22: 4) rather than through the state's recruitment channels as was often the case in the state sector.[26] By doing so, Stone had effectively broken the *iron rice bowl* that had characterized the employment system among state-owned-enterprises, for the wages and salaries of its employees were no longer guaranteed by the state budget.

The extra-budgetary (outside central-planning channels) nature of finance and personnel laid the foundation for managerial autonomy, as manifested on two fronts. First, it was Stone's management, not the bureaucrats at various state agencies, who made the company's business decisions, including decisions concerning investment and production as well as personnel. Under central planning, it had been the planning authorities. This independence in decision-making was a logical extension of financial independence, for if government agencies made the business decisions for enterprises, they should also bear the financial consequences of that decision. It is worth while to point out that managerial independence in making business decisions was important from the point of view of integrating strategists into the process of innovation—a key factor that characterizes many innovative enterprises in Western economies (O'Sullivan 1996).

Second, unlike state-owned enterprises where wages and salaries have to follow a national standard wage-and-salary scheme without much room for adjustment at the enterprise level, Stone's management was able to structure its internal payment schemes as it saw fit. The management-devised payment schemes partially tied wages to performance of business units and individuals. Such payment schemes alleviated the free-loader problem that can result from excessive egalitarianism in the pay structure. The latter was characteristic of the state sector, 'where every one earns roughly the same wages, no matter how hard they work, or don't work' (Furst 1988).

2.2.2. Rules governing the distribution of financial returns

The four autonomies had clear implications for the enterprise's operations. Stone's management characterized their employment system as a *'clay rice bowl'*, meaning that their livelihood was no longer guaranteed without hard work. It used this sense of insecurity as a lever to mobilize employees. The argument was made that the *clay*

---

[26] The budgetary recruitment channel worked like this: Every year enterprises that needed to increase their workforces made requests to the personnel bureaux for white-collar workers or to labour bureaux for blue-collar workers. After collecting all the requests, the personnel and labour bureaux reported the total to the planning committee. The planning committee balanced the demand with its overall budgetary plan, and made the final decision. The personnel bureaux and labour bureaux then executed the hiring plan through either passing new hiring quotas to neighbourhood committees for middle-school or high-school graduates (often hired as blue-collar workers by labour bureaux) or channelling new college graduates to enterprises as white-collar workers (by personnel bureaux). An important aspect of this process was that once a person was hired, there would be a corresponding wage-and-benefits budget. This incited enterprise managers to hoard labour because the wage-and-benefits budget was granted directly from the state budget, independent of the enterprises' performance. This was also an important reason behind the over-employment problem in the state-owned enterprises, which surfaced after the government started to tie wage-and-benefits budgets to the financial performance of the state-owned enterprises in the course of economic reform.

rice bowl at Stone could be more secure than the *iron rice bowl*. The reason was simple. To quote Wan, Stone's former president:

We think the *clay rice bowl* will be more solid than the *iron rice bowl*. Why? Because everyone thinks that since the iron rice bowl is made of iron, it would not break. No one would take care of it, no one would work hard to maintain it. As time goes by, the rice in the bowl will be getting thinner and thinner, and finally, nothing will be left in the bowl. In contrast, the content in the clay rice bowl depends on how hard we work. If we don't commit ourselves, if we don't maintain it wholeheartedly with our sweat and intelligence, we would be left with nothing to eat. So we all feel the imperative to work hard. As a result, the *clay rice bowl* could turn into a *gold rice bowl* (STR 75: 4).

In fact, Stone has been paying out wages and salaries to its employees about twice as high on average as those of state-owned enterprises.[27] These higher returns to employees were partly due to the superior financial performance of the company, and partly due to the autonomy that the management had in determining payment schemes within the company.

Nevertheless, Stone could have paid out even higher wages and salaries given its unusually high profit rates in its early years of operation. As we can see from Table 2.2, in comparison with profits, wages and salaries were very small. Obviously, the company management had refrained from paying out even higher wages and salaries. The source of this discipline was the company's collective nature.

As mentioned before, the company was initially set up as a collective enterprise under the jurisdiction of Evergreen Township. Although, as a rural township collective enterprise, Stone did not have to follow the strict rules set for state-owned enterprises, it still had to follow the rules set for collectives in general and for rural township collectives in particular. According to accounting procedures, there was an upper limit for the amount of wages or salaries per person that was allowed to enter into the cost structure. The accounting term was 'before tax wage allowance' (*jishui gongzi*). It was set at around the national average for wage-and-salary levels. Wages and salaries paid beyond that limit were counted as part of profits and subject to enterprise income taxes. Thus, the incentive to pay higher wages and salaries could be held in check if the company income-tax rate was high. However, apart from the first year of operation when the company paid a 30 per cent income tax on its profit, according to the rate set for rural township enterprises, it had been exempted from paying income tax until 1992 (with an exception in 1988 due to an interim policy

---

[27] Because the wages and salaries have been changing constantly in recent years, partly due to the increase in general income levels, partly due to changes in payment schemes both within Stone and among the state enterprises, it is very hard to make an accurate comparison. The estimate above was given by the head of the personnel department of Stone, who has been involved in the company's human resource management since its early days, and was constantly monitoring payment and welfare benefits across industries for benchmarks in making human resource policy decisions. She said, according to her best estimate, 'taking all the benefits (both visible and hidden) into account, including wages, salaries, housing, medical care, etc., the average income at Stone is about twice as high as an average income in society at large. The ratio also varies. It was a bit higher in the early days, and has lowered in recent years' (personal interview). Her estimate is in agreement with the first newspaper report on Stone that appeared in the English-language *China Daily* on 26 June 1985. The newspaper reported: 'The company's pay scale is two or three times higher than average Chinese wages'.

TABLE 2.3. *Estimates of bonus pay-out at Stone* (currency figures in 1,000 RMB)

	1984	1985	1986	1987
1. Sales	9,760	32,200	123,580	317,130
2. After-tax profits	1,430	4,250	9,340	25,000
3. Bonus funds (20% of after-tax profit, 10% for 1984)	143	850	1,868	5,000
4. Number of employees (year end)	67	113	246	417
5. Average number of employees (estimate)	34	90	180	332
6. Pre-tax wage allowance	33	86	173	319
7. Paid wages (including bonuses)	136	302	558	661
8. Paid bonuses	106	216	385	342
9. Paid bonuses as % of the bonus fund	74.1%	25.4%	20.6%	6.8%

Source: Yu 1988: 159.

discontinuity).[28] Therefore, the limit of the 'before tax wage allowance' should not have been an effective constraint on the company to pay out higher wages. It only served as a benchmark, against which the company could assess its own wage policy. The wage-and-salary level, therefore, depended on the rules governing the distribution of the profits.

As mentioned before, as a result of the initial negotiation between the founders of Stone and the Evergreen Township following the rules set for rural collectives, 20 per cent of the profit was initially set as the remittance to Evergreen Township, with another 40 per cent earmarked for the enterprise development fund, 30 per cent for the employee welfare fund, and 10 per cent for the employee bonus fund (*China Daily*, 26 June 1985). After the township withdrew from the company in mid-1985, company management reset the proportions to 50 per cent, 30 per cent, and 20 per cent for enterprise development, employee welfare, and employee bonus funds respectively. The 5:3:2 ratio of profit disposition reflected a balance between collective rationality (the long-term development of the enterprise as a collective) and individual rationality (current earnings of the employees) with the employee welfare fund as a binding mechanism between the individual and the collective.

Since the company's profits were so high, if it had dispersed all the bonus funds (20 per cent of net profit), the income of Stone's employees would have been unusually high compared with the vast majority of the employees at other enterprises. Stone actually had paid out only a fraction of the bonus fund in the early years (Table 2.3).

[28] Tax exemption privileges were granted to companies in the high-tech industries. It was initially granted by the local government within the scope of its jurisdiction until 1988, and after 1989 by the central government. This was part of the government's industrial policy for promoting high-tech industries. It created a vital institutional environment for Stone as well as other high-tech enterprises including Legend and Founder to develop.

There were two constraints on the payment scale at the time. One had to do with the moral obligations the company held towards society at large. Because the company paid much higher wages and salaries to its employees, it caused jealousy among employees in the state sector, who were used to enjoying high status in society. The mayor of Beijing once made a personal appeal to the president of Stone, and urged him to consider his 'neighbours' (meaning employees of other enterprises) in determining the pay levels for its employees. The mayor could not order him to do this because Stone was not a state-owned enterprise.[29] Nevertheless, responding to societal pressures, the management at Stone refrained from paying out high wages. Part of the reason was that the company's management did not want to cause controversy over its highly independent organizational behaviour, which was exceptional amid a sea of traditionally run enterprises. In an editorial in the company's internal newsletter on 24 July 1987, the management justified why it did not pay higher wages: 'Only this way, could we secure a good social environment for the healthy development of the company', it said (STR 36: 2–3).

A more effective check on the levels of wages and salaries later came from a new income-tax code. In a move to solve the increasing income disparity arising in the course of economic reform, the state council issued a temporary statute on personal income tax on 25 September 1987. It substantially lowered the minimum level of income subject to personal income tax.[30] Because it was a progressive tax with very sharp increments, a very high proportion of the increase in income would be taxed away. People at Stone, just like everyone else in China, were not used to the idea of giving money to the state for free.[31] Besides, the money, if not paid out, would be there in the company. The state would not take it away as would be the case in the state-owned enterprises. The sizeable undistributed bonus fund, together with the welfare fund, was accounted for as debts to employees on the company balance sheet. The company used these funds as interest-free working capital.[32]

It would appear that these regulations set constraints on the company's autonomy. However, they did not necessarily inhibit the development of the enterprise. After all, people had given up their job tenure in the state sector hoping that Stone would be an alternative where they could fulfil their personal potential and enjoy higher incomes and job security. The high proportion of profit being dedicated to the enterprise developmental fund was required to provide the capital accumulation that would enable the company to endure. The welfare fund was necessary because there

[29] Personal interviews with a former vice-president of Stone in Apr. 1996.

[30] The first personal income-tax law was implemented in 1981. The minimum monthly income exempted from personal income tax was RMB 800. At that time, there was only an extremely small percentage of people in China that had a monthly income exceeding that figure. The majority of people had monthly incomes of less than RMB 100. It was rare to hear of someone paying personal income tax at that time. The new income-tax code lowered the minimum taxable monthly income to RMB 400.

[31] There was no personal income tax in China previously.

[32] The accumulated welfare fund was later turned into the employee housing fund and placed under individual employee's accounts. Employees were allowed to use it to buy houses. Part of the bonus fund was later used to buy the company's stocks at its initial public offering on the Hong Kong Stock Exchange. It was then distributed among employees according to certain rules relating to rank and seniority. The total of these stocks was about 2.5% of the company's outstanding share issues.

was no alternative social safety net outside of the state sector.[33] Besides, the extra capital the company derived from the welfare funds and the undistributed bonus funds was certainly helpful in accelerating its capital accumulation.

2.3. Indigenous Innovation, Learning, and Capability Acquisition: Progressive Integration of R&D, Marketing, and Manufacturing

The aforementioned new institutional arrangements are relevant for two dimensions of the institutional structure of enterprise governance, namely, who makes the decisions and how the financial returns are distributed. The next question is what type of investments were made under the new organizational framework. In other words, given the managerial autonomy and the constraints on the allocation of financial resources, what learning and investment strategy had the company pursued to build momentum for growth? This section is intended to show that, to a large extent, the organizational principle under which Stone operated shaped company strategies with regard to the acquisition of organizational capabilities. It is by no means a coincidence that company management chose a strategy that finally resulted in its domination of the product market for the integrated Chinese word processor.

2.3.1. Trade and high-tech-product 'forward engineering'

Because the start-up capital of Stone was very small, even negligible, management's first priority was to accumulate capital if it wanted to accomplish anything. Without relying on government grants, the only way of accumulating capital was through trade. To quote two of the founders of Stone:

Stone was initially named Stone New Industry Development Corporation, because we wanted to set up our own high-tech manufacturing plant. When I was working in the state-run computer manufacturing plant, we already knew there were lights-off plants in advanced industrial nations. However, we were still making computers manually. We knew the gap was huge. One of the reasons to set up our own company was to catch up. Why couldn't the Chinese do it? But as soon as the company started, the dream was broken instantly. High-tech manufacturing needs a huge amount of capital. Who will give you the money? We were only a small rural township enterprise, and no one would take us seriously. So the first thing was to accumulate capital.[34]

For enterprises that rely on government grants, capital is not a big issue. For us, because we did not receive a penny from the state, the only place to get the money was the market. How do we make money in the market place? The answer is: selling technology. Stone makes money by selling commodities that embody our technologies (STR 75: 5).

---

[33] The necessity of setting aside a large welfare fund was due to the housing situation. Housing was not commercialized at the time. In the state sector, employees' housing was usually built by enterprises out of state budgetary grants and distributed according to seniority and rank. Employees only paid a symbolic amount of monthly rent (about 2–5% of monthly income). The non-governmental enterprises were responsible for providing housing for their employees, which was a large expenditure.

[34] Interview with one of the founders, currently a vice-president of Stone, in Apr. 1996.

Indeed, what distinguishes Stone from a conventional trading company is the high technology content of the commodities, which makes heavy demands on both before- and after-sales services. Furthermore, the commodity often embodies technology functions resulting from R&D efforts because many imported high-tech products have to be adapted to local conditions.

This activity is often called 're-engineering or forward engineering' (*erci kaifa*), which is derived from the term 'reverse engineering'. The difference is that 'reverse engineering' refers to a technology development strategy that imitates and replicates technologies embodied in imported goods, while 're-engineering' here refers to a process that adds new technological functions to imported products and tailors them to local specifications. It often entails substantial R&D efforts. This is particularly the case for a computer information-processing system because almost all imported computer information-processing systems are general-purpose systems that are not designed specifically for the Chinese market and have to be re-engineered before they can process Chinese information.

It was typical for new S&T firms at the time to conduct trade with general-purpose high-tech commodities. Because of high demands on imported computers and peripherals, on the one hand, and special skills involved in before- and after-sales service for these products, on the other, a company could generally do well by specializing in high-tech commodity trade. Stone did market imported computer systems and peripherals and had set up one of the largest and most complete trading centres for imported electronic components in Beijing. However, Stone's real 'hits' on the market were its re-engineered products.

As mentioned before, in the wake of a wave of large-scale imports of IBM PCs and compatibles in the early 1980s, there existed high demand for computer printers as output devices. The standard printer that was designed for printing Chinese fonts was the Toshiba M-3070 printer. The product was imported by the State Electronic Product Import and Export Co. under the Ministry of Electronics Industry and was very expensive—its import price was US $1,400, and was resold in China at RMB 9,000 (STR 63: 5). While other models were also available in the market, they could not handle Chinese fonts, particularly when connected to an IBM/PC—the most widely used brand of personal computers in China. Stone decided to re-engineer a new generation of the Japanese-made printer—the Brother M-2024, which was sold at a lower price (less than US $800), and was capable of printing Chinese fonts from an IBM/PC. Stone worked out a Chinese font driver (software) and corresponding hardware specifications. It basically solved three key technological issues with respect to handling Chinese fonts from IBM/PCs: (1) the issue of missing the ASCII code when communicating with an IBM/PC; (2) the issue of transferring graphics between an IBM/PC and the printer; (3) the issue of inputting Chinese fonts from the computer to the printer.[35] Stone then went to the printer's dealer—the Japanese trade giant Mitsui Trading Company to buy the printer directly from Japan. Due to the high market potential of the product, Stone was able to negotiate a sufficiently low

---

[35] From the company's brochure issued on 1 Oct. 1986.

purchase price (US $500) and sell it in China at a wholesale price of RMB 4,500 after adding the Chinese font driver and changing one wire connection in the printer.

The financing of the operation was based on short-term bank loans. In this case, the first order of printers was financed by an RMB one million short-term bank loan from the Haidian District branch of the State Agricultural Bank. The source of the hard currency needed to import the product was from an extra-budgetary source. In this case, it was from the retained hard currency of the State Construction Materials Import and Export Company under the Ministry of Construction (arranged exchange rate was US $1 to RMB 3.7—the official rate was 1 for RMB 2.8).[36] Because the printer was priced at only half of the prevailing Toshiba M-3070 model, with equivalent functions and more compact size, it became an instant best-seller. The first 200 printers were sold out within three days after arriving from Japan. Stone was able to pay back the short-term bank loan on time. The quick turnaround of stock eased the constraint of capital, and quickened the pace of capital accumulation.

Stone sold more than 2,000 of the printers in its first year of operations, and earned a comfortable profit (a net profit of close to RMB 1.5 million). In the second year, Stone re-engineered another printer model. In addition to a Chinese font driver, it added a special Chinese font generator, speeding up the printing process considerably.

Because of the added technology content, the proportion of value-added from re-engineering is very high. According to an estimate between the difference of wholesale prices of the re-engineered printer and the cost of importing the product, the percentage of gross value-added could be as high as 60 per cent. Thus, the two re-engineered products became the major sources of profits for Stone in its first two years of operation. Stone was able to accumulate sizeable capital that laid a foundation for further expansion into R&D and manufacturing.

An important ramification of integrating trade and R&D is that it helped to build market consciousness. It made the decision-makers at Stone more keenly aware of market needs. Research and development activities closely followed the market. Over time, a mutual enhancement mechanism between marketing and R&D was established. That is, the market became the compass for R&D activities; and R&D reinforced the firm's market position.

2.3.2. From 'forward engineering' to system design: The breakthrough innovation of the integrated Chinese word processor

Besides building marketing capability and accumulating capital, the early R&D activities associated with re-engineering in the area of Chinese font printing tech-

---

[36] Under strict central planning, all the hard currency from export goods had to be submitted to the central government. The State Import and Export Company had no independent hard currency reserves. The planning agencies allocated hard currency to the enterprises when they needed to import goods. As an initiative of reforming the foreign trade system, mainly for stimulating incentives for export, state-run import and export companies were allowed to retain a certain portion of the hard currency under their own disposition, even though the use of the funds was still heavily regulated. Thus Stone was able to get access to these funds through an arrangement with the State Construction Materials Import and Export Company. For a comprehensive account of the reform of the foreign trade system in China from 1978 to 1988, see the chapter by John Kamm in Vogel 1989.

nology became the starting point for Stone to build its core competence in Chinese word-processing technology. Stone moved from Chinese font printing technology to the integrated Chinese word processor, of which printing technology was an indispensable part. The R&D strength of Stone finally brought it to dominance in the integrated Chinese word-processor market.

The prelude toward developing the integrated Chinese word processor   The idea of developing an integrated Chinese word processor originated during a dinner conversation between a Hong Kong businessman Charles Liu and Stone's president, Wan Runnan, in January 1985. Liu suggested that Stone develop an integrated Chinese information-processing system that could function as a Chinese word processor, a printer, and a telex. The suggestion was to re-engineer the American-made COLEX brand laptop computer, of which Charles Liu was a distributor, into a Chinese word processor. Charles Liu would be responsible for resolving the payment problem resulting from importing the computer from abroad. Stone organized a research team of four people, all of whom were employees of various state institutes. The team was led by Wang Yuqian from CAS's Institute of Computing Technology. In fact, the development process was conducted in the Institute of Computing Technology without the heads of the institute even being aware of it. Wang and his team had completed the re-engineering process by mid-April. However, due to changes in Charles Liu's trading conditions, he was no longer able to balance the payments in hard currency, and the project was aborted.

Instead, Stone's management put its major R&D effort into re-engineering the second printer, the M-1570, after the technology know-how of the first re-engineered printer was no longer profitable due to lack of enforceable software protection measures in China. The major advance Stone made in re-engineering the M-1570 was to develop a Chinese font add-on card in addition to a font driver (software), accomplished by Wang Jizhi, who later became the system designer of the integrated Chinese word processor.

Before the breakthrough of the new integrated Chinese word processor, Stone already possessed sufficient technological capability. Table 2.4 shows the trajectory of technology accumulation, as embodied by the three members of the development team, that led to the breakthrough innovation of the integrated Chinese word processor.

Partnership in product development—the role of Mitsui   Although the first attempt to develop a Chinese word processor had been abandoned, the idea of specializing in Chinese information-processing technology became clearer as sales of the second re-engineered printer, M-1570, increased. The project was put on the agenda again in mid-1985 when an opportunity came.

Of course, the task of re-engineering is relatively easy with respect to manufacturing. To re-engineer the M-2024 printer only required changing one wire connection in the hardware. The Chinese font driver is software, and as such does not require manufacturing capabilities. The Chinese font add-on card for the M-1570 is also a stand-alone part. When it came to producing a whole system, the manufacturing

TABLE 2.4. *The experience of the three key members of the development team for Stone's integrated Chinese word processor*

The three members of the R&D team	State work units before joining Stone	Experience from state work units	Experience with Stone before the integrated Chinese word processor	Contribution to the development of the MS-2400 integrated Chinese word processor
Wang Jizhi	Metallurgy Automation Institute	Developed a preliminary Chinese word-processing system	Chinese font generator add-on card for M-1570 printer	System design and system software development
Wang Yuqian	Institute of Computing Technology	General computer technologies	Chinese word-processing system on COLEX computer; Chinese font driver for M-1570 printer	Suggestions on key technology choices, including choosing Intel 8088 series CPU rather than Z80 series, using computer simulation technology as a development environment; the printing module of the system software
Sun Qiang	Capital Steel	Developed a Chinese accounting software system	n.a.	The Chinese font generator

Source: Synthesized from interviews and company documents.

technology in China at the time was not sufficient. Therefore, it was necessary to have a foreign partner before serious efforts to develop the product could be launched. In fact, the strategy that the Chinese should develop the software and foreign companies should provide the hardware had long preoccupied Wang Jizhi, who would later become the system designer of the integrated Chinese word processor, as a possible short cut for China to develop high-tech industries.

The opportunity came when the Japanese trade giant Mitsui & Co. invited the top managers and engineers of Stone to visit Japan in June 1985, as a result of the successful co-operation between the two companies in promoting the first re-engineered printer, the M-2024. The purpose of the visit was to explore further collaborative opportunities beyond the mere purchasing–supplying relationship. The project of developing the Chinese word processor was agreed upon during the two-week visit. The two sides agreed that Stone would work on the system specifications and develop the system software, the application software, and Chinese font generator while Mitsui would assume the task of hardware engineering design and manufacturing. In August, Stone came up with the system design and the hardware specifications. Because Mitsui is a trading company, the actual development of the hardware was subcontracted to a Japanese contract manufacturer, Alps Electronics Co., Inc. In March 1986 Alps provided the product prototype. The three members of Stone's development team went to Japan, jointly testing the product with the Alps' team. Alps also became the manufacturer of the product after the product tests were completed.

By July 1986 the product had been supplied to the Chinese market in quantity. The Chinese had long been waiting for a product like this to replace the heavy and extremely inefficient mechanical Chinese typewriter, plus it had an advantageous performance/price ratio in comparison with a Chinese word-processing system made up of a personal computer and a printer (RMB 8,000 vs. RMB 20,000–30,000). The product was widely welcomed in the market, and demand was so high that 6,200 orders had been placed within one month after the product was announced to the market. This demand was certainly beyond the expectations of both Stone and the Japanese companies. Many orders were filled late because of underplanning in the production and organization of supplies (STR 4: 1).

It should be noted, however, that without the Japanese designing and manufacturing the hardware, it would have been impossible to put the product onto the market in such a short time with reliable quality and at a reasonable price. In response to critics that Stone was helping the Japanese earn money in China, the system designer and the chief engineer of Stone, wrote:

Word-processing software like WordStar had been popular abroad for years. In Japan, integrated word processors have also entered households. The invention of the Chinese word processor is a natural result of technology development. When we were developing the product, there were actually several foreign companies developing the product too. If we had not occupied this market, others would have. According to the current level of manufacturing technology in China's domestic electronics industry, it is impossible to manufacture a completely indigenous Chinese word processor with 100 per cent domestically made parts and components. So what we have done is to prevent foreign companies from profiting more from China. Besides, from our foreign partners we can learn about technology, production management, quality control, etc. I believe, for China, that international collaboration is a short cut in developing high-tech products (STR 87: 4).

Indeed, the development team did learn a lot from their Japanese counterparts in the process of jointly developing the integrated Chinese word processor. To take one example, they learned about market awareness in product development—knowledge that Chinese scientists and engineers, who were used to grants from the state budget for research and development, usually did not have. Again, to quote the chief engineer:

We all came from state research institutions. We think of product development only from a technological point of view. Our philosophy is to have functions as complete as possible and to use parts and components of the best quality possible. We hardly ever consider costs or manufacturability. As a result, the prototype might look nice, but it would not be marketable because of its high cost. Now we learned to start from the market. Before developing the product, we will estimate first what is the highest market acceptable price, calculating the highest acceptable cost, based on profit rate. We then allocate R&D expenses, production costs, costs of parts and components within the limit. Instead of using high-quality, high-priced parts and components, we use parts and components with satisfactory quality. This way, the product itself would not necessarily represent the highest level of technology, but it would be the best in terms of value for price (STR 87: 4).

One concrete case was given by a member of the development team:

When we were developing the product, we had thought about exporting it to the US for use in the United Nations headquarters because we know Chinese is a required language there. So we raised the issue of designing the product to meet the American URL [Uniform Resource Locator] standard. Our Japanese counterparts convinced us not to do this because to meet that standard, it might increase the cost by 10 per cent. Unless there is a large market demand in the US to spread out the cost, it is not worth while. We did know that the demand at UN headquarters was limited.[37]

An important matter in this kind of collaboration is how to keep technological independence; that is, how to avoid being controlled by the technologically more advanced partner. The people from Stone were keenly aware of this problem. According to another member of the development team:

There was no Chinese word processor at the time. We were all new to the product. The company was very poor, provided only with a 8088 computer as development tool. There was no office space for research and development either; we all did the work at home. The hardware part of the MS-2400 was provided by Japan's Alps Inc., we did the system design and software development. Between March and April 1986, we went to Japan to do the joint testing of the system with the Japanese team. One important issue was what kinds of testing equipment to use. The Japanese used a VAX 730 mainframe computer under a multi-user environment. That was very advanced. But we insisted on using the IBM/PC. We built a debug card on the IBM/PC as a testing tool. If we had used the VAX environment, we would have been controlled by the Japanese technologically because we would not be able to do anything independently from the Japanese. Since we did not use the advanced testing equipment provided by the Japanese, but rather insisted on using domestically available equipment, we had to overcome lots of extra difficulties.[38]

As will become clear in the following sections, maintaining technological independence was crucial for Stone to be able to develop new models of the integrated Chinese word processor independently at a later stage.

2.3.3. From outsourcing to in-house manufacturing: Acquiring production technologies through joint-venture arrangements

As indicated above, Stone outsourced its first model of the integrated Chinese word processor to the Japanese contract manufacturer Alps Inc. via Mitsui. The arrange-

---

[37] Personal interview in Apr. 1996.
[38] Transcript of interviews by the company's internal research unit; see also STR 158: 2.

ment is a mixture of original equipment manufacturing (OEM) and original design manufacturing (ODM). In the sense that it was Stone that provided the system design, the arrangement could be categorized as OEM; however, since the Japanese provided the hardware design, it could be categorized as ODM. At any rate, out-sourcing could be a preferential choice under the circumstances of either a shortage of in-house manufacturing facilities due to capital constraints or of production involving only re-engineered products, that is, the manufacturing task is not com-prehensive. As capital accumulated coupled with the progress of the firm's R&D from re-engineering to system design, backward integration into manufacturing came onto the agenda.

It had long been the goal of the company founders to get into the area of high-tech product manufacturing. It had been envisaged from the very beginning that the company would pursue an integrated strategy of R&D, trade, and manufacturing. It became clearer in the early days that the proper sequence for implementing the strat-egy was to start with trade, and then enter manufacturing, with R&D as the under-lying propeller.[39] The strategy of backward integration into manufacturing was referred to as 'industrialization' (*chanyehua*). The rationale behind this strategy was not so much to reap profits as to build up organizational capabilities in the long term. As a vice-president of Stone pointed out straightforwardly: 'Trade is just a means of capital accumulation, but only manufacturing is the root of an enterprise'.[40]

Yet in order to get into the field of manufacturing, an important precondition is the size of the market, which can permit economy of scale in production. The two models of the re-engineered printers and the first model of the Chinese word pro-cessor, the MS-2400, had opened a new market for Chinese word-processing prod-ucts. Unlike traditional state-owned enterprises, which often relied on separate and also state-run distribution channels, Stone had developed its own distribution net-works in the process of selling its traded and re-engineered high-tech products. By mid-1987 Stone had built a nationwide distribution network and an excellent reputation in the Chinese information technology industry, with a comprehensive organizational structure consisting of headquarters, subsidiaries, and branch com-panies across the country (cf. Fig. 2.1).

With the increase in the firm's marketing capability, the time for starting manu-facturing was ripe. The next step was how and where to get the manufacturing tech-nology. That was crucial because the market could only be sustained by quality products. There were three possible ways for Stone to acquire manufacturing capa-bilities. One choice was to collaborate with state-owned enterprises. Some state-owned enterprises had imported state-of-the-art manufacturing facilities and were able to produce goods of an acceptable quality. However, due to conflicts in organi-zational principles, collaboration with state-owned enterprises at the time could be problem-ridden. Besides, given the level of indigenous production technology, most of the parts and components had to be imported anyway. The second choice was

[39] At the company meeting on 5 Aug. 1984, Wan, the then president of the company, further clari-fied the company's strategy as such (company archives).

[40] Personal interview in Apr. 1994.

self-reliance. Because Stone started from high-tech commodity trading, it had no experience in manufacturing, and it could have taken years to develop the capability independently. The third choice was through joint-venture arrangements with foreign multinationals. As in product development, joint ventures in manufacturing were believed to be short cuts to reach world-class manufacturing capabilities as well as to have access to managerial know-how. Stone had chosen the last approach, and established a joint venture with Japan's Mitsui & Co.

The Stone–Mitsui joint venture grew out of their early collaborations. More specifically, it evolved around the development of the integrated Chinese word processor. As mentioned before, encouraged by the success in the collaboration with Mitsui in supplying the M-2024 printer, Stone came to an agreement with Mitsui to jointly develop the integrated Chinese word processor. In 1986 Stone and Mitsui (through Alps) successfully developed the first model of the integrated Chinese word processor, the MS-2400. Unable to manufacture it, Stone outsourced the production to Alps. However, this first model of the integrated Chinese word processor was more like a market-test product. Because it was the first such product in China, both sides, particularly the Japanese partners involved, were not sure about the market prospects of the product. The product design was based on the minimum requirements for functionality. Alps did not even make a plastic die for the case: it was made out of sheet metal. Because market demand was underestimated, production was underplanned. As a result, the MS-2400 was in short supply all the time. Only a total of 8,000 units were produced in one year (compared with the 6,200 units ordered in just the first month).

It was clear that the market demand for the integrated Chinese word processor in China was large. It prompted the two sides to develop a second model of the integrated Chinese word processor, the MS-2401, incorporating more features and functions. Meanwhile, Stone and Mitsui agreed to set up a joint venture to produce this new product. The proposal for setting up the joint venture—Beijing Stone Office Equipment Technology Co., Ltd. (Beijing SOTEC)—was submitted to the planning committee of the Beijing Municipal Government on 24 March 1986. It was approved on 27 May by the State Industry and Commerce Administrative Bureau. The fact that it had taken only two months and three days for the project to be approved was unusual, given the complexity of procedures in setting up a joint venture in China at the time.[41]

More unusual was the equity structure of the joint venture. According to the joint-venture agreement, its purpose was to apply the advanced electronics technology of the Japanese partner and the word-processing technology of the Chinese partner to the process of jointly developing and manufacturing office automation equipment (mainly integrated Chinese word processors). The total investment was US $4 million, of which Stone's share was 75 per cent and Mitsui's 25 per cent. Details of the equity structure are as follows:

---

[41] In fact, it was one of the fastest approved joint-venture projects in Beijing to that date. That certainly reflected the impact of Stone as a leading new S&T enterprise, as well as the capacities of Stone's top management to mobilize political resources within the government.

Stone:

Total investment: US $3 million (75% of total); of which:

   technology know-how: US $1.2 million (30% of total);

   plant site usage fee: US $1.07 million (28% of total);

   cash: $0.73 million (17% of total).

Mitsui:

Total investment: US $1 million (25% of total);

   all in cash.[42]

Note that Stone's technology know-how accounted for a 30 per cent share of the total investment. This was unusual, because it is often the case that it is the foreign partner in a joint venture who is the sole technology supplier. The 30 per cent share of equity granted to Stone for its technology know-how indicates the weight of Stone's indigenous technology capability in the collaboration.

It was Stone's intention to use the joint venture as a vehicle for acquiring product design, manufacturing, and management know-how from its Japanese partner. This was reflected in the article on mutual obligations of the partners in the joint-venture agreement. According to that article, the joint-venture partners assumed the following duties and obligations respectively:

Stone:

1. systems design and software development;
2. marketing the products in China and Hong Kong;
3. providing managers, technicians, and workers for the joint venture;
4. providing market information on China and Hong Kong.

Mitsui:

1. supplying parts and components;
2. developing hardware;
3. marketing the products in places other than China and Hong Kong;
4. providing manufacturing and testing technologies, training Chinese managers and technicians;
5. providing market information on parts and components.

The most important provision in the above list is the obligation Mitsui assumed to provide manufacturing technology and train Chinese managers and technicians. Because the joint venture was basically run by the Chinese (Mitsui only dispatched an associate general manager, who flew in from Japan once a month), technological and managerial training became indispensable to assure the quality of production. From the very first year of operations, various training programmes were implemented according to a mutually agreed comprehensive training plan. Almost all the line operators had been sent to Japan once. At the middle-management level, line managers and staff personnel in functional departments were sent to Japan for training according to a schedule of four people per course, twice a year. At the highest level, the Japanese provided training opportunities for two people per year. Through the frequent visits at all levels, the joint venture successfully transferred the

---

[42] From Beijing SOTEC charter, Article 11 (Beijing SOTEC Archives).

Japanese management model, including job category, operations layout, quality standards, quality inspection, and just-in-time production, etc. (STR 141: 4).

The comprehensive training, to a certain degree, paved the way for a process technology transfer from Japan. The joint venture started with the assembly of the new model of the integrated Chinese word processor, MS-2401 on the SKD basis. Mitsui first purchased parts and components according to the specifications set by the hardware design engineers at Alps. It then let Alps assemble the parts and components into semi-knocked-down condition. Mitsui then supplied the SKD kits to the joint venture in Beijing.

The process of internalizing manufacturing capability in the joint venture includes two interrelated aspects. One is moving from SKD-based production to CKD-based production. The second is localizing parts and components.

The issue of localization was imperative right after the start of the production, because of the hard currency balance of payments problem. On the one hand, the government had set very strict rules for joint ventures with regard to the ratios of domestically made parts and components and exportation of the final goods for consideration of the balance of payments at the macroeconomic level. On the other hand, the joint-venture partners both had incentives to raise the content of domestically made parts and components. Because the major market for the integrated Chinese word processor was in China, given the fact that most of the parts and components were originally supplied by the Japanese while only very few final products found their way in the international market, balance of payments became one of the key issues right after production started. As one of the assistant managers at SOTEC recalls, 'One of the biggest headaches was locating hard currency. I remember I spent a lot of time going to the Beijing Municipal Bureau of Foreign Exchange Administration, negotiating with state-owned companies for hard-currency quotas. There always seemed to be a danger that we would not be able to come up with the hard currency needed to pay for the next bulk of supplies'.[43] Obviously, any increase in the ratio of localization would reduce the balance of payments burden for the joint venture. It also reduced costs of production because domestically made parts tended to be cheaper.

A team consisting of high-level managers and engineers from Stone was sent to Japan shortly after the start of production, exploring the possibilities of localization of parts and production. They visited production lines and spoke to Japanese engineers about technology specifications and production perimeters for the localization of parts and components as well as production. However, although Mitsui had certain incentives for localization, the contract manufacturers did not, for they did not want to sacrifice their business. Therefore, the team had only limited success in getting technology information from their Japanese counterparts. Nevertheless, the engineers at SOTEC did manage partially to localize the floppy driver, the printer head, and the case and frame.

It was clear that as long as the production was on an SKD basis, the localization rate would be limited. The most expensive part of the product was the motherboard, and if the motherboard was supplied in semi-assembled condition, there would be no sharp increase in the rate of localization. Mitsui had an incentive for supplying the motherboard in its entirety, because the gain from supplying the motherboard at a high price would more than offset the loss in profit from the joint venture. Besides, Mitsui only had a minority interest in the joint venture.

In contrast, Stone as the major stakeholder of the joint venture had a strong incentive to move from SKD- to CKD-based production. Not only would it make localization easier, but also it would open up the possibility for Stone to master a wide range of manufacturing technologies. However, given the reluctance of Mitsui to give up control of the supply of parts and components, the only way for Stone to move into CKD-based manufacturing was to acquire a hardware design capability and to develop a new generation of integrated Chinese word processors independently.

2.3.4. Completing the learning cycle—internalizing product development capability

The idea of developing a new model of the integrated Chinese word processor independently was raised by the top management of Stone in October 1987, three months after the joint venture went into operation. The key for Stone to be able to develop the product independently was the capability of hardware design. Without the assistance from its Japanese partners, Stone had to seek out the technological capability domestically. Again, the state sector became the source of the technologies. This time, it was from a military-related research institute, more specifically from the state rocket technology programme.[44]

The central figure in this regard was a Ph.D. candidate,[45] Qiu Gang, at the Cybernetic Research Institute under the Ministry of Aerospace Industry. Qiu was working for the state satellite positioning and control technology project during his Ph.D. programme. What he was doing at the time was designing a task-specific computer system, processing real-time data to control the position of the satellite at launch time. Because of this work, he had a unique combination of both software development and hardware design capabilities. His saga with Stone started when he bought an M-1570 printer—Stone's second re-engineered printer. Qiu bought this printer for printing out satellite trajectories from his computer. He wrote a program that could turn the dot-matrix printer into a plotter. He demonstrated this program to the people at Stone, and his talent caught the attention of the top managers and senior engineers. The company hired him as an outside technology consultant for RMB 120 a month (that was more than twice as high as Qiu's stipend as a graduate student). Stone also bought his programme for RMB 1,500, and integrated the program into the printer driver.

Qiu missed the development of MS-2400 because he had to work on a satellite launch at the time, so Stone invited him to develop the MS-2401. He assumed the task of developing the printer control module for the system software. The software

---

[44] The information for this section comes mainly from two telephone interviews with Qiu in Oct. 1996.

[45] Chinese postgraduate education follows the Soviet model: apart from universities, research institutes also assume the task of training graduate students.

was written so neatly that it greatly improved the printing function of the integrated Chinese word processor over the first model. When the time for the independent product development came on the agenda, Qiu had already earned his reputation as a star among both the top managers as well as the senior engineers within Stone.

Qiu was assigned as the head of the R&D team for developing a fourth-generation model of the integrated Chinese word processor—the MS 2406.[46] The development process started at the beginning of 1988. The whole development team was sent to Hong Kong in mid-1988 to take advantage of direct access to new and up-to-date parts and components, as well as chip design facilities in Hong Kong, where Stone had already set up a subsidiary as the group's overseas purchasing centre.

Qiu transferred the multi-processor, multi-task computer system technology he learned in developing the task-specific computer for a satellite control system into the development of the MS-2406. Thus, the MS-2406 adopted a two-CPU architecture enabling word processors to edit and print at the same time.

Anticipating the production of the newly designed product, Stone set up a manufacturing plant in Shenzhen's Special Economic Zone, just across the border from Hong Kong in April 1989. The manufacturing plant was initially set up as a branch of Beijing SOTEC. It was called the Shenzhen Branch of Beijing SOTEC. The project was an integral part of the firm's overall strategy of building a manufacturing base in southern China, near Hong Kong, to take advantage of the favourable business environment there, as well as to build a base for future overseas operations. Shenzhen SOTEC started producing a jointly developed third-generation model of the integrated Chinese word processor—the MS-2403—in preparation for the production of the independently designed MS-2406. The production of MS-2406 started in early 1990. Production was conducted on a CKD basis from the very beginning. Because of the independent design, Stone was able, for the first time, to source parts and components independently from Mitsui. As a result, the localization rate of MS-2406 reached 43 per cent in terms of value at the beginning (STR 100: 4). By 1992, except for the CPU and some key components that China could not produce at the time, most of the parts and components were domestically sourced (STR 135: 2).

In 1991, as part of the overall strategy of backward integration, Stone formed another joint venture with Mitsui and Fujitsu to produce printer heads for the integrated Chinese word processor. The joint venture was set up again in Shenzhen. The total investment was US $3 million, of which Stone's share was 51 per cent, Mitsui's 25 per cent, and Fujitsu's 24 per cent. The joint venture, named Shentong, licensed the most advanced 24-pin dot-matrix printer-head production technology from Fujitsu. It began full production in December 1991. Thus, Stone had internalized almost all the key manufacturing technologies for its integrated Chinese word processors.

The combination of Stone's advanced Chinese word-processing technology with the strength of the Japanese manufacturing technologies ensured the high function-

---

[46] The third-generation integrated word processor, MS-2403, was still a product of joint development between Stone and Mitsui and followed the same pattern as the MS-2400.

ality and quality of the MS-series integrated Chinese word processors. Stone's share of the market has remained above 80 per cent ever since the product was launched. As a first mover, Stone's position in this market has never been challenged by its followers, including the Japanese company Ricoh that designed and manufactured a competitive product, trying to cash in on this high-profit market.

The integrated Chinese word processor was the major source of profit for the company. Sales of integrated word processors manufactured by the company accounted for about 40 per cent of the company's total sales, and the gross profits attributable to the integrated word processors for about 60 per cent of the company's total profits.[47]

2.4. From a New High-Tech Venture to an Industrial Going Concern

By 1992, after more than seven years of high-speed growth, Stone had formed a group organizational structure with Sino-foreign-equity joint ventures as R&D and manufacturing bases, group headquarters and subsidiaries as distribution centres, and a nationwide sales and service network with dozens of branch companies and service centres and hundreds of dealerships. The company had been, for five consecutive years, listed as number one in terms of sales among Chinese electronic enterprises. However, further company expansion faced two constraints: the first one was related to employee incentives. The second one was related to the funding of long-term capital investment.

The company had been following a profit distribution scheme that led to most of its after-tax profit being accumulated as collective assets. By 1992, the assets' net worth had reached more than RMB 200 million. However, the relationship between the company's assets and its employees was not clearly defined. In the past, it had not been a major problem because wages and salaries at Stone were among the nation's highest. As time went by, however, the wage advantage of Stone's employees was rapidly decreasing. On one hand, the wage-and-salary levels at some large-scale state-owned enterprises had been rising steadily as their performance improved in the new market environment. On the other hand, there were hundreds of newly established S&T enterprises operating in the same region that offered competitive wages and salaries. More serious was the competition from foreign multinational companies rushing into China since 1992 that drove up wages and salaries for Chinese talent.[48]

Stone had attracted many talented people in the past due to its reputation as a leading Chinese high-tech enterprise. Its employees were highly regarded in the new market for human resources. Stone started losing its capable employees, mostly middle managers and technological personnel, to other companies—especially foreign

---

[47] The remaining sales and profits were mainly from distributing and trading imported computers and peripherals through its nationwide distribution network in the process of distributing and selling the integrated Chinese word processors, see 'New Issue' 1993: 1.

[48] From 1992 foreign direct investment in China suddenly grew tenfold (from RMB 2 to 3 billion a year to RMB 20 to 30 billion a year) as it became clear at the time that China was not only a source of cheap labour but also a huge potential market by itself. The salaries that they paid local staff could easily be several times, if not ten times, higher than those in local Chinese enterprises.

ones. Under strong pressure to raise pay levels, it faced a difficult choice: as a high-tech enterprise, it is necessary to invest continuously in products and processes, which meant that there were competing needs for financial resources. Drastic increases in wages and salaries were detrimental to the company's long-term development; but without them the company ran the risk of waning incentives among employees. Determining the appropriate allocation of returns became a major challenge.

This challenge was compounded by a second one. About 40 per cent of the company's profits had been derived from developing, manufacturing, and marketing its own MS series of integrated Chinese word processors and other products, but Stone was still considered to be more a high-tech product trading company than a high-tech industrial concern, because 60 per cent of its sales revenues were derived from mere distribution of traded (mainly imported) computer electronics products. Therefore, boosting the content of its own manufactured products became another major challenge.

In 1992 a new corporate strategy took shape, called 'industrialization' (*chanyehua*). More specifically, the goal was to transform Stone from an R&D-and-marketing enterprise into an 'industrial going concern' (STR, 15 June 1991: 1–2). Yet the strategy's implementation faced a major challenge in raising capital. Large-scale manufacturing projects need long-term capital investment. In the past, Stone had only relied on short-term loans from the local branches of state banks to meet its needs for working capital. Its internally accumulated capital was fully absorbed in its existing lines of business, and there was no extra cash available from inside for large-scale, long-term industrial investment. On the other hand, long-term loans for capital investment were still directly controlled by the central planning authority. Being a non-governmental enterprise, Stone was not, and would not be willingly, subject to central planning.

As it turned out, both challenges could be met by reorganizing the company into a joint-stockholding company—a measure that was called 'corporatization' (*gufenhua*) in China. It was believed that distributing shares of the company's productive assets among individual employees could solve the incentive problem. It was also expected that the company could raise money for long-term investment from the stock market through a public offering. In fact, reorganizing the company into a joint-stockholding company had been a managerial goal since 1986.

2.4.1. Early experiments with joint-stock measures

In 1986 Stone's management attempted to create a new ownership structure. As we have seen, Stone was initially registered as a collectively owned rural township enterprise under the jurisdiction of the Evergreen Township. After the township gave up its supervisory as well as ownership rights over Stone's assets, the company became a stand-alone enterprise without direct administrative attachments. Yet the company still followed the profit distribution policy in accordance with the rules governing township enterprises, accumulating the majority of its after-tax profits as collectively owned assets. As a result, the company itself as a collective became the de facto owner of its productive assets. However, there was no clear law at the time defining collective assets. Past experience suggested that collective ownership tended to evolve into quasi-state-ownership in the traditional central planning system in the sense that assets were subject to the discretion of government agencies. Stone's management wanted to experiment with new organizational arrangements to clarify control over the company's collective assets. They felt that reorganization into a joint-stock company could serve its purpose.[49]

At a company meeting announcing the joint-stock reorganization on 20 June 1986, Stone's president explained to company employees:

As a collectively owned enterprise, we should have the real characteristics of collective ownership. Nowadays, a collectively owned enterprise is not very much different from a state-owned enterprise. So-called collective ownership means, in fact, owned by no one. The gains and losses of the enterprise have nothing to do with individual employees. We would like to link individual interests with the performance of collective assets by creating employee-joint-stock ownership. Raised to a theoretical level, we would like to create something new in China in terms of ownership structure (STR 3: 2).

As an experiment, the company issued 4,000 shares with a face value at RMB 100 per share. About half of the employees bought the shares, spending from RMB 100 to 12,600 with an average of RMB 1,855 per person. The stock issue raised a total of RMB 449,100.

However, this first attempt was more experimental and symbolic than substantial. The amount of capital that had been raised was insignificant, and it amounted to less than 1.5 per cent of the company's total accumulated assets, which had already reached about RMB 30 million by the end of 1986. The money raised was used as only a supplement to working capital. The employee-shareholders could derive up to 20 per cent dividends per year. However, there was no market for trading the stocks, so that the value of the stock did not vary accordingly, making it more like a high-interest corporate bond than a stock. As a result, the stock measure had no significant effect on employee incentives. The company soon stopped the experiment because of the lack of a clear legal framework.

At the same time, the company was still growing at an extraordinary pace. Its net assets had reached RMB 80 million by late 1988. Company management felt an increasing need to clarify the legal rights over these accumulated assets. Meanwhile, as theoretical debates and empirical experiments evolved, China's reform theorists and practitioners had reached a deeper understanding of the joint-stock company as an organizational alternative. One of the major economic advisers to Stone's

---

[49] Joint-stock measures in China in 1986 still caused suspicion among the policy-makers because of their capitalistic origin. The first suggestion of the systematic adoption of joint-stock measures as a way of reforming state-owned enterprises appeared in China in 1983 in an internal governmental policy paper written by two young economists. Sporadic experiments of joint-stock measures appeared in the state sectors from late 1984. The aforementioned paper was published on the front page of China's major economic newspaper, the *Economic Daily*, on 3 August 1985. It nevertheless indicated that the idea had jumped into the mainstream of policy debate over reform in China (Steinfeld 1996; 1998). From various aspects, Stone's experiment was still considered pioneering.

president wrote an article in the 17 November 1987 issue of one of China's leading economic newspapers—the *World Economies Herald* (*sijie jingji daobao*), entitled 'Market, Stockholding System and Stone'. In that article he claimed that joint-stock ownership could be the best measure for aligning individual employee's interests with the interest of enterprises on the one hand, and maintaining the enterprises' collective nature on the other. The article provided the theoretical underpinnings for experimenting with joint-stock organization at Stone.

A joint-stock proposal was once again put on the agenda in 1988. This time it was not simply a matter of issuing stocks to internal employees. The goal was to restructure the company into a publicly held joint-stock company. In order to gain legitimacy and authority for the new experiment, the company invited experts from the State Council's Research Centre for Economic, Technological and Social Development—a major government think-tank—to design the restructuring plan.

The proposal was to erect a new joint-stock company, with total equity of RMB 100 million, divided into 100 million shares. The group would transfer the assets of its major subsidiaries and branch companies into the joint-stock company, amounting to about 50 per cent of the group's total net assets (RMB 40 million out of RMB 80 million). In exchange, the group would hold 40 per cent of the joint-stock company's outstanding shares. All employees would be counted as founders of the new stock company and would be entitled to 10 per cent of the total shares (RMB 10 million) for free, as capitalization of their intangible human resource assets. These shares would be distributed among all employees who joined Stone before 31 December 1988, according to seniority and merit. The remaining 50 per cent of shares would be issued to the public.

The management's original intention was to distribute all the accumulated assets as shares to individual employees. The argument was made that since Stone had started with no equity capital (the RMB 20,000 used for registration was a loan from Evergreen Township), all its assets were sheer accumulations of retained earnings. They were attributable only to the efforts of the company's employees. However, the government did not agree with its argument, partly because there was no precedent, and partly because a substantial part of the company's assets could be attributed to the tax privileges the company had enjoyed.[50] The 10 per cent shares devoted to employees was the upper limit that the government regulatory authorities would accept.

The proposal was approved, and the new stock company, named Stone New Technology Industry Co., Ltd., was registered on 7 December 1988. However, the restructuring process and the planned public offering were suspended due to the 1989 student democratic movement after which the government halted its policies toward

---

[50] Stone had enjoyed its income-tax exemption granted by the local Haidian District government under its policy of promoting high-tech industries. Normally, income tax for state-owned enterprises and urban collectives ran at about 55%. For rural townships and village enterprises, it was 33%. However, the actual tax rate varied from enterprise to enterprise, due to the implementation of various reform measures at the time, especially the enterprise contracting system. For case studies about the enterprise contracting system, see Steinfeld 1996; 1998.

economic reform. More serious for Stone, the company's president, Wan Runnan, was forced to leave the country after the crackdown on the student movement because of his heavy involvement in it. For months the company had been investigated by a team from the Beijing Municipal Government and party authorities. It eventually survived the storm. The company's high profile as a leading enterprise in Chinese economic reform certainly helped, as did the rational forces that still existed within the government. For one thing, the leaders at the top did not want to give the world the impression that China had reversed its policy of economic reform, even though there were de facto retrenchments on all fronts. On 14 December 1989 the new chairman of the Stone Group, Shen Guojun, who was also one of the company's founders, along with several other senior managers, held a news conference that was sponsored by the Haidian District government. The press conference was organized in response to a request from the international journalists' club in Beijing. They announced that Stone would continue its business as usual (STR 92–3: 5–7).

In May 1990 the company reorganized its subsidiaries into divisions of the new joint-stock company (cf. Fig. 2.1). However, other measures, including the 10 per cent earmarked as employee shares and the public offering, were put on hold indefinitely—the political environment was simply not favourable for new institutional experiments at the time.[51]

2.4.2. Going public on the Hong Kong Stock Exchange

In 1992 the political environment in China took a dramatic turn due to the famous 'Deng's Trip South' in the spring of that year.[52] Organizational and institutional experiments were, once again, encouraged. The joint-stock organization became a policy priority for reforming state-owned enterprise. Experiments of 'corporatization' of state-owned enterprises had been extended. Regulations regarding joint-stock reorganization and public listing were drawn up. Two stock exchanges (one in Shenzhen, the other in Shanghai) were opened, and an institutional infrastructure was being put in place.

Stone resumed its effort of reorganizing into a joint-stockholding company. The company's net assets had reached RMB 200 million from RMB 80 million in 1988. The number of the group's employees had increased from about 600 to about 3,000. Corporatization had been joined with the company's new strategy of 'industrialization'. The latter became a new impulse in its rationale of going public.

---

[51] This account on stock measures is drawn from company archives as well as local government documents.

[52] Deng's 'Trip South' was a peculiar political strategy used by top Chinese leaders. The strategy was to mobilize regional political forces to tip the balance of power at the centre, particularly when the leader at the top felt he was losing control over the bureaucrats at the centre. Mao used this strategy to initiate the 'Cultural Revolution' and regain his control at the centre, although the result was disastrous. Deng's 'Trip South' to Shenzhen in the spring of 1992 was his last effort to push China onto a fast track of economic reform at a time when the new generation of leaders was clearly becoming more conservative about economic reforms in the aftermath of the Tiananmen incident. He succeeded. Afterwards, he gradually receded from China's political scene and became more and more a symbolic figure.

Meanwhile, the motivation for clarifying ownership rights of the collective assets among individual employees became stronger. Stone faced strong pressure to raise its pay levels. Otherwise, it would continue to lose capable employees to other companies. Stone did raise its pay level once in 1992, but, because of the high personal income-tax rate, two-thirds of the newly increased wages and salaries went to the government. In comparison, it was a commonplace in China that small companies were audited or monitored less and could easily avoid paying personal income taxes.[53] Therefore, the cost was much higher for Stone to raise wages and salaries than for small companies. Furthermore, as a high-technology company, Stone had to invest continuously in research and development in its existing products, let alone invest in new processes and products as planned in its new strategy. Simply raising wages and salaries was contradictory. Therefore, it hoped that corporatization could solve incentive issues by at least distributing a portion of the collective assets among employees.

For the pure purpose of raising capital, it would have been more lucrative to go public in domestic stock markets. According to one estimate, Stone could easily have raised RMB 600 to 700 million through a public offering on the Shanghai or Shenzhen Stock Exchanges.[54] However, as it became clear to the Stone's management that high technology is a global business, and major technologies and markets for high-tech products were outside China, in pursuing its industrialization strategy via joint-venture arrangements with foreign multinationals, Stone's management felt a need to restructure Stone according to international standards. By doing so, it hoped to acquire international legal, financial, accounting, and managerial skills. So, it chose to pursue a public listing on the Hong Kong Stock Exchange instead.

After a year of preparations, including evaluation and auditing by international accounting, auditing, and legal firms under the strict listing requirements of the Hong Kong Stock Exchange, the Stone Group reorganized its core business into a joint-stock company named 'Stone Electronic Technology Limited' and went public on the Hong Kong Stock Exchange on 16 August 1993. The total of outstanding shares offered was 600 million, of which the Stone Group as an investment holding company held 58 per cent. This percentage corresponded to the net asset value of the group's core business that was transferred to the stock company. Another 17 per cent of the shares were placed with corporate or institutional shareholders, including Mitsui.[55] The remaining 25 per cent of shares were issued to the public.

According to the regulations of the Hong Kong Stock Exchange, company

---

[53] For reports on employees who left Stone because of lower salaries, see the 22 Mar. and 7 May 1993 issues of *Guangming Daily* and the 24 Mar. 1993 issue of *Chinese Youth Daily*. Both are major national newspapers.

[54] From Stone's 1988 proposal for restructuring into a joint-stock company. Source: the Office for Enterprise Stockholding Restructuring of the Haidian District government.

[55] The exact amount of shares that Mitsui and other institutional investors got was listed in the new issue prospectus. Mitsui held 12 million shares, which accounted for 2% of total outstanding shares. In all, there were six institutional investors. Their percentages of the shares ranged from 2% to 5.5% of the total (see the 'New Issue Prospectus' of Stone Electronic Technology, Ltd., 1993: 168–9).

employees could buy up to 10 per cent of the publicly issued shares. The company used its past undistributed employee bonus fund to purchase 10 per cent of the shares (a net worth of 18,900,000 Hong Kong dollars at the listing price), and distributed them among the employees of the new joint-stock company. The employee-held stock accounted for about 2.5 per cent of the total outstanding shares.

The 58 per cent of shares that were held by the Stone Group under the title of Stone Holding were kept intact as collective assets, as were the group's remaining unlisted businesses. Thus, management's goal to create an employee-owned, joint-stock company had only remotely succeeded. This was because the government's regulatory bodies insisted on keeping the company's collective assets intact as a condition for approving Stone to go public. This restriction strongly resembled what had happened during the approval of the company's first public offering proposal in 1988. The difference was that, in 1993, there already existed a legal statute that governed the urban collective enterprises. The statute clearly stated that collectively owned assets should be kept intact, any attempt to partition them into private hands was illegal.[56] This was why Stone used its accumulated bonus fund to buy the stock and distribute it to its employees. The company's employees were entitled to the bonus fund, which had been kept undistributed to avoid high personal income taxes.

Nevertheless, the Hong Kong stock market accepted the concept of collective ownership from China without any particular problems. This was evident from the high volume of trading and increasing prices of the company's stocks after the public listing.[57]

The restructuring that resulted from the initial public offering on the Hong Kong Stock Exchange streamlined the company's business operations. The resulting corporate structure is shown in Fig. 2.2.

The ownership structure was arranged to ensure the firm control of Stone Group Corp. (Stone Holding as it was legally defined with respect to the listed company) over the listed company and its subsidiaries. This was also reflected in the organization of the governance body of the joint-stockholding company. Of the five executive directors, four were senior managers of Stone Group Corp., and only one was hired from a Hong Kong accounting firm as chief financial officer. Two outsiders were placed as independent non-executive directors. One was the managing director of the company's major stock underwriter, Peregrine Investments Holdings Limited, who was also a director of a number of companies listed on the Hong Kong Stock Exchange. The other was the chairman and managing director of Mitsui & Co. (Hong Kong) Limited.[58] Obviously, the latter two were mostly symbolic and played minor roles, if any, in the company's strategic decision-making processes.

---

[56] The legal statute governing urban collectively owned enterprises is the Law Applicable to the Urban Collectively Owned Enterprises of the PRC. It was issued by the State Council on 9 Sept. 1991.

[57] On the first day of public listing, the stock price of Stone went up 110% (see *Hong Kong Economic Daily*, 17 Aug. 1993).

[58] From Stone's 'New Issue Prospectus', as well as 1994 and 1995 Annual Reports.

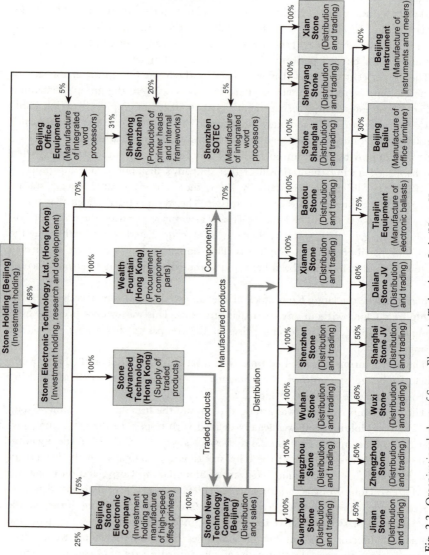

Fig. 2.2. Organizational chart of Stone Electronic Technology, Ltd. (Hong Kong)

Source: 'New Issue Prospectus' of Stone Electronic Technology, Ltd. (Hong Kong), 1993.

2.4.3. Industrial investments under a new corporate structure

The company raised about HK $300 million in cash from both direct placements and the public offering.[59] The arrangement of the majority ownership by Stone Group Corp. enabled the top management of the group to make investment decisions with the proceeds in line with its overall strategy of 'turning the company from a high-tech trading company into an industrial concern'. According to the new issue prospectus, the company planned to use 'approximately HK $75 million towards establishing Sino-foreign joint ventures for the purpose of building manufacturing facilities for computers, computer software and electronic cash registers; approximately HK $74 million towards expanding the group's distribution and service outlets to approximately 2,000 and to establish approximately 50 regional management centres'. The remaining fund would be used as additional working capital.[60]

The first major area of investment was to restructure and expand the company's nationwide distribution and sales network, one of the largest in China. Company management knew that its past success was, in a large part, due to its outstanding marketing and distribution capabilities. The increase of the company's marketing and distribution capabilities would ensure an outlet for future manufacturing goods. An enlarged distribution and sales network could also increase the volume of traded goods, which was a stable, if not high-margin, profit source. It could serve as a cushion for other high-margin, but also high-risk, investments. The management planned to increase the number of distributors from 1,053 to 2,000 to reach every county in China. By 1994 the number had already reached 1,700. To increase control over the distribution network and to improve after-sales service, the company spent several dozen million RMB to set up regional management centres in major cities.

The second major area of investment was 'building manufacturing facilities for computers, computer software and electronic cash registers'. On the computer manufacturing side, the company formed a joint venture with Compaq to produce personal computers in June 1994. The initial investment was RMB 22 million, of which Stone's share was RMB 2.2 million. The joint venture launched production in August 1994. It is said that it was Compaq's first joint venture ever in its global operations. However, regardless of the high growth potential of the production of the joint venture, the joint venture's contribution to the Stone Group's overall strength was limited because Stone held only 10 per cent of the equity. In fact, Stone only sent one senior manager to the joint venture as an associate general manager (STR 203: 7–10).

One big project the company had been acting on, however, was developing an electronic cash register. The company had already started the project in 1990, in anticipation of the eventual decline of sales of the company's major product—the

---

[59] The exchange rates at the Shenzhen Swap Centre of one RMB against the Hong Kong dollar for 1991, 1992, and 1993 are 0.752, 0.980, and 1.118 respectively. The exchange rates have stabilized around 1.1 since 1993 ('New Issue Prospectus' of Legend Holdings, Ltd., 1994: 6).

[60] 'New Issue Prospectus' of Stone Electronic Technology, Ltd., 1993: 53.

integrated Chinese word processors—due to increased competition from personal computers with Chinese word-processing software (STR 104–5: 1). Given the large number of retail stores in China and their eventual computerization, the electronic cash register was expected to be in huge demand in the near future. Management had high expectations that the electronic cash register would replace their Chinese word processor as the company's main cash generator. The company developed its first generation of electronic cash register by the end 1990 and marketed the product starting in 1991 (STR 119: 1–2), leading this market in technology, products, and sales (STR 137: 4; 208: 7).

In 1994 the development of the electronic cash register added a new twist. China had just implemented a new value-added tax (VAT) system. The government needed VAT cash registers installed in all stores in the future to record and calculate VAT. Given the importance of the VAT cash register, the government decided to regulate the development, manufacture, and distribution of the product. In May 1994, under the direct involvement of the relevant government ministries, a VAT cash register research and development joint venture was formed, in which Stone held a 20 per cent interest. Other joint-venture partners were Great Wall (the largest state-owned computer enterprise), the state-owned Qingdao TV Manufacturing Plant, and Japan's Omron (the world's largest cash register producer). Because Stone was already in a leading position in developing and manufacturing electronic cash registers in China, it actually bore the task of developing the new VAT cash register, which it success-fully did by January 1995. The total development cost was US $5 million, and was shared by the joint-venture partners. Stone produced 20,000 units of cash registers in 1995. It was expected that China would need 20 million VAT cash registers installed over the next eight to ten years, and Stone was aiming to provide 30 per cent of that demand (*China Industrial and Commercial Times*, 4 January 1995).

The above projects were financed out of the proceeds of the initial public offer-ing. However, the Stone Group as the major shareholder of the joint-stock company also collected a major part of the dividends. In addition, with a public company as a subsidiary, it made it relatively easy for the group to get bank loans. Added together, the financial resources of the group were greatly enlarged and permitted the group to pursue two large-scale industrial investments outside the structural framework of the listed company.

The first one was a new product line of energy-efficient lighting equipment, fix-tures, and fittings. It was a joint venture between the Stone Group (40 per cent), Matsushita (52 per cent), and Mitsui (8 per cent). The total investment was US $40 million and Stone financed its part with a RMB 100-million long-term loan from the Beijing City Co-operative Bank (STR 154: 1). Production of the products began in mid-1994 and full production was reached in December 1994. The joint venture created the largest manufacturing plant for lighting and related products in China and also was the most advanced in terms of both product and process technologies, which originally came from Japan.

The second large-scale investment was a joint venture with a state-owned phar-maceutical enterprise, the Anhui Number Two Factory of Pharmaceuticals. It was a kind of merger and acquisition. The main product line of the state-owned enterprise was raw Vitamin C for export. Stone's management decided to diversify into the pharmaceutical industry through the joint-venture operation.

2.5. Concluding Remarks

Stone was very successful in creating a new organizational structure to turn technology potential accumulated in the state sector into commercial reality. In an interview with a group of college students in early 1988, the company's president at the time, Wan Runnan, attributed its rapid success to two major factors. The first was the managerial autonomy that permits the company to fashion its own business strategies. The second was the strategy of pursuing progressive integration of R&D, manufacturing, and marketing. As Wan put it:

One of our biggest advantages is our market-oriented R&D, trade, and manufacturing integrated business strategy. State-run research institutions, for which we all worked for a considerably long time, actually have very strong technology capabilities, but they only focus on research, not on marketing or manufacturing capabilities—while trading companies only focus on distribution, completely ignoring research and manufacturing; state-owned manufacturing enterprises only focus on production with no concern for product sales. As a real enterprise, it is necessary to integrate R&D, trade, and manufacturing with the market as an end. This way, it could form a virtuous circle. We made money through integrating technology into trade. With the return from trading high value-added technological goods, we could either reinvest in manufacturing, pursuing economy of scale, or invest in research and development. This way, we could continuously come up with new products, continuously scale up production, continuously get into new businesses. This is the secret behind our success (*Guangmin Daily*, 15 January 1988).

The process of capability acquisition at Stone was self-enhancing. New capabilities were built upon and were complementary to the existing capabilities, all of which were in line with the firm's core technological capabilities. One outstanding factor that was not mentioned specifically in the above quotation was the high rate of capital accumulation resulting from the profit distribution scheme. Without the high proportion of net profit being designated to company development funds, the implementation of the strategy would have been doubtful, given the company's financial self-reliance.

After the company went public, however, both its resources and productive opportunities were greatly enlarged, as reflected in its aggressive investment activities in recent years. Nevertheless, the effort of transforming the company from a high-tech venture into an industrial going concern was not an easy task. Both the institutional and market environments had changed dramatically in China after a decade of economic reform and open-door policies. Managerial autonomy was no longer a unique feature of Stone, as state-owned enterprises also adopted the practice. Competition had intensified from all directions: from awakening, resource-rich, state-owned enterprises and giant foreign multinationals.

In a speech in 1996 the current president of Stone, Duan Yongji, spelled out the rationale underpinning the company's current strategy of transforming itself into an industrial going concern:

As a completely non-government-owned S&T enterprise, Stone is different from both the state research institute's S&T enterprises and the university-run S&T enterprises. Both have privileges to be included in the state budgetary plan, and get preferential investment loans and favourable treatment, as well as having direct access to the latest technologies and continuous in-flow of high-quality personnel. We still have difficulty getting into large-scale government investment projects. Under these circumstances, we have to explore new avenues to survive and develop. Our strategies are, in the areas of general purpose technological products, that we will 'go with the giants', that is, forming joint ventures with multinationals, leaping forward in our capacity resources; while in application-specific areas, we will develop products with our own proprietary technologies. In short, our strategy comes from careful consideration of our unique status and circumstances' (STR 209: 4).

It is still too early to tell whether the new strategies will work. Whatever the outcome is, Stone, as a pioneering company, has carved out a historic role in opening up new avenues in China's high-tech industries. Its success has had general repercussions on China's economic reform and particularly on China's S&T system reform. It has induced new experiments within the state S&T system. The two types of S&T enterprises mentioned in Duan's address—the state research institute's S&T enterprise and the research university-run S&T enterprise—testify to the effect of the 'Stone phenomenon'.

3

The Legend Computer Group Company: A Model of 'One Academy, Two Systems'

> In part, what we are seeing now is a real shift in the locus of technological development and dynamism, away from the bureaucratic (state-run), traditionally administrated research institutes. The trend instead is more towards high-tech oriented computer companies, something akin to joint stockholding companies. These companies are outside the stranglehold of the Chinese bureaucratic organizations. They are keenly aware of technological developments outside of China, and they are trying to plug into them. And they are more attuned to market dynamics, including maintenance, service and product differentiation.
>
> Dennis F. Simon, veteran China watcher, 1988.[1]

In the May 1996 issue of the Chinese version of *Computer World*, Legend was listed as the largest enterprise in the Chinese information technology (IT) industry. Its revenue reached RMB 7 billion in 1995, 70 per cent of which was generated from overseas. That year, the Legend Group (Hong Kong) supplied some five million computer motherboards and add-on cards to the world market, making it the world's fifth largest supplier of these products. In China, the Beijing Legend Computer Group had become the number one domestic PC maker. It was number three in market share in China after AST and Compaq and ahead of IBM and other international and domestic PC makers.

Legend is a company that grew out of the Institute of Computing Technology (ICT) under the Chinese Academy of Sciences (CAS). It is an export-oriented high-tech enterprise, specializing in developing, manufacturing, and marketing computer products. The company is also a multinational enterprise group, consisting of Hong Kong Legend Computer Group Co. and Beijing Legend Computer Group Co., with a corporate structure that integrates technology, industry, and trade.

Officially, the company describes itself as a new type of state-owned enterprise that has emerged from China's economic reform, particularly the reform of the science

---

[1] From Furst (1988).

and technology (S&T) system. In an interview with a group of Chinese journalists in 1993, the three top executives of the company gave their self-assessment of the company (Wen 1994: 39):

First, the company provided a successful model for China's science and technology system reform. More specifically, it had adopted an organizational form that is based on the principle of 'state-owned, non-government-run' (*guoyou minying*), with a balance between state-ownership on the one hand, and managerial autonomies in finance, personnel, planning and management on the other. It opened a new avenue for state-run research institutions to be integrated into China's industrial development. This organizational model was referred to as 'one academy, two systems', that is, symbiosis between the system of scientific research and the system of technology commercialization under one organizational roof—in the Legend case, it was the Chinese Academy of Sciences.

Second, the company had combined the two steps of globalisation and industrialisation (backward integration into manufacturing) in one stroke. It had established a world-wide business operation, headquartered in Hong Kong, with R&D centres in Silicon Valley, Hong Kong, Shenzhen and Beijing, two dozen overseas branch companies as sales outlets, and a large-scale manufacturing base in Southern China. Its QDI brand-name computer motherboard and add-on cards became well established in industrial circles. Among its clients were companies such as Gateway of the United States.

3.1. Early History

Legend was founded in November 1984. Two important developments at the time underpinned the decision to set up the company. First was the new government initiative to reform the national science and technology system. Second was the rise of new non-governmental science and technology enterprises in the Zhongguancun region of the Beijing Haidian District, where ICT, along with dozens of other research institutes of CAS, was located. As one of the co-founders, now a senior executive vice-president of the group, recalled:

The circumstances at the time were like this. The Institute of Computing Technology was funded 100 per cent under the state science and technology budgetary plan before the reform. After the initiation of economic reform, especially the S&T system reform, it was proposed that research grants for applied scientific research institutions be cut at a rate of 20 per cent per year starting in 1985. Worse for ICT was that it was finishing up its last large-scale state-funded computer project, the 757 super-computer project. No new project was put forward. So ICT was changing from a fund-rich institute to a poor one rather quickly. Life became rough for the computer scientists in the institute. The labs in the institute started to make money from conducting small commercial R&D projects or doing consulting to supplement their research funds and bonus funds. Meanwhile, as part of reaction to the government reform initiatives, dozens of new non-governmental science and technology enterprises mushroomed in the surrounding area. Among them were enterprises set up by research institutions. All these firms profited mainly from doing computer business. However, ICT was the forerunner in the field of computer science and technology in China. The people from the institute played important roles in these new S&T enterprises. Why does the institute not set up a company of its own? The director was anticipating that, as a result of grant cuts, lots of people in the institute would have nothing to do. The director's initial concern was to find a way out.[2]

Thus, the company was set up as an 'institute-run enterprise' (*suoban gongsi*). It was, in fact, named after the Institute, as 'New Technology Development Company of the Research Institute of Computing Technology of CAS', or simply the Institute of Computing Technology Company (ICT Co.). The eleven founders of the company were all from ICT, and ICT even loaned RMB 200,000 as start-up capital to the company. The institute was 100 per cent state-funded at the time, so it was not sup-⌉ posed to have extra money for business investments. However, setting up companies was considered to be one of several organizational experiments in the effort to reform the existing science and technology system. In fact, according to one account, the money was a bank loan, which was secured by the eleven founders through personal connections, and was put onto the institute's balance sheet. The latter, in turn, 'loaned' the money to the company. ICT also provided office space, utilities, etc., in kind at the beginning. ICT also continued to maintain and manage the state-employee status and the professional ranks for those who moved to the company, and paid base salaries to them. Thus, the company, as its name indicated, was the institute's company.

Due to its non-profit nature, the institute was not able to provide financing beyond the initial RMB 200,000 loan. Instead, the director of the institute assured the eleven company founders that the institute would give the company three types of preferential treatment. First, the company would be given full autonomy in managerial ⌉ decision-making, financial budgeting, and employee recruitment—designed to ⌋ mimic the non-governmental S&T enterprises such as Stone in the region. Second, the company would have full access to the institute's rich science-and-technology resources, whether they were tangible or intangible. Third, the company could use the name of the institute in making business deals.

Though this might lead one to believe that all was carefully planned from the beginning, in fact the company's beginnings were more chaotic. The company's founders were eleven ordinary research fellows out of the ICT's more than 1,500 employees (mostly research fellows). They found the first several months tough and confusing, for the eleven entrepreneurs tried to sustain themselves financially without any prior business knowledge. They tried everything, even resorting to selling roller skates. Fortunately, by chance, they learned that the science equipment supply department of CAS had imported 500 personal computers. It needed a company to help install and test the computers, train operators, and provide maintenance—precisely their area of expertise. So ICT Co. bid for the project, and got it. Although the work involved only labour services, it permitted the company to accumulate a crucial capital for the amount of RMB 700,000. Meanwhile, the management team realized that the company's long-term prosperity depended on the development of its own commercially viable products. At this point, the organizational ties to the institute became invaluable.

[2] Personal interview, Aug. 1996.

The Research Institute of Computing Technology under CAS had the greatest concentration of IT talent in China. As a science and technology institute, it was typical of the old system. Among the institute's 1,500 employees were about 200 senior scientists and engineers, more than 400 full-time research associates, and hundreds of support technologists. In its thirty-plus-year history, the institute had built two vacuum-tube computers, two semi-conductor computers, one IC computer, and one LSIC vector computer. They were all products of large-scale national science and technology projects. Most of them were the first and often the only ones of their kind in China. However, all of them were built for scientific purposes, particularly for defence-related projects. None had ever been turned into a commodity.

It did not take long for the managers of ICT Co. to identify a Chinese word-processing technology developed by a key scientist in the institute. They decided to commercialize it by transplanting it onto an IBM personal computer. As mentioned before, in the early 1980s there had been a computer frenzy in China as a result of an extensive nationwide discussion of the rapid development of information technologies overseas.[3] Government agencies, public institutions, and business enterprises all jumped on the bandwagon of buying microcomputers (often imported) without careful consideration of how they would or could be used. As a result, thousands of microcomputers that were installed were underutilized, the bottleneck being the lack of adequate Chinese-language processing technology. Commercialization of the Chinese word-processing technology was certainly promising. With the assurance of full access to the institute's resources from the director of ICT, the company invited the original developer of Chinese word-processing technology, Ni Guangnan, to join the company. This invitation would prove to be a turning point for the company.

Ni, one of the most promising computer scientists in the institute, had worked as a key scientist in various large-scale national computer projects. He had participated in China's first vacuum-tube computer project. He was also among the first Chinese computer scientists to work in the field of computer pattern recognition. His first achievement in this cutting-edge technology field was the 'written Chinese-language recognition system'. The project received CAS's Breakthroughs in Science and Technology Award in the early 1970s. Later, to overcome one of the major barriers for computerizing Chinese-language processing—the Chinese character input system—Ni and one of his colleagues came up with the idea of applying artificial intelligence technology to the Chinese character-input process. The idea was to let the computer automatically come up with the words most likely to follow according to context, therefore, raising the efficiency of the input process. It was called associative Chinese-character inputting technology. The first implementation of the technology was on a minicomputer in 1975. The resulting system—'the 111 Computer Chinese Information Processing System'—was one of the earliest computerized Chinese word-processing systems. For that, Ni got a second Breakthrough in Science and Technology Award. However, whatever its scientific merit, the system was ex-

---

[3] See Ch. 2.

perimental, with far more development being required before it could have practical usage.

In 1981 Ni went to the Canadian Academy of Sciences as one of the first Chinese scientists to visit Western research institutions after China opened its doors. During twenty-one months in residence, he successfully developed a 3-D high-resolution graphic display system on an M68000-based personal computer. The performance of the PC-based system reached the level of a workstation at the time. He presented his result at several international conferences and received considerable attention. He was also invited to give talks at several other foreign universities.

His achievements made him confident that China's general backwardness in the area of industrial sciences and technologies was not because of Chinese scientists' inherent inability but because of the organization of the science and technology system. The structure of the existing science and technology system insulated their activities from industry.

Upon his return from Canada in late 1982, Ni noticed a dramatic increase in the installation of computers nationwide and their underutilization. So he decided to continue his earlier work on Chinese word-processing technology. He successfully transplanted the Chinese input system from the domestic 111 mini-computer to an imported 8-bit personal computer system. The resulting system was called 'LX-80 associative Chinese-graphic microcomputer system'. He then went on to commercialize it. He had discussions concerning the system's production with three state-owned electronics enterprises. After a series of tough negotiations, one of the enterprises agreed to produce the system on a trial basis. Just around that time, a new 16-bit microcomputer was introduced into China, making the 8-bit system obsolete, and the production plan was abandoned (LXZR 1992: 303).

On reflection, Ni felt the need for a team that could closely monitor the trends of technological development overseas and would be committed to the commercialization of the technology. To this end, he signed contracts with two new science and technology enterprises. The managers of ICT Co. came to him after learning that he was working on commercializing the word-processing technology. By promising him that they would follow through on commercializing it, they persuaded him to join the company.

The commercialization of the technology entailed developing an add-on card and supporting software for the then widely used IBM PC and compatible machines. Ni devoted most of his time, including weekends and holidays, to the project. The first product was out for test marketing in the summer of 1985. In November, on the company's first anniversary, the commercial version of the product passed technological as well as market testing, and was out on the market in full scale. The product was called the Associative Chinese Word-Processing System, Version I.

Originally, it was not the only Chinese word-processing add-on card on the market; however, it soon became the dominant one, with more than 50 per cent of market share. This result stemmed from the company's commitment to the product's continuous improvement (through upgrades). Its stellar performance gave it the edge over competing products, particularly because of its incorporation of artificial

TABLE 3.1. *Legend's financial performance—the early years (not including Hong Kong Legend)* (currency figures in 1,000 RMB)

	1985	1986	1987	1988	1989	1990	1991
No. of employees	44	86	199	318	363	507	630
Sales revenues	3,000	18,000	70,140	134,000	220,000	250,000	680,000
Taxes*	210	2,425	6,246	4,879	10,398	23,213	42,376
Remittance to ICT	1,200	1,200	1,200	1,200	1,200	1,200	1,200

* Including sales tax and income tax.

Sources: LXZGBD, 1993; Legend Group (Hong Kong), Fifth Anniversary Brochure, June 1993.

intelligence. More than one-third of the company's revenue in its first three years of operation was brought in through the sales of this product.

The company had also commercialized other technologies—a total of 156 technologies by 1988, 27 of which were profitable. Products directly or indirectly associated with these technologies accounted for 80 per cent of the company's sales, and its revenue grew exponentially (Table 3.1).

The company's surprising market performance created a momentum of growth. It started setting up branch companies in major Chinese cities, and in April 1988 entered the world market by establishing a major joint venture in Hong Kong— Legend (Hong Kong) Co. By that time, the company had built its own R&D capabilities and had set up two of its own R&D centres.

In October 1988 under the administrative sponsorship of ICT, ICT Co. was reorganized into the Legend Computer Group Co. The director of ICT became the chairman of the board of directors, and the former general manager of ICT Co. became the president. The group consisted of two major subgroups: Beijing Legend Computer Group Co. and Hong Kong Legend Computer Group Co. The two Legends conducted complementary businesses. Beijing Legend provided one-third of the initial capital, plus R&D and managerial skills and a back-up market for Hong Kong Legend. With the support of the international marketing skills and financial resources of its Hong Kong partners, Hong Kong Legend got into the business of PC-motherboard and add-on card manufacturing. By 1994 Hong Kong Legend became the world's fifth largest supplier of PC motherboards and add-on cards. As sales expanded, Legend built a manufacturing base in south China that is said to be the largest production facility for PC motherboards and add-on cards in East Asia.

Building on the technological competence of Hong Kong Legend in PC-motherboard and add-on card manufacturing, Beijing Legend was able to shift from developing, manufacturing, and marketing Chinese word-processing add-on cards to developing, manufacturing, and marketing personal computers under its own brand name. By 1993 Beijing Legend had surpassed the largest traditional state-owned computer manufacturing enterprise, the China Great Wall Computer Co., to become the largest domestic PC maker in China, trailing only AST and Compaq in the Chinese market.

A very successful enterprise, Legend was, and still is, categorized as a state-owned (whole-people ownership) enterprise because it was set up by a state research institute. What set Legend apart from the traditional state-owned enterprises, according to the president of Legend, Liu Chuanzhi, is the kind of operational principles that Legend learned and implemented from non-governmental S&T enterprises such as Stone (LXZR 1991: 130). He maintained that 'the three autonomous rights' granted to Legend by ICT in the early years were equivalent to the 'four autonomies' of Stone. The granting of these autonomies led to Legend's categorization as a 'state-owned non-government-run' (*guoyou minying*) S&T enterprise. It will become clear in the following sections that the nature of state ownership in the Legend case is different from that of the traditional state-owned enterprises.

3.2. Technological Resources and Managerial Autonomy: Relations with the Institute of Computing Technology

As indicated above, Legend was established as a reaction by a state research institute to the changes in the state's science and technology policy, especially with regard to the financing of science and technology research projects and to the challenges posed by newly emerged non-governmental S&T enterprises in the Zhongguancun region. A big difference between Legend and Stone is that the eleven founders of Legend were all from CAS's ICT. In addition, they continued to be counted as employees of ICT. They derived their base salaries from ICT, and they maintained the option of returning to ICT, should the business venture fail.

Playing a role analogous to that of the Evergreen Township to Stone, ICT loaned the seed capital and provided office space and other in-kind resources to Legend in the early days. The fact that the company was initially named after ICT, the New Technology Development Company of the Research Institute of Computing Technology, was an invaluable intangible asset to the company because ICT was the nation's leading research institute in computer science and technology. As one of the co-founders put it, 'initially, people came to the company because they were confident in ICT'.[4] Not until 1989, when the company had established itself on the basis of the Legend brand Chinese word-processing add-on card did the company reorganize itself into the Legend Group Company.

The value of its close ties with ICT was also evident from the fact that the first major contract the company picked up was from CAS through internal contacts. One of the co-founders described in flowery details the contract's importance: 'the first contract was great, you know. The paper was snow white. Each character was written with artistic style. At the time, we had no money. We could do nothing. It was really distressing. The first contract was so precious! It brought money to the company. You would never forget that!' (LXZR 1991: 324). The contract helped the company

---

[4] Personal interview, Aug. 1996.

accumulate a crucial RMB 700,000 of initial capital that, in turn, enabled it to launch its first major product—the Chinese word-processing add-on card.

Also indispensable for the company's rapid success was its ready access to the rich technology resources of ICT. Besides the Chinese word-processing add-on cards, there were several other technological products that were developed either by people who had transferred to the company from ICT, often with prototypes of the products, or that were developed directly in the institute's labs under contract arrangements with the company.

Despite this direct support from ICT, the company remained fully independent. ICT would not, and did not, interfere in the business affairs of the company. In other words, Legend was given full business autonomy. It was not surprising that the company president attributed its rapid growth to two fundamental conditions: the strong technological back-up from the institute and the managerial autonomies the company enjoyed.

As Legend grew, the relationship between ICT and the company also evolved. By 1986, it had paid back the RMB 200,000 loan to ICT, and had started to pay rent for office space and scientific instruments as well as the cost of utilities. The company also started to reimburse the base salaries of the employees who were still attached to ICT. In addition, during the first three years of its existence, the company paid ICT an extra RMB 3,650,000. From 1988 on, this payment was fixed at RMB 1,200,000 per year. The company had also been paying an overhead fee of RMB 120 per person to the institute for managing the state-employee status of the people who originally came from the institute—a total of 128 employees to date.

The institute continuously provided indispensable administrative support to the company at a time when vertical administrative ties still provided the major organizational channels to gain access to resources. In 1989 the company was granted an administrative rank equivalent to ICT under CAS, thus giving the company direct access to the administrative resources of CAS, which itself is ranked at the ministry level.

In 1995 CAS authorized Legend to run the institute of Computing Technology as a further experiment to reform CAS, with the intention of fully integrating ICT into the company. The president of Legend Group Co. was appointed as director of the institute, reversing the administrative relationship between the institute and the company. The company was started as a subsidiary of the institute, and ended up as its supervisory body.

3.3. Technology Commercialization and Market Expansion

Without a direct investment grant from the government, ICT Co., like Stone, had to find a way of accumulating capital. As we have seen, the great advantage that ICT Co. had was its direct access to the institute's rich technological resources, with its thirty years of experience in designing and building computers. What the company did was to commercialize technologies accumulated in ICT within an innovative organizational framework.

Starting with the Chinese word-processing technology, the company developed hardware and software products that turned a personal computer from a general-purpose information-processing system into a system capable of processing Chinese-language information. This technology development strategy, which was akin to Stone's 'forward engineering', helped the company develop its core competence in the area of Chinese-language processing technology. Note that Legend took a different path from Stone in developing Chinese word-processing technology. Although both companies specialized in Chinese-language processing technologies, Stone focused on developing a stand-alone integrated Chinese word processor—a device equivalent to an electronic typewriter—while ICT Co. focused on adding Chinese-language processing functions onto general-purpose computer systems. Based on this and other proprietary technologies, ICT Co. was able to accumulate capital rapidly for further expansion.

Two practices of the company were particularly noteworthy. First, like other new S&T enterprises, ICT Co. integrated R&D, manufacturing, marketing, and services into a coherent business structure. Moreover, the management had put unusual emphasis on before-and-after sales service. The company was able to upgrade the product according to the user's needs. Second, the company used its market for Chinese word-processing systems as leverage to drive the sales of complementary traded computer products, thereby expanding its market capability quickly and accelerating the process of capital accumulation.

3.3.1. Service-centred product development strategy: The case of commercializing a Chinese word-processing technology

To reiterate, there were several competing Chinese word-processing systems in the mid-1980s. At that time, a Chinese word-processing system was a combination of a PC add-on card and system software. Only recently has it evolved into a pure software system as the processing and memory capacities of the personal computer have been dramatically enlarged. By developing both the necessary hardware and software, ICT Co.'s Chinese word-processing system dominated the market within a short period of time.

The company's success was in large part attributable to its commitment to the continuous improvement of the product. As the president of Legend later recalled:

What were our major competitive advantages? Other Chinese word-processing add-on cards were mostly developed by research institutes. These institutes did not have the kind of marketing capability that we had. I remember at a product contest in early 1986, there were at least several Chinese word-processing add-on cards, the quality and performance of which were as good as ours. Why did they lose? It was because they did not have the organizational capabilities to derive ideas from the market and act accordingly. We had an advantage in this regard.[5]

In the early 1980s most Chinese were computer illiterate. To sell computer systems, it was also necessary to teach them how to use them. To do so, the company used several methods, with a strong emphasis on technological services.

[5] Liu's address at the opening of the group's Daya Bay manufacturing base in Nov. 1995. From company archives.

First, the company placed highly trained technical personnel on the front line of sales. Several senior research fellows from ICT joined the company's sales force. As one of the senior managers, who was among the few who bore the title of senior research fellow (the equivalent of a full professor) at the time, recalled:

I joined the company after helping with a trade show in 1985. There was a shortage of personnel. I was borrowed by the company from ICT to be a product demonstrator. At the time, it was still not positively regarded for senior research fellows to staff a trade show, but I felt all right with it. After all those years being insulated in the computer labs at ICT, I was delighted to have some fresh air. The company's exhibition booth was located at the entry at the centre of the hall, very noticeable. However, when I first arrived at the show, I felt a little bit embarrassed. You know what, the product demonstrators for other companies were all good-looking young men and women, all dressed up. Only there were two old people in our booth. Professor Chang, who was even more senior than I, was an old man. I was an old lady, not attractive at all. But soon things changed, other company's booths were only scattered with visitors. Our booth was always crowded. The main product on exhibition was the Chinese word-processing system. At the time, the level of computer literacy in China was indeed very low. People were curious about the inner working of the computer. They asked you: What is a computer? How does it calculate? They wanted to understand basically how computers worked. That was my area of expertise, so I did my best to answer all the questions. To be honest, the Chinese word-processor add-on card at the time was very crude, made of three printed circuit boards connected with naked wires. It did not look like a decent commercial product. Yet people were interested very much in the product, asking a lot of questions. I patiently explained to them and that led to even more questions. Each day at the closing time, the organizers of the show had to expel people from our booth. They then moved to outside and continued asking questions. Even though it was very exhausting, I was very happy. I felt I had some direct value for society. I transferred to the company soon after.[6]

She became a sales manager of the Chinese word-processing add-on card, and led the sales team that was so successful that she was awarded the title of 'best salesperson' (LXZR 1992: 331).

Second, under the influence of these 'scholars-turned-salespersons', it became routine in the company for a sale to start with an explanation of the inner workings of the product, and end with a free after-sales service package. A standard after-sales service was a free training class. The company's training centre turned out on average 3,000 to 4,000 operational technicians for clients each year.

Third, the company sponsored a Legend Chinese Word-Processing System Users' Association with 500 institutional or corporate members, which regularly distributed technological materials to its members. The members, in turn, actively provided feedback about the products, becoming a unique source of inspiration for product improvement.

Fourth, to reach out to more consumers and clients, the company held regular technology fairs, twice a year from 1985. It mobilized top computer scientists from inside the company and from ICT to talk about trends in almost all areas of computer technologies, covering topics ranging from CPUs to peripherals, and power

[6] Personal interview, see also LXZR 1991: 328.

supplies to networking. The fairs attracted more than 5,000 people per year, and became a big event among computer users (LXZR 1992: 57–8).

The close linkages with the users served as a source of ideas for future improvements and product upgrades. In fact, members of the product development team were also actively involved in service practices. For example, the company's chief engineer, the inventor and designer of the Chinese word-processing add-on card, Ni Guangnan, not only served as the major speaker at the company's annual technology fairs, but also often personally acted as a salesperson at the company's trade show and retail centre. By listening to customers' needs, he could get a better idea about how to improve the Chinese word-processing system.

In the first several years, the company had put one-third of its technological personnel, including six senior scientists, in the team that integrated development, manufacturing, and marketing of the Chinese word-processing add-on card system. The organizational structure that integrated R&D, manufacturing, marketing, and after-sales service made it possible for the company to react quickly to market needs (LXZR 1989: 3). As a result, the hardware had been upgraded three times and the software seven times within the first three years. Table 3.2 shows the evolution of the product.

TABLE 3.2. *The technological evolution of Legend's Chinese word-processing system*

Time and Version	Features
July 1985, Version I	Supporting IBM PC/XT, AT, mono display; introduced the Direct-Writing-Onto-Screen Technology for the first time; commercialized Chinese character input technology for the first time, greatly increased the efficiency of the Chinese character input process, putting to rest the debate on the inherent disadvantages of pictographic language in the computer age
Oct. 1986, Version II	Supporting CGA display; compatible with almost all Western-language software
Oct. 1987, Version III	Supporting EGA and other high-resolution graphic display devices
Oct. 1988, Version V-1 and V-2	Supporting VGA display; compatible with graphic application software; due to its contribution to promoting computer use in China, as well as its technology superiority and market dominance, the technology was awarded the National Technology Progressing Gold Medal, the highest award for technological innovation in China
Mar. 1990, Version VI and VII	Version VI is a Chinese word-processing system based on pure software; Version VII is a miniaturization of the PCB-based card into an ASIC chip
Oct. 1991, Version IX	A collaborative product with US Trident Corporation; combined Chinese word-processing card and the TVGA card into one
Aug. 1993	A second Chinese word-processing system based on pure software

Source: LXB 96: 2.

3.3.2. Technology-led market expansion

By 1987, as a result of the company's commitment to technological services as well as continuous technological upgrading, the ICT Co. had established its position as the number one developer of Chinese word-processing systems. As indicated before, from a marketing perspective, the product was a computer add-on card with a software package. It could be installed into any IBM or compatible personal computer to form a Chinese-language processing system. It sold for about RMB 2,000 apiece and could be sold either alone, or with a basic computer system. The sale of an RMB 2,000 Chinese add-on card could actually drive the sale of a computer system worth RMB 20,000.

At the time, the Chinese domestic PC market was in its infancy. It lacked good-quality, reasonably priced personal computers. After an extensive survey, the company chose AST as the standard machine for its Chinese word-processing system. It signed a contract with AST and became the sole distributor of AST personal computers in China (LXZGBD 1993: 8), thus laying the foundation for AST to become the leading brand in the Chinese PC market for several years.

The integration of the AST machines with the sales of Chinese word-processing add-on cards greatly enlarged the company's sales volume. Sales revenue jumped from RMB 70 million in 1987 to more than RMB 130 million in 1988, and then again to RMB 220 million in 1989 (cf. Table 3.1). Profit increased significantly, even if not proportionately (because traded goods yield lower profit margins than goods based on proprietary technologies).

The process of commercializing the Chinese word-processing system became a template for future efforts. The company took the development of proprietary technologies in the form of 'forward engineering' to boost sales—a strategy other high-tech firms also pursued but without the technological strength that ICT Co. derived from its close ties with ICT. Using the same strategy, the company commercialized dozens of technologies in its first several years, either through the use of personnel transferred from the ICT as in the case of Ni, or by subcontracting R&D projects to the labs within ICT (LXZGBD 1993: 6). As a result, the company derived over 80 per cent of its revenues from either products with its own proprietary technologies or products that integrated parts of those technologies.

For example, in 1988 the IBM PS/2 computer had been in the Chinese market for two years. Because of the lack of a complementary Chinese operating system, it did not sell well in China. By developing a Chinese operating system, the company made sales of US $1 million worth of PS/2s in one year. In comparison, other companies in the same region had difficulty selling the computers. The technology that ICT Co. developed made the difference. Another example, also in 1988, was that the company developed a Chinese-language software interface for a networked system. The new technology drove sales of network products worth RMB 10 million. The two products combined accounted for close to 15 per cent of the company's total revenues for that year (LXZR 1993: 164–5).

The integration of forward engineering with trade not only enlarged the sales revenue, and accelerated capital accumulation, but also helped to build a nationwide sales and service network. In 1988 the company established four branch companies in four major provincial capitals (Harbin in north-eastern China, Zhengzhou in northern China, Wuhan in central China, and Fuzhou in southern China) and twenty-four service and maintenance centres all over the country (LXZR 1992: 163–4). By 1989 the number of branch companies had increased to fourteen and service and maintenance centres to thirty-six (LXZR 1992: 84).

3.4. Internationalization and Industrialization

The company's ultimate goal was to develop, manufacture, and market its own computer systems. In a formal meeting with the president of CAS in 1987 concerning the mission of the company, the ICT Co.'s management team stated that they wanted to make their own brand-name computers that could compete anywhere in the world in terms of price and performance.

However, in China the manufacture of PCs was monopolized by a handful of large-scale traditional state-owned enterprises under the Ministry of Electronics Industry (MEI). Since ICT Co. was a new enterprise outside the turf of MEI, it was not given a manufacturing licence. After all, the Chinese domestic PC market was in an early stage of development. The size of the market was only a fraction of one per cent of the world's total. Company management judged that the market was too small for large-scale ventures (LXZR 1992: 108–9).

These circumstances prompted the company's management to seek overseas expansion. The company had been trading imported computer goods for several years. In the process, it had gained knowledge about business operations in Hong Kong. In addition, through his father, who was chairman and general manager of a Chinese government concern in Hong Kong, the general manager of the company had learned how to set up companies in Hong Kong.

The management designed a three-step multi-year overseas expansion plan. First, the company would form a trading company in Hong Kong; second, it would build an industrial base that integrated R&D, manufacturing, and marketing; third, it would establish itself as a major concern by going public on the Hong Kong Stock Exchange.

3.4.1. Complementary strengths: Building a joint venture with Hong Kong partners

Two specific goals in setting up a trading company overseas were: first, to accumulate capital, and second, to break into market niches. The general manager of ICT Co. explained:

Just because we have set up ICT Co., we have been able to get to know the needs of our clients and consumers, and develop products accordingly. So this was our purpose in setting up a trading company in Hong Kong. We have learned our lessons. For example, in 1987 we developed a computer add-on card that could connect PCs with fax machines. We called it FAX-PC. We only sold 300 in China. In fact, a similar product had not yet appeared in the world market. Only after we brought it to a technology trade show in Hong Kong, did we realize that there was a large market out there for similar products. However, we designed the products according to the specifications of the most widely used brand of Ricoh fax machines in China, a model that was already obsolete overseas. When our design engineers considered redesigning the product, we had already lost the market opportunity. Had we known things like this earlier, we probably would not have missed these kinds of market opportunities (LXZR 1992: 29, 85, 187).

ICT Co. took on Daw, a small Hong Kong-based computer trading company, as a business partner. Together with China Technology, a Hong Kong-based Chinese government-backed company, ICT Co. formed an equity joint venture in Hong Kong. Each side invested an equal share of the initial HK $900,000 equity. The composition of the joint venture was designed to take advantage of each partner's unique business strength.

Daw was founded in February 1980 by several young Hong Kong businessmen who had graduated from Imperial College in London with computing science or mathematics degrees. The company was set up to develop business application software and distribute computer electronic products. It was one of the first authorized distributors for IBM personal computers in Hong Kong and China. At the time, Daw had been doing business with ICT Co. for two years. Daw's general manager, Lui, got to know the people in ICT and ICT Co. in 1985 in the process of distributing a computer terminal simulation card. In 1986 he had a chance to take a look at ICT's 757 mainframe computer—a computer that was very advanced even by international standards. More striking to Lui was that it was designed and built independently by the scientists and engineers in ICT with domestically made parts and components at a time when China was still very much insulated from the outside world. He was particularly impressed by the high level of R&D and design capabilities at ICT (LXZR 1992: 214).

In 1987, when ICT Co. chose AST personal computers as the standard for its Chinese word-processing add-on card, Daw, as an authorized distributor for AST personal computers, became the major supplier for ICT Co. In the process, the managers of the two companies got acquainted with each other. Lui and his partners at Daw wanted to expand their business but were constrained by their limited financial resources and technological capabilities. When the general manager of ICT Co., Liu Chuanzhi, suggested that they form a joint venture in Hong Kong in the summer 1987, Lui responded enthusiastically. Lui had confidence in the capabilities of ICT and saw the business potential of collaborating with ICT Co. He knew from his personal experience that ICT was exceptional among Chinese enterprises and institutions, the majority of which Hong Kong business people found very difficult to deal with.

China Technology was incorporated in Hong Kong in 1987. It was a joint venture among major Chinese government-backed business concerns in Hong Kong, including China Patent Agent (H.K.), Ltd., China Everbright Holdings Co., Ltd., China Resources (Holdings), Ltd., Bank of China Group Investment Co., Ltd., China Patent Technology Development, Ltd., and China National Technology Import and Export

Corporation.[7] The strength of China Technology lay in its deep financial pockets and international legal expertise. Liu Chuanzhi, the general manager of ICT Co., had personal connections with this company. Liu's father was the chairman and general manager of one of the major shareholders of China Technology—the China Patent Agent (H.K.), Ltd.

'Why China Technology?' one of the senior vice-presidents of the Legend Group recalled:

Lui and his partners at Daw did not have a strong financial background in Hong Kong. They were not rich Hong Kong people. We, the people at ICT Co., were just a bunch of poor 'country uncles' in the eyes of Hong Kong people. No one in Hong Kong would take us seriously enough to loan us money. Without money, how would we do business? China Technology was different, however. The Bank of China was one of its shareholders. Among other shareholders were Everbright and China Resources—all big Chinese government concerns. If China Technology was a part of the venture, it would make it a lot easier to get loans from banks. This was the strength of China Technology. The strength of Lui and his partners at Daw was their familiarity with international marketing, their fluent English, and knowledge of local customs and culture. Our strength was having strong technological and manufacturing capabilities, and a large domestic market.[8]

After several months of negotiations and preparations, the joint venture was formally incorporated in Hong Kong in March 1988 (LXZR 1992: 162). It was named Hong Kong Legend Technology Inc., after ICT Co.'s 'Legend' brand Chinese word-processing add-on cards. Lui and his partners at Daw merged their entire business into the new joint venture. Daw ceased to carry on any business other than the holding of interests in the joint venture. The general manager of ICT Co., Liu Chuanzhi, became the chairman of the board of directors. The former general manager of Daw, Lui Tam Ping, was appointed as general manager. In addition, each of the three joint-venture partners appointed an associate general manager.

Hong Kong Legend started operations on 1 April 1988. Its business was a merger of Daw's and ICT Co.'s existing trading businesses in Hong Kong and China respectively. However, it operated on a much larger scale. As was mentioned above, ICT Co. had already built a nationwide sales network for distributing the Chinese word-processing add-on cards and AST personal computers. It provided a large back-up market for Hong Kong Legend. One senior vice-president illustrated the operation of this back-up market: 'if the Hong Kong market could sell 500 PCs per month, Hong Kong Legend would order twice that amount, for we knew that if the extra 500 could not be sold in Hong Kong, they would be sold in China in the following month'.[9] In

---

[7] All these companies were typical Chinese government-run enterprises in Hong Kong. They played more active roles in Hong Kong's economy after China and Britain had signed the accord returning Hong Kong to China. However, their major business activities were in the service sectors; for example, banking, real estate, import-export, etc.

[8] Personal interview, Aug. 1996.

[9] He added that 'the computers were not yet fresh fruits that were not storable. One or two months in storage was OK at the time.' Interview with a senior vice-president of the company. See also the transcript of the address of the president of the Legend Group at the opening of the company's Daya Bay manufacturing base in 1995 (from collections of the company's internal documents).

fact, more than 60 per cent of the sales revenue of Hong Kong Legend was generated from the Chinese market, mainly through distribution channels of ICT Co. in its first year of operation (LXZR 1992: 186). The enlarged order lowered the purchasing prices, and increased the company's profit margins as compared with smaller Hong Kong trading houses.

The financial resources for the larger orders were secured with loans guaranteed by China Technology. In fact, the loans for the initial transactions were borrowed directly out of the internal reserves of China Patent (H.K.), Ltd., where Liu's father was the chairman and general manager.

The result was a profitable and fast-growing business. It went so well that the joint-venture partners literally recouped their initial investment within three months.[10] By the end of 1988, after nine months in operation, the revenue of Hong Kong Legend had reached US $11.74 million. Net profit was three times the initial investment, well beyond the initial expectations of the joint-venture partners (LXZR 1992: 34).

The general manager of ICT Co. described this Hong Kong–China partnership as 'a blind man with strong muscles carrying on his shoulder a sharp-sighted cripple', meaning that ICT Co. had very strong R&D muscles but was blind in the international market place due to lack of experience. On the other hand, Daw had strong international marketing capabilities but was crippled by its lack of R&D and financial resources. The complementary strength of the Hong Kong–China joint venture would be even more fully revealed when it began to develop its own products.

3.4.2. Breaking into the world PC motherboard market

With the steady inflow of revenues from the trading business, the management of Hong Kong Legend ventured onto the second stage of its overseas expansion, that is, to build an industrial concern abroad. It started by acquiring a small Hong Kong manufacturing plant, Quantum Design Inc. (QDI).

To some extent, the acquisition was a coincidence. On one occasion, the general manager of Hong Kong Legend, Lui, met the owner-manager of QDI, Jiang Guohui, at a dinner party. Lui was becoming well known in the Hong Kong small-business circle for his successful joint venture with mainland partners. Jiang admired Lui for being able to turn his fortune around with the help of a mainland concern. Lui mentioned the meeting with Jiang to Liu, the chairman of Hong Kong Legend, adding that Jiang was willing to merge his company into Legend. QDI was a typical small owner-managed Hong Kong manufacturing company with only several dozen workers, designing and manufacturing PC motherboards. Liu saw the acquisition as a point of entry into PC manufacturing, and promptly responded. Thus, in August 1988, just four months after its founding, Hong Kong Legend acquired 80 per cent of QDI's shares. The original owner-manager retained 20 per cent and stayed on as the general manager.

---

[10] Based on the financial data from April to Sept. 1988 see LXZR 1992: 163.

The acquisition marked the starting point for Hong Kong Legend to get into the PC manufacturing business. Soon after, the chairman of Hong Kong Legend, who was also the general manager of ICT Co., along with several top managers, attended COMDEX, the world's largest annual computer trade show in Las Vegas. The mission was to 'fathom' the market for computer products in the United States. Liu and his associates spent a total of twenty-six days visiting major US cities. They were impressed by the huge size of the US market for computer products. The chairman of Hong Kong Legend recalled:

We found that the computer market was visibly divided into high-end and low-end products. The high-end products were mainly made by large US corporations, such as IBM, HP, AST, etc. There was a big price gap between these products and low-end products. The low-end product market was basically taken by Taiwanese companies. The markets for these products were small businesses, families, or individual users. Taiwanese products had indeed taken a big chunk of the US market.

On reflection, we felt that the technological capability at ICT was strong. We had our top computer scientists such as Ni Guangnan and his cohort. We also had a new generation of computer scientists. Our team in China was among the best. However, were we able to compete directly with the world's best in areas such as super-computers or mini-computers? Definitely not. But with our best Chinese team, we could compete in the low-end of the high-tech products. We certainly had a chance.

Therefore the management elaborated a product development strategy in line with the famous Chinese 'horse race' parable[11]—using the best horse to compete with the rival's second best (LXZR 1992: 89). The company started by developing a motherboard for the 286 personal computer. The 286 microprocessor was in its last stage of the product cycle at the time. Large companies had already shifted to 386 or higher models, and the market was filled with products made by companies in South Korea, Taiwan, and Hong Kong. ICT Co.'s management knew that the company was technically strong enough to compete at this level. The chief engineer of ICT, Ni Guangnan, and his team were sent to Hong Kong to develop the product. After comprehensive reverse engineering of existing 286 machines, the R&D team adopted the most advanced design idea, coming up with a product prototype that performed much faster than equivalent models. The company sent the product to CeBit in Germany, one of the largest computer shows in Europe, in spring 1989. The product's high performance and low price won ICT Co. orders for several thousand units per month.

However, only after getting into the business did the management realize how competitive and risky the international PC markets were. Management soon found out that the production at QDI's existing plant could not come up with products to design specifications and the defect rate was as high as 80 per cent. It was

---

[11] The 'horse race' parable was from an ancient Chinese war strategy book, 'The Art of War' by Sun Bing (not to be confused with the book by Sun Zhu sometimes used in American business schools). It is about a horse race between kings of two ancient Chinese states. The strategist advised one of them to match his first best horse to the second best of his rival, the second best to the third best, and the third best to the first best. The result was two wins out of three.

impossible to fill the orders brought back from the computer trade show. The market was lost. Parts, components, and semi-finished products were stockpiled. The whole company was in a state of disarray. The situation was so dreadful that even the general manager, who was the former owner of the QDI, lost confidence (LXZR 1992: 90, 390).

The chairman of Hong Kong Legend, who was running ICT Co. in Beijing, was called to the rescue in June 1989. He found that it was basically a production management problem: the top managers were unable to co-ordinate production effectively. So he called a board meeting. This led Hong Kong Legend to buy out all the remaining shares from the then-general manager of QDI. The top management then completely reorganized QDI's management team. Several production managers and engineers from Beijing were sent to the plant.

The reorganization process was not easy. As the chairman of Hong Kong Legend recalled:

Production management was not new to us. Chinese word-processing add-on cards represented a successful case. This seemingly easy task was not easy in Hong Kong because of the language barrier. The people sent to manage the plant from Beijing did not understand the local dialect. Plus, there was a shortage of labour in Hong Kong. The turnover rate was very high. The wages at QDI were not particularly high. Workers constantly came and went. A small number of local workers, who took advantage of the language barrier, formed a small circle that isolated new workers. It made the workforce even more unstable. We discovered the problem and fired these guys. After all, we were the bosses. We gradually cultivated a stable core of workers. The one-time perfect rate increased from less than 30 per cent in June to 80 per cent in July, then to more than 95 per cent after two months (LXZR 1992: 91).

Then there came a second crisis. One of the most important reasons why the 286 machine received a large amount of orders in the computer shows was its low price. In 1988 the price of one of the most widely used RAMs in personal computers, the DIP RAM chip, increased from four- to fivefold. The design team at QDI adopted another kind of chip called SIM RAM instead. The price of the SIM chip was only half of the DIP chip. The lower priced chip brought down the cost of the whole system, generating a lot of orders. However, the orders had not been filled in time because of the quality problem. By July, when the quality of the product was finally stabilized, the market no longer existed. Within only four months, the price of the DIP chip had been lowered several times. As a result, the price advantage of the 286 with the SIM chip had completely disappeared. It was a big blow to the company.

But it came up with an innovative response. The company chairman recalled: 'Our development team was indeed very strong. They started all over again, changing design, doing CAD, prototyping, starting a small pilot production, then regular production. At the same time, we carefully planned the timing of purchasing parts and components and of marketing. In less than one month, at the end of August, we started advertising and sending letters to our clients. Each time we sent 20,000 to 30,000 letters. By mid-September, the product quality in batch production was stabilized. We started shipping out the products. This was a first test of our capability of adapting to sudden and unforeseen changes in the international PC market.'

The members of the product-development team were all very happy with the volume of production and sales of their own products. However, very quickly, another blow came. One user complained that the computer did not function properly with the Oki-brand memory (RAM) chip. Such a problem seemed hardly possible. There were several dozen companies manufacturing RAM chips. All were supposed to follow the same industrial standard, and therefore, the product development team did not conduct an exhaustive compatibility test. Nevertheless, the problem did exist, and further in-house testing confirmed that. At the time, the chief product designer, Ni had already gone back to Beijing. The people in Hong Kong did not know the exact causes. Again, the chairman of Hong Kong Legend recalled:

It is hard to describe how desperate we were. We just felt it was most likely that the problem was not going to be fixed. We already had made about 3,000 sets of motherboards. To fix the problem, we had to add wires on the circuit board. That was not acceptable to the market. There were a lot of motherboard products out there; no one would buy ours. Adding separate components to correct it was not acceptable either. Clients would think our product was not mature. With these restrictions, even if Ni was a genius, how could he fix it? We had absolutely lost hope. It was not a matter of throwing away several thousands of motherboards. It was a matter of reputation. We had just started. We really wanted our clients and customers to get to know us. We spent so much on advertising, sent so many letters, all for the purpose of letting people know us. Now, we had to tell them that our product did not work with the Oki chip. It was like telling them 'don't buy our product'. If we were not going to reveal the problem to our clients, the problem would reveal itself. Then, our reputation would be completely ruined. Our clients would ask for refunds. It would get out of control (LXZR 1992: 98).

Besides, it was also a matter of trust with their Hong Kong partners. At the time of QDI's reorganization, the major Hong Kong partner, Lui Tam Ping, was very supportive. He trusted the technological abilities of the people from ICT. The first incident with the DIP chip had been understandable; however, here was another technological mistake in such a short time. It was very hard to convince him as well as his sales force that the company would make it. With a sinking feeling, the chairman of Hong Kong Legend made a long-distance call to Ni at 8 p.m. Two hours later, at 10 p.m., Ni called back saying he had found the cause—the Oki chip was indeed different from all the other chips. He had yet to find a solution. At 11:30 p.m. Ni called again, to say that he had solved the problem.

It turned out that the Oki chip had an extra logic gate—a very rare occurrence as all logic gates were usually occupied in the design process. Relying on his profound knowledge of the computer's inner workings, Ni miraculously fixed the problem without adding any extra wires or correcting components.

Thus, in October 1989, one year after acquiring the QDI, Hong Kong Legend finally had a foothold in the world market for PC motherboards, shipping a steady volume of 3,500 per month.

3.4.3. Creating a competitive edge: Integration of R&D, trade, and manufacturing across borders

After weathering a series of breathtaking crises in the process of breaking into the PC motherboard manufacturing business, Legend's management had learned a great deal about doing business in the international market place, and had a clearer idea about their strengths and weaknesses.

The first lesson they learned was how intense competition was in the international market. The chairman of Hong Kong Legend reflected on the Oki-chip incident:

If it had happened in China, it definitely would not have been that serious. We could have always made up at a later stage, based on our good relations with our clients. In the international market, everything is serious. You just could not take chances (LXZR 1992: 98).

Management had reached a new level of understanding of the nature of market competition. To quote the chairman again:

In the past, we criticized the research institutes for only focusing on research and ignoring the market, and so we established ICT Co. to address the market. We learned how to develop products according to market needs in China. Now we know, after our first round of competition in the international PC motherboard market, that the bottom line in market competition is still technology (LXZR 1992: 98).

The management had more confidence in their technological strength, not only because the R&D team could quickly solve unforeseen problems, but also from directly observing the technological capabilities of small Hong Kong manufacturers.

There had been two young in-house engineers at QDI before the acquisition. One was a student returning from studies in the US, the other was a graduate from Hong Kong Polytech. They were responsible for product design and development at QDI. 'According to our observations, they were not as good technically as our graduate students. Though they knew more about international product markets and getting information quickly, they were far from being on the same par as our young technologists. Our technologists, like our chief engineer, Ni, had all gone through the complete design cycles of several different computer models. His graduate students were all chosen from the best universities in China.[12] We held a definite competitive edge in technological capabilities (LXZR 1992: 96–7).[13]

Travel restrictions between Hong Kong and China created a barrier for dispatching R&D personnel from Beijing to Hong Kong. That was partially a cause of the Oki incident. In the process of developing the first 286 motherboard, only Ni and several of his assistants went to Hong Kong. Ni basically developed the product by

[12] Again, elite research institutes in China are part of the postgraduate education system alongside graduate schools in universities. Senior research fellows at research institutes are often advisers to graduate students. The chief engineer, Ni, advised several graduate students each year as a senior research fellow at ICT. Other senior research fellows who transferred from ICT to ICT Co. did so as well. These graduate students often worked on R&D projects and were more likely to be hired by the company after completing their degree. They became the major source for R&D personnel at the company.

[13] The two former QDI engineers left for other companies soon after the technologists from Beijing were sent to QDI.

himself, and product testing was conducted by his assistants. That was unacceptable. 'No matter how rigorous a person is, the development process is so complex, mistakes are always possible. Testing has to be done independently', to quote the company chairman. However, this problem could be alleviated through better organization of technological resources in Hong Kong and mainland China. In this case, testing could be conducted in Beijing where the abundance of technological personnel allowed a more thorough testing of new products.

In contrast, there was a financial advantage in establishing a manufacturing business in Hong Kong. The success of QDI in breaking into the PC manufacturing business was in a large part due to the financial support from its mother company, Hong Kong Legend. Top management at Hong Kong Legend used the profits from the trading business to sustain the R&D and other product development activities at QDI. This financial commitment made it possible for QDI to weather the series of crises. The computer trading business of Hong Kong Legend, in turn, was sustained by a large back-up market in China, which was organized by ICT Inc. in Beijing. As mentioned before, about half of Hong Kong Legend's trading business was done in China via the distribution channels of ICT Co. Therefore, as is illustrated in Fig. 3.1, there was a considerable degree of integration of business activities across the Hong Kong–China border between ICT Co. and Hong Kong Legend.

To take advantage of the complementary resources across the border, it was decided to reorganize overseas and domestic businesses into a group and so Legend Group Co. was formed in November 1989. The Legend Group Company consisted of Hong

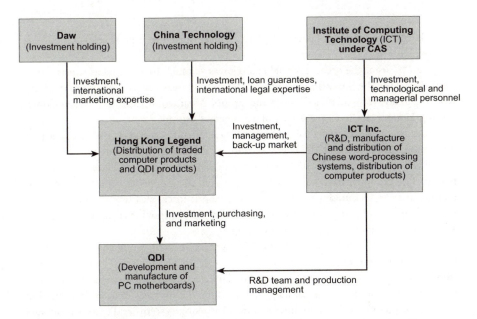

Fig. 3.1. Organizational relations between ICT Co., Hong Kong Legend, and QDI

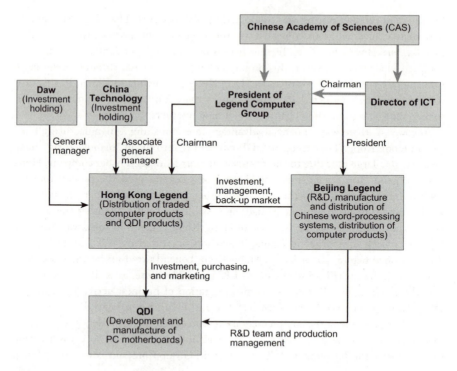

Fig. 3.2. Organizational and managerial structure of Legend Computer Group

Kong Legend and Beijing Legend (ICT Co.'s successor). The organizational structure is shown in Fig. 3.2.

As can be seen, the organizational change was as much managerial as it was structural. Basically, the general manager of ICT Co., who was also the chairman of Hong Kong Legend, rose to preside over the group. Meanwhile, ICT Co. was renamed Beijing Legend as the Chinese part of the Legend Group.

Under the new structure, the group's overseas operations and domestic operations were more fully integrated. The structure enabled top management to allocate resources and co-ordinate R&D, manufacturing, and trade more effectively across the border. The group realized significant competitive advantages as a result of the complementarity of technology strength, a large labour force, and low production costs within China, and international product market access, quick market feedback, and abundant financial resources in Hong Kong.

For example, the group formed two R&D centres in Hong Kong and Beijing, both under the direction of the group's chief engineer, Ni Guangnan. There was a division of labour between the two centres. The Hong Kong centre focused on the development of PC motherboards and add-on cards for the overseas market. The Beijing centre focused on developing Chinese word-processing systems and systems software for the Chinese domestic market. In addition, a product testing centre was established in Beijing for testing new products developed at the Hong Kong R&D centre (LXZR 1992: 110–11).

To take advantage of an ample labour force and inexpensive manufacturing facilities (mainly cheap land) in China, the group established an equity joint venture, Shenzhen Legend, as the group's manufacturing base in the Shenzhen Special Economic Zone.[14] QDI owned 45 per cent, Beijing Legend 45 per cent, and Shenzhen Science and Industry Park Corporation the remaining 10 per cent ('New Issue Prospectus' of Legend Holding Limited, p. 136).[15]

The R&D team in Hong Kong took advantage of quick access to market information, new parts and components, and other R&D facilities in Hong Kong to develop new products.[16] It then sent the prototype of a newly developed product to Beijing for testing. The product was not only tested by a troop of in-house testing engineers at Beijing testing centre; it was also sent to local users for real-time tests. The testing results were fed back to the Hong Kong R&D centre. After revisions based on the testing results, the product was sent to a pilot plant in Hong Kong for a trial production run. After the processing technology was stabilized and the quality of the product met the requirements of overseas clients, it was quickly moved to the group's manufacturing base in Shenzhen for large-scale production.[17] Table 3.3 lists the spatial allocation of the group's R&D, manufacturing, and marketing activities.

The spatial allocation of the development tasks across the border, with R&D and pilot production in Hong Kong and testing and large-scale production in China, substantially lowered the development cost, and also accelerated the process of new product development. The group moved from 286 to 386 and then to 486 microprocessors in less than one year, with an average of one new model every one to two months (LXZR 1992: 53). By late 1990 it had almost synchronized its product development cycle with the pace of the latest technological developments in the world.[18]

[14] In China, joint ventures in manufacturing are exempt from income tax for the first two profit-making years and are entitled to a 50% reduction in income tax during the next three years (cf. the Sino-Foreign Equity Joint Venture Law). Shenzhen, as one of the 'Special Economic Zones' located in the Guangdong Province, provides preferential income-tax treatment for Sino-foreign joint ventures, better than that offered in other regions of China (for an account of the inception of the Shenzhen Special Economic Zone, see Vogel 1989).

[15] The Shenzhen Science and Industry Park Corporation is owned by Guangdong International Trust and Investment Corporation, the Chinese Academy of Sciences, and Shenzhen Municipal Government, with each of the partners contributing an equal share ('New Issue Prospectus': 43).

[16] R&D had to be located in Hong Kong because of an information advantage. There was a six-month gap in new product development between the US and Taiwan or Hong Kong, and a much longer one in China. That, and the easy access to the latest parts and components in Hong Kong, were crucial conditions for quick new product development.

[17] It became a common practice among Hong Kong manufacturing companies to have their pilot production plant in Hong Kong and large-scale production plants in China to take advantage of low-cost and high-quality labour there. For a case study of the division of labour between a plant in Hong Kong and a plant in Shenzhen, China, within the same Hong Kong electronics manufacturing company, see Lee 1995.

[18] An indication of the effectiveness of Legend's new R&D and marketing integrated system as compared with that of the central-planning mechanism was that when Legend had its 486 model on the market in 1990, the government had just incorporated the development of the 486 machine in its next five-year plan in 1991–5.

TABLE 3.3. *Spatial allocation of R&D, manufacturing, and marketing in the Legend Group*

	Hong Kong	China
R&D	R&D and product development	New product testing, Chinese word-processing system and software development
Manufacturing	Pilot production	Large-scale production
Marketing	International sales and purchasing	Domestic sales and services

This organizational integration also enlarged the risk-bearing capacity of its most precarious business, motherboard manufacturing. One example is particularly illustrative: In the spring of 1991 a price war between the two computer CPU manufacturing giants, Intel and AMD, caused the market for CPUs, the most expensive components in computer motherboards, to become extremely volatile. In the months between March and June, Hong Kong Legend's motherboard business suffered a loss of HK $17 million, close to HK $200,000 a day.[19] At the time, no one knew when the storm would end. Management, on one hand, moved all the remaining manufacturing from Hong Kong to Shenzhen, China, to lower production costs. On the other hand, it mobilized financial resources from all of the group's operations, including Beijing Legend, to withstand the losses.

When Legend finally emerged from the storm three months later, the market for its products had enlarged several-fold. Before the storm, the company only had four overseas sales offices (branch companies). The number increased to ten afterwards. The sales of manufactured products increased four times within one year, jumping from HK $79 million in fiscal year 1990 to HK $322 million in fiscal year 1991.[20] The reason was that large numbers of small manufacturing companies in Hong Kong went bankrupt.[21] Most were Legend's direct competitors.

To meet the sudden increase in market demand, the company expanded its in-house production capacity at Shenzhen Legend by purchasing extra industrial sites and facilities. Meanwhile, it fully utilized the abundant manufacturing facilities of a large pool of state-owned electronics manufacturing enterprises in the Shenzhen Special Economic Zone. It kept the more complex motherboard production in-house, and contracted out the manufacturing of less complicated computer add-on cards to the state-owned enterprises.

Management referred to this way of organizing production as a 'reservoir method', in the sense that the production volume could easily be adjusted to unforeseen market

---

[19] To better understand the magnitude of the loss, Hong Kong Legend's whole year's profit in 1990 was HK $25 million (LXZR, 1992: 141).

[20] The group's fiscal year runs from 1 April to 31 March of following year. Data from 'New Issue Prospectus': 45.

[21] The high risks in the manufacturing business might explain why few, if any, Hong Kong-based overseas private ethnic Chinese business groups expand through manufacturing (Redding and Tam 1993).

TABLE 3.4. *Hong Kong Legend's production volume of computer motherboards and add-on cards* (in 1,000 pieces)

	1990	1991	1992	1993	1994
Motherboard/Add-on cards	30	330	2,300	2,400	5,000

Sources: 'New Issue Prospectus': 37; China Electronics Industry Yearbook 1992; LXB 87: 1; 103: 2.

TABLE 3.5. *Sales of the group's manufacturing products, 1990–1995* (by fiscal year)

	1990	1991	1992	1993	1994	1995
Sales (1,000 HK $)	78,822	322,335	870,127	1,000,000	1,926,022	2,486,768
Increase (%)	—	309%	170%	15%	93%	29%

Sources: 'New Issue Prospectus': 45; Annual Report 1994–95: 20. The exact figure for all of 1993 is not available due to the company's reorganization for the listing. However, it could be estimated indirectly from the group's total production figure, RMB 1.17 billion, equivalent to HK $1 billion (exchange rate of RMB 1 to HK $1.1, Shenzhen swap market, Sept. 1993).

changes, just like controlling the level of water in a reservoir. Through contract manufacturing, in-house production capacity could be kept low, lowering the probability of capacity underutilization. The method not only effectively lowered production costs, but also further enhanced the company's risk-bearing capacity in manufacturing.

As the result of the group's technological strength in R&D, and the cost advantage in production, the company's market expanded rapidly. Table 3.4 shows the increasing production volume of the group in computer motherboards and add-on cards. Table 3.5 shows the sales of the group's manufacturing products from 1990 to 1995.

3.4.4. *A round trip: Introducing the 'Legend' brand computer back into China*

With the PC motherboard development and production capabilities at Hong Kong Legend and a nationwide PC distribution and service network of Beijing Legend in China, the group started to introduce its own brand name of 'Legend' personal computers in China in 1990.

The Legend brand computer was an extension of the development of motherboard and add-on cards. The motherboard is the heart of the computer system. Once the motherboard and other add-on cards are developed, system integration is the next step forward. Although Hong Kong Legend initially developed the Legend brand computer for the international market, it found that it was more difficult to establish a new brand in the international consumer market. On top of that, it was even harder for a Chinese company because there were virtually no Chinese products in the international PC consumer market. That is why it focused on marketing motherboard and add-on cards instead.

However, the situation in China was different. Legend had established itself as a leader in computer technologies and products with its successful introduction of Chinese word-processing products. Plus, the group had already built a nationwide sales and service network in the process of distributing its Chinese word-processing add-on cards and companion computer systems (mainly AST computers). Its high name recognition and comprehensive network made it easier for Legend to introduce its own brand into the Chinese market.

At the beginning, Hong Kong Legend handled the design, production, and supply of the motherboards and add-on cards, and also purchased other components and peripherals. It then assembled them into semi-knocked-down (SKD) form. Beijing Legend assembled the SKD kits into complete units, and then distributed them through its sales network in China.

With this division of labour between the two Legends, Beijing Legend started shifting from distributing mainly AST machines to distributing its own computer brand in 1990. In the first year 2,131 units of Legend computers were sold, which represented about half of all the computers Beijing Legend had sold that year. In the second year the number jumped to 9,000. By 1993, the unit sales of the Legend Group had surpassed the largest state-owned computer enterprise under MEI, the Great Wall Group Computer Company. Its market volume increased steadily in tandem with the overall expansion of the Chinese PC market. Table 3.6 shows the sales growth of the Legend brand PC over the years and its share in the Chinese domestic PC market.

The entry of Legend into the Chinese domestic PC market was a boost for China's domestic computer industry. At the time, competition in the Chinese domestic PC market was just heating up. For several years the market had been dominated by Great Wall, a state-owned enterprise under the MEI. Imports of personal computers were restricted (less than 30 per cent of total personal computers installed). In 1991,

TABLE 3.6. *Sales of Legend's PC and its share of the Chinese domestic market by volume*

	1990	1991	1992	1993	1994	1995
Total units sold	85,000	100,000	250,000	450,000	718,000	1,080,000
Legend PCs	2,000	9,000	18,000	27,000	60,000	100,000
Legend's share	2.4%	9.0%	7.2%	6.0%	8.3%	9.3%

Sources: Quantity: Electronics Industry Yearbook, 1995: 369; Annual Report, fiscal year 1995–6: 14. Total Computers sold in China: see 'New Issue Prospectus' (Founder): 29. Market share: 1992: 'New Issue Prospectus': 23; Annual Report 1995–6: 12.

TABLE 3.7. *Domestic production of personal computers and imports in China* (units)

	1985	1986	1987	1988	1989	1990	1991	1992
Total output	35,700	39,200	47,500	53,300	69,700	80,100	93,400	82,500
Great Wall	n.a.	n.a.	20,456	13,594	20,544	15,606	18,000	15,000
Imports	18,700	20,400	22,500	26,700	20,300	24,900	111,300	167,500

Note: Great Wall Co. was formed in 1987.

Sources: CCID; see also 'New Issue Prospectus' of Stone: 21–2. Great Wall: 1991 Company Report.

however, there was a sudden jump in PC imports—the volume was four times higher than the year before. As a result, major international computer makers dominated the Chinese PC market almost overnight (Table 3.7).

A fundamental reason for the dramatic shift was that, after a decade of high economic growth, China had been transformed from a mere low-cost manufacturing site to a potential large market in its own right. The worldwide economic recession at the time accelerated the speed of major PC makers entering into the Chinese market. Major PC makers, especially US firms, were suffering from eroding profits or operational losses due to the recession. There were deep price cuts of computer products. China, as the only major economy that was growing at a high rate at the time, became an outlet for these low-priced products. The market leaders, AST and Compaq, held more than a 40 per cent combined share of the market (Table 3.8). The import shock was a setback for the Chinese domestic PC manufacturing industry, as manifested by the decline of domestic PC production in 1992.

The advantage of leading international PC makers lies in their superior technological capabilities, deep financial pockets, and large-scale production. The latter was particularly crucial. The worldwide production of major international PC makers usually topped more than a million units per year, while the largest Chinese domestic producer at the time, the Great Wall Corporation, produced less than 20,000 units per year.[22] PC manufacturing is a low-margin business, with the bulk of costs going for parts and components. Labour costs are only a very small fraction of total costs. Major multinational PC makers enjoyed deep discounts through large-volume purchases of parts and components. In addition, the high labour cost of international PC makers was spread over large units of production, leading to lower unit labour costs. Thus, Chinese PC makers were all at a cost disadvantage vis-à-vis the major international PC makers in terms of production costs, let alone quality and technology.

Facing competition from international PC makers, the Chinese PC manufacturers suffered from declining profits or losses. The survival of the domestic PC

---

[22] According to a World Bank report, the optimal scale of production is 200,000 units per year. The production of Great Wall was only one-tenth of that figure ('1992 Report of the Great Wall Computer Group Co.').

TABLE 3.8. *Shares of the Chinese domestic PC market in 1992 by volume*

Domestic Brands	33.9%	Foreign Brands	66.1%
Great Wall	11.2%	AST	26.9%
Legend	6.5%	Compaq	18.5%
Langchao	4.3%	Acer and other Taiwanese brands	5.9%
Changjiang	3.5%	IBM	5.2%
Yunan Electronic	2.8%	Olivetti	2.9%
Others	5.6%	Others	6.7%

Note: the Legend PC share here is slightly different from Table 3.6. Two factors might have caused the discrepancy: first, they are from different sources; second, there is a difference in the periods over which the data were collected—because Legend's fiscal year is from 1 Apr. to 31 Mar. of the following year, Table 3.6 is based on Legend's fiscal year data, while this table is based on the calendar year.

Sources: International Data Corporation (IDC), also 'New Issue Prospectus' of Legend: 23.

manufacturing industry was put into question. Suggestions were made that China should give up producing computer systems, focusing instead on parts and peripherals such as computer cases, floppy disks, keyboards, low-resolution monitors, etc. News that major Chinese enterprises, such as Great Wall and Stone, had entered into joint-venture arrangements with leading international PC makers such as IBM and Compaq was interpreted as a sign that domestic PC makers were conceding to international competition.

Like other domestic PC makers, Legend also had a disadvantage in production costs upon entering the market in 1990, due to its small production scale, and the resulting high costs in purchasing parts and components. However, Legend did enjoy a major advantage in the Chinese market—its nationwide sales and services network.

As previously indicated, Beijing Legend had adopted the AST machine as the basic system for its brand of Legend add-on cards. It built a comprehensive nationwide PC sales and service network in the process. By 1990, it had fourteen branch companies and thirty-four service and maintenance centres in major cities all over the country (LXZR 1992: 109). The sales and service network lowered the entry barrier for Legend, making it possible for the company to introduce its own brand of computers.

As Legend developed complementary capabilities in technology, production, and marketing across both domestic and overseas businesses, it started gaining competitive advantages in many respects.

First, the group established labs and R&D centres in Silicon Valley, Hong Kong, Shenzhen, and Beijing. With a lab in Silicon Valley to monitor the latest technological trends, and the abundance of highly qualified personnel in China, the group was able to keep its product development current with the world's latest technological developments.

Second, the group's business of PC motherboards and add-on cards at Hong Kong Legend had gained a significant share of the world market since 1991. The cost of the motherboards had been lowered significantly. While the computer system was being upgraded to higher versions of products, the value share of motherboards and add-on cards in the whole system increased significantly, from around one-third to one-half of the complete system.[23] With its in-house supply of the motherboards and add-on cards, the group was able to control the cost of the whole system.

Third, as China increasingly became a major supplier of low-tech computer peripherals such as cases, power units, keyboards, and monitors to the world market, the group was able to purchase quality parts, components, and peripherals other than motherboards and add-on cards locally instead of importing them, further lowering their costs. As a result, the cost disadvantages in production had diminished and had even been reversed.

Combining low costs in R&D, management, marketing, and services, Legend started enjoying a significant competitive edge vis-à-vis major international PC makers. In fact, by 1994 the Legend's brand-name PC could undersell comparable AST and Compaq models by an average of 10–20 per cent, and still enjoy a 6 per cent net profit margin, which was above industrial average. Relying on high quality and low pricing, the group was able to gain market share in the increasingly competitive Chinese PC market.

Through this so-called 'round-tripping' through Hong Kong, Legend finally had a foothold in domestic Chinese PC manufacturing. The group was even designated by the MEI in 1992 as one of the national computer manufacturing bases, and its production was included in the national production plan (LXZGBD 1993: 10).

The successful launch of its own brand-name personal computer boosted the revenues of Beijing Legend. Sales jumped from RMB 250 million in 1990 to more than RMB 680 million in 1991 (LXB 93: 1).[24] Legend brand computers replaced Legend Chinese word-processing add-on cards as the company's major revenue and profit generator (Table 3.9).

3.5. Continual Expansion

With the success of the QDI motherboards and add-on cards in the international market and Legend computers in China, the group had fulfilled its goal of internationalization and industrialization under one coherent strategic plan. By 1993 the group had created an organizational structure that integrated R&D, manufacturing, and trade, with revenues roughly generated half from trade and half from manufacturing in both domestic and overseas markets. It had successfully completed the first two steps of its overseas expansion plan. To fulfil the managerial goal of building a big business concern, the group set forth to expand further by converting Hong Kong

---

[23] The weight of motherboards as percentage of total cost for 386/40, 486/25, 486/66, Pentium/66 were 36%, 38%, 43%, and 52% respectively (LXB 93: 3).

[24] One-third of the 680 million sales in 1991 was derived from the sales of Legend brand PCs (Legend Group Archive 1996: 29).

TABLE 3.9. *Performance of Beijing Legend* (currency figures in millions RMB)

	1989	1990	1991	1992
No. of employees	363	507	630	705
Sales revenues	220	250	686	1,039
After-tax profit	1.08	1.54	2.69	4.03
Remittance of taxes and profit*	1.04	2.32	4.24	5.39

* Including sales tax, income tax, and remittance to the Institute of Computing Technology.

Sources: 1989–90 figures: LXZGBD 1993: 20–1; LXZR 1992: 130. 1991–2 figures: China Electronics Industry Yearbook 1993: VII-20. 1994 figures: LXB 103: 2.

Legend into a public company and investing in new businesses with financial resources from the initial public offering (IPO).

3.5.1. *Going public on the Hong Kong Stock Exchange*

To prepare for the public listing, Hong Kong Legend went through a series of corporate reorganizations. First, a holding company was created in Hong Kong as a private limited company under the name of Legend Holdings Ltd. on 5 October 1993. The company issued and allotted shares to the Beijing Legend Group, China Technology, and the former owner-managers of Daw. The composition of the shares is listed in Table 3.10, column 2. The new holding company, Legend Holdings (Hong Kong), Ltd., then 'acquired' all the existing businesses of Hong Kong Legend. At an extraordinary general meeting on 18 January 1994, it was decided that Legend Holdings, Ltd. would be converted into a public company. The authorized share capital was increased to HK $100,000,000 divided into 1,000,000,000 shares. Of the new shares, 492,257,250 were issued to existing shareholders in proportion to their existing shareholdings in the company. That was equivalent to a 1,000-fold increase in the amount of shares for the existing shareholders. 182,250,000 shares were to be offered as new issues at a price of HK $1.33 per share, of which 13,500,000 were placed with Feng Ming Investment, a subsidiary of the Bank of China, Hong Kong Branch, and 168,750,000 shares were to be issued to the public; 325,000,000 shares remained unissued.

The resulting ownership structure is listed in Table 3.10, columns 2 and 3. Of the three founding partners, China Technology had dramatically lowered its shares in the company in the process of reorganization. The shares of Daw in the company were divided among its individual owners. The only one left intact was Beijing Legend Co., which held a controlling amount of the shares.

The restructuring ensured Beijing Legend's firm control over the listed company and was also reflected in the governing body of the company. Of five executive directors, three were from Beijing Legend, two were former owners of Daw, and the President of Legend Group (Beijing) became the chairman.

TABLE 3.10. *The ownership structure of Legend Holdings, Ltd.*

	Shares before IPO	Shares after IPO	Percentage
Beijing Legend (Group)	261,800	261,800,000	38.8
China Technology	15,034	15,034,000	2.2
Lui Tam Ping	81,106	81,106,000	12.0
Ng Lai Yick	81,106	81,106,000	12.0
Cheung Nap Kai	28,116	28,116,000	4.2
Cheng Kwok Lap	17,699	17,699,000	2.6
Other individuals	7,889	7,889,000	1.2
Feng Ming Investment	n.a.	13,500,000	2.0
New issues to the public	n.a.	168,750,000	25.0
Total issued shares	492,750	675,000,000	100.0
Total authorized shares	1,000,000	1,000,000,000	

Note: The named individuals were former owners of Daw. Other individuals were mostly minority share-holders of various subsidiaries of Hong Kong Legend. Feng Ming Investment was a wholly owned subsidiary of the Bank of China, Hong Kong Branch. 325,000,000 shares remained unissued at the initial public offering.

Source: 'New Issue Prospectus' of Legend.

It was intended that the control structure of the listed company could not be readily altered after the company went public, as was indicated in the following statement in the New Issue Prospectus: 'Without the prior approval of the members in a general meeting, no issue of shares (with regard to the unissued shares) in the capital of the company will be made which would effectively alter the control of the company' ('New Issue Prospectus' 1994: 126). The organizational structure of the listed company is illustrated in Fig. 3.3.

3.5.2. Expansion through vertical integration

The initial public offering raised a total of HK $220 million in cash. With the majority control of the listed company belonging to the group, top management was able to pursue investments according to a coherent strategic design.

It is well known that the IT industry is among the most competitive industries, marked by fast-changing technologies and cut-throat price wars. However, profit margins vary widely along the supplier chain. With systems integration on one end, semiconductors (mainly CPUs and memory chips) on the other, and manufacturing of motherboards and add-on cards in the middle, the profit level at the various stages of the supply chain exhibits a U-shape. Manufacturing motherboards and add-on cards has the lowest profit margin.

Fig. 3.4 shows a more detailed illustration of the supply chains of the IT industry. Systems integration as a knowledge-intensive business is protected by local

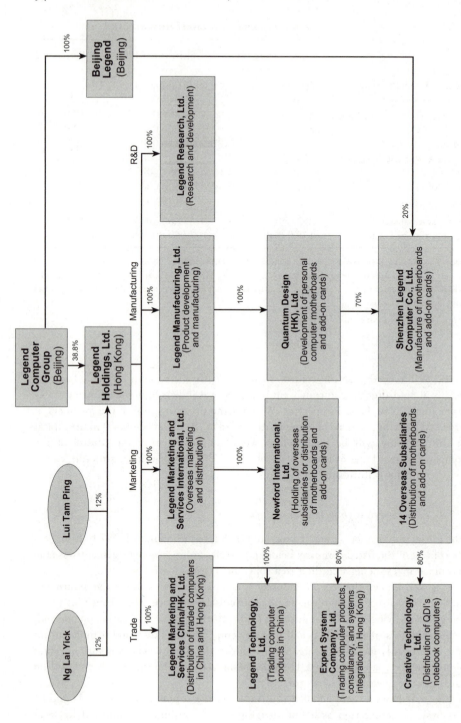

Fig. 3.3. Organizational chart of Legend Holdings, Ltd. (Hong Kong)

Source: 'New Issue Prospectus' of Legend Holdings, Ltd., 1994.

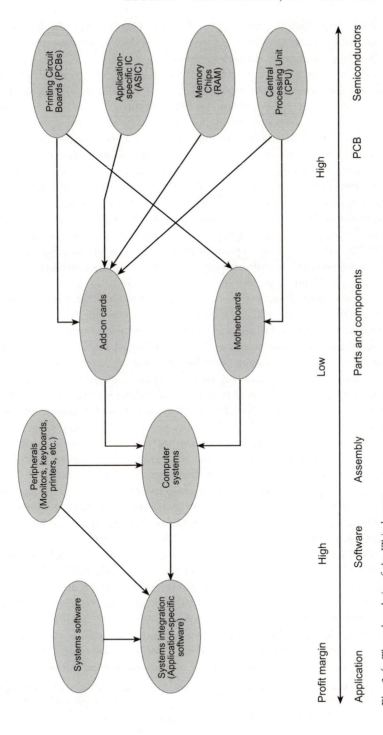

Fig. 3.4. The value chain of the IT industry

specific knowledge, hence competition is limited. That explains the high profit margin of the business. On the other end, semiconductor devices represent the highest level of technology in the computer industry. A high-input, high-yield, but high-risk business, manufacturing semiconductors is both capital and knowledge intensive, with tremendous entry barriers. The cost of development and production facilities can easily top US $ billions. Without substantial knowledge as well as capital accumulations, it is not feasible for new enterprises to enter this product market. Manufacturing mostly involves assembly, and the technologies are relatively mature. It has been increasingly concentrated in East Asian newly industrialized regions. In a sense, the success of Legend was a reflection of this general trend.

Nevertheless, Legend's management seized the low-margin motherboard manufacturing business as a platform from which to enter the high-margin part of the business. It was understood that two things are fundamental for an enterprise. One is a manufacturing base, the second is a distribution channel. The president explained: 'No matter how low the profit margin would be, manufacturing was indispensable for any product'. By cultivating a worldwide distribution network for large-scale manufacturing products, the company was building up basic resources for entering systems integration, on the one hand, and semiconductors, on the other.

On the systems integration side, the group acquired a majority (80 per cent) share in Expert System Solutions, Ltd., a local Hong Kong company, in the process of corporate restructuring for a public listing. This Hong Kong-based computer company aimed to offer turnkey solutions in computer information systems to major Hong Kong corporations and institutions. A large tender contract awarded by the Hong Kong government to the company in early 1994 marked the full launch of the group's systems integration business in Hong Kong.[25] The company won a consecutive tender from the Hong Kong government in 1995. Sales to corporate end-users grew rapidly. In addition, the Expert System obtained the international quality accreditation, ISO9002, in 1995. All these indicated that the group had established itself as one of the major players in Hong Kong's systems integration market.

As China continues to open up and upgrade its information technology infrastructure, systems integration has become an increasingly significant business. The group established a wholly owned subsidiary under Hong Kong Legend Holding—Legend Advanced Systems, Ltd.—targeting the systems integration market in China. Within three years, the group had successfully established a broad client base in China, with clients from a diverse range of commercial and industrial sectors, including government bureaux, international and local banks, public utility providers, retailers and manufacturers. Revenues of this subsidiary had increased more than tenfold within three years, from millions to dozens of millions of RMB.[26]

Recognizing the increasing importance of being able to provide total solutions and quality services, the group established a software development centre in Shenzhen for customized software, and a comprehensive local support network

[25] 'New Issue Prospectus' 1994: 52, 58, 130; Company Annual Report 1994–5: 15, 55; Company Annual Report 1995–6: 15–16.   [26] Legend Group Archive (1996).

including service centres in eleven major cities in China staffed by a team of more than 250 professionals. It successfully developed and launched Chinese-language software for inputs, communication, and printer drivers for minicomputer systems, which are indispensable for large information systems.[27]

The local knowledge base, especially its expertise in the development of Chinese-language software systems, was certainly an advantage for the group in competing with major international information technology providers in China's market for systems integration. A notable example was the group's successful bid for a large Chinese national information technology tender in 1996. In an open international bid for more than US $100 millions' worth of systems integration projects of the Chinese State Economic Information Centre, financed by loans from the Japanese government, Legend out-competed all major international information technology providers, winning more than US $20 millions' worth of contracts.[28]

On the manufacturing side, the first thing Legend management did after the initial public offering was to consolidate its manufacturing base and expand into printed circuit board (PCB) production. As mentioned previously, the group was using contract manufacturing to meet increasing market demand for its motherboards and add-on cards, a strategy that was described as the 'reservoir method of production'. This flexible production organization avoids large-scale fixed capital investment, while maintaining the ability to meet increasing market demand for motherboards and add-on cards. Since the group's client base was not stable, the flexible manufacturing arrangement could avoid investment risk. However, by early 1994, the company's in-house production capacity had reached 140,000 motherboards per month, and its subcontractors produced 580,000 add-on cards per month. At peak times, more than a dozen state-owned manufacturing enterprises were involved in subcontracting manufacturing. The group's QDI brand-name motherboards and add-on cards had become well established on the world market. A worldwide sales network had been put in place with a total of twenty-one overseas sales subsidiaries (Table 3.11). Regular clients had increased to several thousand. With the newly available financial resource from the IPO, Legend considered it time to expand and upgrade its production capacity.

A significant move of the group in this regard was the acquisition of a 71,830-square-metre industrial site and building, the Legend Science and Technology Park in Huiyang, China, a city near Shenzhen and less than fifty miles from Hong Kong. The acquisition cost HK $108 million. The Beijing Legend Group, Lui Tam Ping, Ng Lai Yick, and several other major stockholders of Hong Kong Legend Holdings, Ltd. subscribed 86 million new issues (12.8 per cent of issued shares), in proportion to their relative shares in the company, at a price of HK $1.25 per share. Hong Kong Legend then invested about HK $15 million out of its internal reserves to upgrade and expand its production facilities. By 1995 the group had twenty-one fully automated SMT (surface mounting technology) production lines. Its in-house production

---

[27] Company Annual Report 1994–5: 13–15; 1995–6: 14–15.   [28] LXB 111: 2.

TABLE 3.11. *Legend Group's overseas sales network*

Regions	Countries (number of sales subsidiaries, 21 in total)
North America (8)	USA (5), Canada (3)
Europe (8)	UK (1), France (1), Germany (1), Netherlands (1), Denmark (1), Spain (1), Austria (1), Sweden (1)
Asia Pacific (5)	Australia (2), Singapore (1), Malaysia (1), Taiwan (1)

Source: Annual Report 1994–5: 14.

capacity reached 250,000 motherboards and 550,000 add-on cards per month.[29] The group's PC motherboard and add-on card manufacturing operation in Shenzhen was subsequently relocated to the park. Centralizing production aimed to achieve a better economy of scale and a higher level of product quality.

The large volume of motherboards and add-on cards provided a basis for the backward integration into PCB production—the first major investment by the group in this higher margin business. It was estimated that the minimum net profit margin could be as much as 15 per cent, compared with the industrial average of 2.5 per cent in motherboards and add-on cards.[30] However, because of the large initial capital investment and market uncertainty, it was not easy for other firms to jump in. The group had been sourcing PCBs for years. As the production volume of motherboards and add-on cards increased, the in-house demand for PCBs became large enough to absorb a sufficient portion of in-house-produced PCBs, reducing the investment risk.

The group set up a new subsidiary—Huiyang Techwise Circuit Co., Ltd. in China in early 1994, and invested RMB 47 million to build the PCB manufacturing facility. The first phase of pilot production was carried out in late 1994. Production capacity had reached 100,000 square feet per month in less than one year. The designed capacity was 400,000 square feet per month. The bulk of the PCB products were intended for internal use, with a portion of the high-end, multi-layer products being sold to the group's long-term business clients.[31]

The large-scale integrated circuit (LSIC) semiconductor chip represents the highest level of technology in the global IT industry. There are only a handful of large companies in the world that can develop and manufacture these chips. The Legend Group has signalled their intention to enter this area. At the group's 1995 Christmas party in Hong Kong, the group president articulated the group's determination to enter the advanced semiconductor manufacturing business: 'Legend is a high tech-enterprise. We work on the low-margin manufacturing part of the IT business only to lay a foundation. We will prudently enter into the semiconductor manufacturing

---

[29] Its actual production in late 1995 had reached 170,000 motherboards and 450,000 add-on cards per month respectively (Company Annual Report 1995–6).

[30] Figures from SBC Warburg Company Report 1995: 4, 6.

[31] The information regarding the PCB business is drawn from: interviews with a senior vice-president of the group; Company Annual Report 1994–5, 1995–6; SBC Warburg Company Report 1995.

TABLE 3.12. *Major investment activities of Hong Kong Legend Holdings, Ltd.*

Areas of investment	Name of subsidiaries	Location	Legend's holding (%)	Investment (millions)
Systems integration	Expert System	Hong Kong	80	HK $1.2
Motherboard manufacturing	Huiyang Legend Computer Co., Ltd.	Huiyang	90	RMB 8
Industrial park	Legend Science Park	Huiyang	100	HK $108
PCB manufacturing	Techwise Circuits Co., Ltd.	Huiyang	75.5	RMB 41
Semiconductors	Valence Holding, Ltd.	Hong Kong	70	HK $2.1

Note: The exchange rate of Chinese RMB to HK $ was about 1.1 to 1 in 1995–6.

Sources: Annual Reports 1994–5; 1995–6.

business. As an enterprise, we will not take it only as a pure technological issue, but as a business system design. We will take marketing, finance, technology, and management all into consideration, and lay out a detailed plan. One thing is clear; sooner or later, we will take a share in that business.'

After the successful launch of its self-designed ASIC semiconductor chips for multiple I/O cards and VGA cards, the group entered into a joint venture for the development, manufacturing, and distribution of semiconductor products in May 1995. The joint venture marked its first formal step towards entering the semiconductor business.

The joint venture was formed under an arrangement similar to the one that Hong Kong Legend originally had with QDI in the business of manufacturing PC motherboards. More specifically, the group had taken a majority 70 per cent ownership in an existing Hong Kong semiconductor design company, investing a total of HK $2.1 million for the controlling share. Valence Semiconductor Design, Ltd., the company's original owner-managers, kept the remaining 30 per cent share.

Valence was one of a few local semiconductor design companies in Hong Kong with ten years of experience in designing chips for multinational companies. The partnership ensured the group's quick start in the business of semiconductor design.

The company started designing and manufacturing semiconductor products through subcontracting arrangements with wafer fabrication plants in Hong Kong, Taiwan, and Japan, and selling ASP-brand integrated circuits (ICs) in the region. It received contracts from customers in Japan, Taiwan, South Korea, Singapore, and Europe, designing customized ASIC chips for PC, telecommunication, consumer electronic, instrumentation, and industrial automation products.[32]

To summarize, converting Hong Kong Legend into a public company had greatly enlarged the group's financial resources for strategic expansion. Table 3.12 is a

---

[32] The information regarding the group's expansion into the semiconductor business is summarized from interviews with a senior vice-president, Company Annual Report 1994–5, 1995–6; LXB 105: 1.

summary of the group's major business investments. The group's scope of business had expanded from computer manufacturing and trading to systems integration, PCB manufacturing, and semiconductors design, manufacturing, and distribution. Fig. 3.5 is an illustration of the group's business operations to date.

3.6. Concluding Remarks

Legend represents both a success story of Chinese S&T system reform, and a new pattern for Hong Kong–China partnerships.

Legend was a flagship in China's S&T system reform: as a research institute-run enterprise under the Chinese Academy of Sciences, Legend created a model that profoundly transformed CAS, the very creature of central planning where rich technology resources had been accumulated but not effectively used during the decades long central-planning era. What Legend had done was to create an organizational framework that was capable of effectively turning technological resources into market successes. As the former general manager of ICT Co. and later the president of Legend, Liu Chuanzhi, once reflected:

There were 120 research institutes and 80,000 employees under CAS. There were numerous research institutes in the nation as a whole. What is the appropriate way to mobilize the state research institutions on the battlefield of economic development in the Chinese context? In other words, what is the most suitable organizational form to do so? I think it is the kind of enterprises like ours. What we have done all these years is to explore an avenue of reforming state research institutions (LXZR 1992: 27, 296).

Legend became a model of what was later called 'one academy, two systems', which was crystallized by the leadership of CAS in conjunction with the strategy of reforming the nation's science and technology system.[33] The goal of the S&T system reform was to shift the majority of the human resources in the science and technology system onto the so-called battlefield of economic development. CAS played a leading role in this process—not only because CAS was the nation's most prestigious science and technology institution and a major repository of high-quality science and technology resources, but also because the leadership of the academy consisted of the most open-minded technocrats in China. They could envision the role of commercial technologies in international competition and were willing to provide support for institutional and organizational experimentation. Under their leadership, CAS and its institutes directly and jointly had set up seventy-two S&T enterprises by 1987—about one-third of the total in the so-called 'Electronics Alley' in the Zhongguancun area of the Haidian District (Yu 1988: 43, 68). As one of the vice-presidents of CAS, Hu Qiheng, explained in 1988:

What do we mean by 'one academy, two systems'? Which two systems? Normally, people would think that one is the research system, the other is development. The latter is nothing but doing

---

[33] The phrase resembles the famous motto coined by Deng Xiaoping regarding China's Hong Kong policy after 1997, e.g. 'one nation, two systems'.

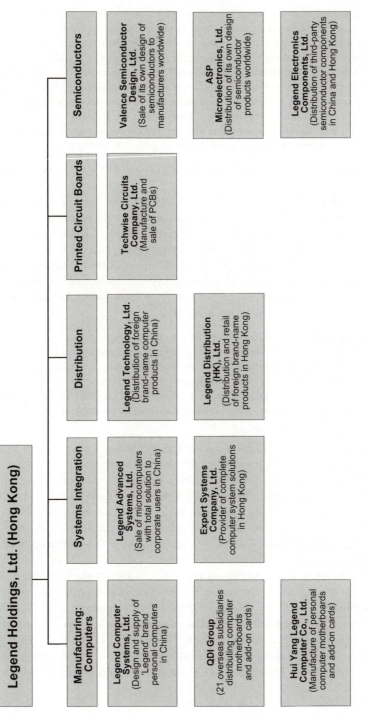

Fig. 3.5. Hong Kong Legend's major business operations

Source: 1996 Annual Report of Legend Holdings, Ltd.

business and making money. It seems in conflict with the mission of the Academy. That is not case. The two systems mean two different mechanisms of progress in science and technology. There are two forces underlying the development of science and technology. One stems from inherent human curiosity about nature. It is rooted in basic scientific inquiries. New technological breakthroughs result from these inquiries. The other stems from the market. Market demand for product and process technologies shapes the research agenda of scientists and technologists, hence becoming a driving force behind science and technology development. Both mechanisms fit the mission of the Academy. That is what we mean by 'one academy, two systems'. In the past, we only focused on the first one, and ignored the second. Now we should build organizational structure to let the second system grow (LXZR 1992: 150).

Clearly, Legend was the successful embodiment of this new science and technology policy.

As for the Hong Kong–China partnership, emphasis has been put on how Hong Kong took advantage of China's cheap labour, incorporating southern China into a coherent economic region, resembling a fifth little dragon.[34] Legend represented a new trend—a recognition of China's quality technological resources rather than cheap labour by Hong Kong business people. The combination of the marketing and financial expertise of Hong Kong and high-quality, low-cost, dedicated science and technology personnel on the mainland proved to be even more viable. As one of Legend's major Hong Kong partners, Lui Tam Ping, said:

The alliance between our two Chinese and Hong Kong enterprises is not simply an alliance of material interests. To a certain extent, it is an alliance of science and technology with market forces, an alliance of Chinese domestic science and technology resources with overseas market forces. The joint venture is the locus that integrates R&D, manufacturing, and marketing across the border. It has accomplished a task of integrating science and technology into the economy—a task Hong Kong and China could not accomplish by acting alone (LXZR 1992: 220).

The connecting point of Chinese science and technology resources with overseas business resources was, of course, the market-oriented system of CAS, as it was represented by the New Science and Technology Enterprises such as Legend. It was because of the organizational affinity between the new Chinese science and technology enterprises and Hong Kong businesses: both operated according to market principles, which made this new form of China–Hong Kong partnership possible.

Nevertheless, institutional differences remained salient. The difference could be seen as a difference between 'individualism' versus 'collectivism'. It was most clearly reflected in the ownership structures of the group. While Hong Kong partners are direct owners of their respective share of the productive assets, the Chinese slice of the assets remains collectively owned or owned by state institutions.

The company had been defined as a state-owned enterprise because it was set up by ICT, which was a state research institute. This was not because the institute provided the initial capital. As we already know, it was, in fact, a loan, and the company returned it once it made money, just like Stone did with Evergreen Township. It was

---

[34] See Vogel 1989: esp. ch. 8.

because the company used the institute's intangible science and technology resources, which were supposed to be the property of the state. It was always understood that the company was nominally owned by ICT, even though ICT had little to do with the business operations of the company other than derive an insignificant amount of fees from the company in the later stage. This meant that the property rights of the company's accumulated assets still remained vague.

As the company grew bigger and the wealth disparity between individual Hong Kong partners and Chinese managers, scientists, and other key personnel increased, the desire of the Chinese management to clarify the property rights of the Chinese part of the assets also increased.

The property at stake was the 40 per cent or so of the assets of Beijing Legend in Hong Kong Legend Holding, Ltd., as well as the productive assets of Beijing Legend itself. The available institutional vehicle to clarify the property rights of the assets was the joint-stock measure, or corporatization as it was called in China, especially after the new corporate law took effect in 1994.[35] Institutions and individuals that would have direct claims over the company's assets were ICT and CAS, the direct supervisory body of both ICT and Legend, as well as the employees of the company as a collective. According to some tentative government regulations based on the new corporate law, a common understanding was reached that Legend is jointly owned by ICT, the employees of Legend, and, to some degree, CAS. The preliminary agreement, resulting from negotiations among the three, stipulated that Legend holds 35 per cent of the share of the equity on behalf of its employees, ICT and CAS hold 45 per cent and 20 per cent respectively. The proposal awaits approval by the newly established Bureau of State-Owned Assets Administration.

As an alternative, the company started setting aside a Founders' Fund from retained earnings to reward 'founding members' of the company. According to a senior executive of the group, the founding members of the company were defined according to their seniority and contributions to the company. Thus, all the employees would be entitled to a share of the company's assets in varying degrees. Management saw this as a possible institutional innovation that would ally the interests of individual employees to the interests of the company.

The aim was that no matter what the outcome of the final approval of the joint-stock measure would be, both CAS and ICT would still be stable, long-term shareholders. Given this and the interests of the employees, management was able to think about the development of the company from a long-term perspective. The newest performance data show that the company has jumped to the leading position in the Chinese PC market It has started selling PCs in Russia and parts of Africa and Asia.[36]

[35] This law took effect on 1 July 1994. It was approved by the Standing Committee of the People's Congress on 29 Dec. 1993.
[36] *Business Week*, 14 Apr. 1997; IDG Market News Service, Hong Kong Bureau, 18 Apr. 1997, from IDG China market news update on the Internet.

4

Founder Group Company: The Changing Organization of Innovation

Innovation is the soul of high-tech enterprises.

Wang Xuan, Director of the Institute of Computer Science and Technology of Beijing University and Chairman of Founder (Hong Kong), Ltd.[1]

Based on a fundamental invention in the technology for processing high-resolution Chinese fonts, and a series of follow-up and complementary breakthrough technological innovations, Founder has been leading the world in pictographic-language electronic publishing systems technology. An indication of this technological leadership is Founder's dominance of the markets for Chinese-language electronics publishing systems, not only in China but also in Hong Kong, Taiwan, Singapore, Malaysia, the United States, and Europe. Furthermore, with its experience in developing sophisticated pictographic font-processing technologies, Founder has developed a series of high-resolution colour electronic publishing systems that enable it to compete head-to-head with the world's leading colour electronic publishing systems developers, such as Linotype-Hell of Germany and Adobe of the United States.

Unlike Stone's integrated Chinese word processor or Legend's associative Chinese word-processing add-on card, Founder's professional high-resolution Chinese electronic publishing systems technology originated in a large-scale government-led industrial R&D project under the central-planning mechanism.[2] The technology had already advanced to the stage of pilot production before Founder took over. Thus, the case of Founder provides a unique opportunity to examine the evolution of the organization of industrial innovation in the process of China's transition from a centrally planned economy to a more market-oriented one.

This chapter documents the changing organization of innovation in the rise of Founder. The central focus is on the transformation of the organization of industrial innovation from government-led to enterprise-centred. As such, Founder's experience

---

[1] Company brochure, 1995.

[2] The three technologies developed by Stone, Legend, and Founder covered the spectrum of Chinese-language information-processing technologies, with the high-resolution publishing system at the high end of the technological spectrum, the integrated Chinese word-processor in the middle, and the Chinese word-processing add-on cards at the low end.

has far-reaching implications for the ability of new Chinese science and technology enterprises to compete in the global information technology (IT) industry.

4.1. The Organization of Large-Scale Industrial R&D under Central Planning

4.1.1. Project 748

As symbolized by Richard Nixon's visit to China in the early 1970s, China resumed its contact with the outside world after more than two decades of international isolation. In 1973, as part of a technology modernization drive, the official Xinhua News Agency (New China News Agency) sent a 'technology study delegation' to Japan, to investigate the applications of new technologies in the publishing and printing industry. The delegation visited the major Japanese news agency, Asahi Shibun, and several leading electronics companies such as Hitachi, NEC, Matsushita, Nihon Shaken, and Toshiba over a period of one month. At Nihon Shaken, members of the delegation saw an opti-mechanical typesetting system. 'The whole workshop looked like a hospital', said one of the members of the delegation. 'Workers all wore white gowns and worked in an air-conditioned environment' (JNWJ 1994). The sharp contrast with the laborious lead-typesetting technology and poisonous work environment in the printing shops back home left a deep impression on the members of the delegation. Elsewhere, they saw other new technologies for computerizing Chinese-character (*kanji*) font processing. This field trip triggered a technological renewal initiative at the Xinhua News Agency.

Meanwhile, from December 1973 to June 1974 the Fourth Ministry of Machine Industry (the predecessor of the Ministry of Electronics Industry, or MEI) had invited technological experts from leading Japanese electronics companies to give seminars on Chinese-font information-processing technologies. In addition, under the direction of Guo Pingxin, the then deputy chief of the Science and Technology Bureau at the ministry, a team of technocrats investigated science and technology advancements in the world computer industry by systematically reviewing the most recent science and technology literature. According to Guo, 'the materials we looked through could be piled up several feet high' (JNWJ 1994: 132).

Computer technology had been developing rapidly in advanced industrial countries while China was trapped in the Cultural Revolution. Digital Equipment Corporation (DEC) had introduced the PDP-8 minicomputer in 1965 and the famous 16-bit PDP-11 in 1970. Database and word-processing software technologies had also matured. These developments pushed the frontier of computer applications from mere numerical calculation to information processing. At the same time, semiconductor technologies had undergone profound development, progressing from transistors to chips. In 1971 Intel announced the world's first microprocessor, the 4004, and in 1972, the much more advanced 8008.

Similarly, in the West the printing industry had made the transition from lead typesetting and lead-plate printing to phototypesetting and offset printing. In 1965

Hell, a German company, had invented a CRT-based third-generation phototypesetting technology.[3] This breakthrough marked the full assimilation of typesetting into the field of information technology. The technology was widely adopted in the industry from the early 1970s. Two Japanese firms subsequently licensed the technology, and developed the third-generation Japanese-language publishing system.

This rapid technological progress around the world created a sense of urgency among Chinese technocrats. It was clear that the computerization of information processing was a general trend. China had started developing computers in the 1950s, producing several generations by the early 1970s. Yet the applications of these computers were still confined to the realm of scientific calculation. The key to making the transition from numerical calculation to information processing in China was to develop technologies that could input and output the complicated Chinese characters.

Moved by this sense of urgency, in mid-1974 the Fourth Ministry of Machine Industry organized a panel of experts from dozens of government agencies and research institutions. The participants concluded that it was time to start a research programme on Chinese-language information processing and digital typesetting. They estimated that, due to its intrinsic complexity and interdisciplinary nature, such a large-scale research project would take more than a decade and cost more than RMB 100 million. It was suggested, therefore, that the Fourth Ministry of Machine Industry, the First Ministry of Machine Industry,[4] the Chinese Academy of Sciences, the Xinhua News Agency, and the State Bureau of Publishing Affairs Administration jointly undertake the initiative. The five agencies submitted a proposal to the State Planning Commission and the State Council on 9 August 1974.[5] They suggested that:

1. a Chinese-language information processing system engineering research project be incorporated into the state's primary scientific and technological research plan;
2. the Fourth Ministry of Machine Industry, the First Ministry of Machine Industry, the Chinese Academy of Sciences, the Official Xinhua News Agency, and the State Bureau of Publishing Affairs jointly form a project body to organize and co-ordinate resources across different administrative jurisdictions;
3. the required technological personnel be mobilized and the requisite electronics equipment, printing equipment, optic parts and components, and chemical materials be jointly arranged by the Fourth Ministry of Machine Industry, the First Ministry of Machine Industry, the Chinese Academy of Sciences, the Ministry of

---

[3] Phototypesetting and offset printing technologies were invented in the US in 1946, to replace the poisonous lead in the printing process. At first, the new printing technology was manually operated. In 1951 another US company, Photon, invented mechanical phototypesetting, subsequently considered to be the second-generation technology. Hell's CRT-based phototypesetting technology represented the third generation of the technology.

[4] The First Ministry of Machine Industry was in charge of the machine-tool manufacturing sector in China, including printing equipment. It was later renamed the Ministry of Machine Industry.

[5] This information comes from the recollections of Wang Baochen, Su Baochuan, and Guo Pingxin in JNWJ 1994.

Post and Telecommunications, the Ministry of Fuel and Chemical Industry, the Ministry of Light Industry, and other related ministries, bureaux, or state institutions.[6]

The State Planning Commission approved the project within a month. It issued an official document on 4 September 1974, incorporating the project into the state's 1975 fiscal year primary science and technology development plan. Like several other large-scale government projects, the project was given a code number based on the date it was initiated. Thus, it was referred to as Project 748 (standing for August 1974). A special office, called Office 748, was set up in the Fourth Ministry of Machine Industry, and assumed the role of organizing and co-ordinating research and development efforts. Guo Pingxin was appointed head of the office.

The project was further divided into three sub-projects: (1) Chinese-language phototypesetting, (2) Chinese-language information database technology, and (3) long-distance Chinese-language information transmission technology. Of the three, the Chinese-language phototypesetting was the most fundamental.

The project was supposed to build on existing technologies already developed in the advanced nations. In the area of phototypesetting, the CRT-based phototypesetting system developed by Hell was the most advanced at the time. The basic principle of the technology was to generate a page layout on the screen of a high-resolution computer monitor, then take a photo picture of the on-screen image, and develop the film for offset printing. The fonts used to generate the on-screen page layout were stored in the memory of the computer in dot-matrix format.

With only several dozen characters and other symbols, font storage and generation in an alphabetic system was not a major problem for third-generation phototypesetting technology. In contrast, one set of font type in a Chinese-language publishing system has close to 7,000 characters. A system that can meet the minimal requirements for application to professional publication needs at least four different types of high-resolution fonts. The memory space required to store these fonts in dot-matrix format is enormous (up to 20 MB). A minicomputer at the time had an internal memory of only 64 kB. It could store information for only six Chinese characters. Although secondary memory devices such as hard drives had larger memories, the access time was too slow to meet the requirements of industrial applications. Besides, the capacity of such hard drives was also limited at the time.[7] The major technological problem then was how to compress Chinese-font information so that it could be stored in the very limited memory space of the computers currently available and then regenerate the fonts without distortion at a high enough speed.

Since the Japanese language also contains substantial numbers of Chinese characters (*kanji*),[8] the Japanese had faced similar problems. The limitations in computer memory space forced them to adopt low-resolution fonts, resulting in a low quality

[6] From 'Proposal for Starting a Chinese Information Processing System Engineering Project', a photocopy in JNWJ.

[7] For instance, the Chinese domestically made minicomputer had only 64 kB of memory space at the time, which was far from being enough to store even one set of Chinese font type.

[8] The Japanese language uses several hundred basic Chinese characters.

of printouts. Thus, although the third-generation technology was already being widely used in the West, the dominant system in Japan continued to be based on second-generation technology.[9] A major technological hurdle had to be overcome to apply the third-generation technologies to a pictographic-language publishing system.

Before 1974 there had been scattered efforts among state research institutions in China to develop phototypesetting technologies for a Chinese-language publishing system. Some targetted the second-generation technologies; others focused on the third-generation technologies. Both had made some progress. It was decided that the development of the phototypesetting technology of Project 748 was to be conducted in Beijing in order to take advantage of the relative strength of the existing research programme in the city's metropolitan area. According to the jurisdiction rules of the time, the Publishing Bureau of the Beijing Municipal Government had authority over the co-ordination of the project from Office 748. The bureau decided to develop a Chinese-language typesetting system based on the second-generation technology. The development task was assigned to a joint research team staffed by a research university and a printing factory that had been working on the second-generation technology for years. The bureau allocated research funds to get the development process under way.

Originally, Beijing University was not a participant in the project. That it later became the leading institution in the research programme was, to a certain extent, a coincidence. At the time, Beijing University had just built a minicomputer, the 6812. Since computing capacity was very limited at the time, the university wanted to utilize the resource as fully as possible. It organized a task force to investigate the scope of the computer's possible applications. Chen Fangqiu, a junior mathematics professor, was sent by her department to join the task force. In the process, she became familiar with Project 748. Her husband, Wang Xuan, was then a junior professor in the Department of Electronics, and hence became familiar with the project as well (JNWJ 1994: 60–4).

Wang Xuan was a gifted computer scientist. He had participated in the design of one of the first computers in China—Beijing University's Red Flag Computer—when he was only a senior college student majoring in applied mathematics at Beijing University in the late 1950s. Upon graduation, he stayed on at the university as an assistant professor. He had been working on projects for developing computer systems for years at Beijing University. The challenge that confronted Project 748—the sheer complexity of generating high-resolution Chinese fonts in a computer system— stimulated his passion. For the next several months, Wang and his wife explored possible solutions to this seemingly impossible technological problem.

A mathematician by training, Wang intuitively looked at Chinese characters in terms of mathematical representations. He soon came up with an idea for compressing Chinese-font information. By mapping the contours of Chinese fonts into different shapes and parameters, the memory space required for storing Chinese fonts could be reduced by several hundred times. It was a brilliant idea.

---

[9] The typesetting system that the Xinhua Delegation saw at Nihon Shaken was a second-generation system.

Some were sceptical, however, that a mathematical idea could solve an intriguing industrial technology problem (BDFZ 22: 3). Such scepticism was warranted. No matter how brilliant the idea, the key to success was implementation. Wang's interdisciplinary background worked in his favour. According to Wang:

It is true that a mathematician might come up with an idea for compressing information content by several hundred times. However, he would face a more intriguing issue of how to regenerate the original information with reasonable speed. The speed of computers in the 1970s, including large computers, was only on the magnitude of tens of thousands instructions per second. It could only generate several Chinese fonts per second. That was far from the minimum requirement for a workable system. A person who has only a mathematics or software background might give up, feeling the barrier too high to be penetrable. The reason that I had the chance to solve the problem was due to an important decision in my life when I was 24 years old. Before that, I had mainly worked on computer hardware. At that time I decided to shift to the software area, working at the juncture between software and hardware when the word 'software' had not yet been coined. Today, it is common to have people who have both computer hardware and software expertise, but at that time, very few people knew both. Chance always favours the prepared mind. With both hardware and software knowledge, I came up with an implementation using a combination of hardware and software technology, raising the speed of font generation by a magnitude of a hundred times (BDFZ 22: 3).

Confident of his ideas, Wang set forth to persuade the key decision-makers in Office 748. In May 1976, after comprehensive testing, including a successful computer simulation, Wang's proposal finally won the support of Office 748. In September, the office issued a memorandum, officially assigning the development task to Beijing University (BDFZ 9: 3). Thereafter, Beijing University took the lead in developing the technology. It assembled a special research team, called Task Force 748, out of which grew the Institute of Computer Science and Technology (ICST).

Wang soon started working on the system's design. In reviewing technological trends in the field, he noticed that a new, fourth-generation typesetting technology was being mentioned in professional journals. The difference between the fourth- and third-generation technologies was in their output mechanism. Instead of using a high-resolution computer monitor or CRT as an output device and then taking a picture of the screen, the new technology directly recorded the page layout onto film using a laser typesetter. Due to the high resolution of laser light, the resolution of the type that had been set could be much higher and more accurate than the images taken from a CRT screen. Monotype, a British electronic publishing systems developer, came up with a commercial laser typesetting system in 1976. However, it was not widely adopted, even in the West, until 1984 when Linotype, a leading German company, developed a similar product.

At the time, there were major technological obstacles to the indigenous development of a high-resolution computer monitor and high-resolution photo-film in China. Yet both were essential for the third-generation publishing system. The manufacture of a high-resolution CRT computer monitor necessitated very complicated electronic and optic devices, while the high-resolution film also involved a very delicate chemical-processing technique. Both were beyond the range of existing

Chinese technological capability. In contrast, there was a much greater chance of developing the required laser typesetter for the fourth-generation system because complementary technological capabilities already existed in China. Wang was told that a state-owned enterprise under the Ministry of Post and Telecommunications had developed a high-resolution newspaper fax machine, the principle of which was close to a laser typesetter. The only difference was that the light source in the former was not laser. Wang saw the machine at a trade show in Beijing in early 1976. He consulted an expert in laser technology in the physics department of Beijing University, asking if it was possible to change the light source to laser. The answer was 'yes'.

The core of the laser typesetting system was a raster image processor (RIP). It was used to generate font and photo images in a dot-matrix format to control the laser typesetter for recording the page layout onto film. The development of the RIP was much more complicated than the development of the control unit for a CRT-based third-generation system, the chances of success seemed higher than those for developing the third-generation technology. It was fortunate for the Chinese printing industry that the decision to skip the third-generation technology and to develop the fourth-generation technology had been made at such an early stage when the technology was just emerging in the West. By following this route, the Chinese printing industry jumped directly to laser printing technology when both Japan and Taiwan continued to rely heavily on the third-generation technology into the late 1980s. But the development of the fourth-generation technology was only possible after Wang's ingenious idea for compressing and generating Chinese fonts, for the laser image recording required fonts at a much higher resolution, and hence, a higher rate of information compressing and a higher speed of font generation.

By late 1977, Office 748 had started to bring in enterprises and research institutes to work on complementary technologies. It assigned industrial prototyping and manufacturing to Weifang Computer Co. (hereafter referred as Weifang)—a state-owned computer electronics enterprise under MEI. Several other state research institutes and enterprises were assigned the tasks of developing complementary hardware, such as a laser typesetter and other computer peripherals. To the enterprise that made the newspaper fax machine went the task of developing the laser typesetter. Industrial testing for the system would be carried out at the Xinhua News Agency. Thus, from early on, the project included research institutes, industrial enterprises, and end-users across administrative boundaries—characteristic of large-scale, state-led development projects.

The Xinhua News Agency initially provided RMB 1.7 million to Beijing University for laboratory equipment (mainly computers) before the state's budgetary money came along.[10] Close to seventy researchers from six state institutions and enter-

---

[10] The figure is from JNWJ 1994: 43. Note that R&D expenses were mostly for research equipment and materials. The cost of R&D personnel was not accounted for as part of the expenses because all the research personnel were directly on the payrolls of their respective work units. In any case, their salaries were exceedingly low when compared with the cost of equipment and materials. Hence, the Chinese R&D cost structure was very different from that in developed countries, where staff salaries constitute the bulk of the cost of R&D.

prises were involved in various aspects and stages of the prototyping process. The first prototype was built in 1979. It printed out a sample newspaper page in the lab of ICST,[11] and then a sample book in the following year. The prototype received technological approval from MEI in June 1981. The system was named Hua-Guang (meaning 'the Light of China'). The prototype was named Hua-Guang I. In 1982 an application was made to patent the technology in Europe.[12]

4.1.2. Indigenous innovation and foreign competition

Although the basic design principle of the system had been proved by means of computer simulation in 1976, it still took four years to complete the first prototype. And there was still a long way to go before industrial application was possible. Besides the intricate difficulties relating to the complexity of generating high-resolution Chinese fonts, there were two major barriers to a fast turnaround.

First, the development of the system entailed a large-scale software development project. It included a multi-user operating system and an on-screen newspaper editing software system. With no suitable high-level computer language tools for Chinese word-processing software development at the time, assembly language—a language that is close to machine language—was the only computer language for coding, thus making it a very time-consuming process.

Second, the software development process was further complicated by the poor quality and performance of domestically made computer hardware and peripherals. Due to the general lag in computer electronics technologies, the domestically made computer system into which the high-resolution typesetting system was integrated was several generations behind those of the advanced countries and unreliable. When errors occurred in the software testing process, it was often not immediately clear if they reflected software-design problems or computer-hardware problems. In addition, the laser typesetter was a high-tech manufacturing product that integrated technologies across precision machining, lasers, and electronics. Due to China's general backwardness in all of these areas, the task of developing a reliable product was as difficult as developing the core technology of the system—the RIP for Chinese-font information processing.

In fact, both problems could actually have been avoided, or at least alleviated, had the development team adopted imported computer systems and a laser typesetter. However, the official policy inherited from the era of China's international isolation was 'self-sufficiency' or 'do-it-all-by-yourself', so that everything in the system had to be domestically made. It was not 'politically correct', so to speak, to use imported parts and components. The balance of payments was certainly a factor, for China was experiencing a severe shortage of hard currency at the time. Nevertheless, the scarcity

---

[11] *Guang Min Daily*, 11 August 1979.

[12] This was perhaps the first patent the Chinese government had applied for abroad since 1949. The patent was granted in 1987 by the European Patent Office (European Patent Number EP0095536) (BDFZ 14: 3). Note that until 1985 there was no patent system in China.

of foreign exchange was not a prohibitive constraint on using some imported equipment to facilitate the development process.

The slowness of the development process in coming up with an industrially applicable system raised doubts in China about its indigenous technology policies and
capabilities. These doubts were further reinforced when suitable products from
foreign companies became available. Meanwhile the demand from the
publishing/printing industries for a reliable industrial system was urgent.

The printing industry in China was still at the stage of lead typesetting. The process
required that workers manually select individual fonts from a shelf of thousands of
Chinese characters, an extremely labour-intensive and time-consuming process. Typesetting thus became the bottleneck of the whole printing process, and the time to
print was painfully long. For example, in one of the largest publishing houses, the
People's Press, which was one of the most well-equipped publishing houses in China,
it would take a year to get a book printed. In China's leading science book publishing
house—the Science Press—it took 500 days to print a book. Some senior scientists
complained that their own work would only be published posthumously. People in
major cities could only read newspapers with day-old news. There was an urgent need
to upgrade typesetting technology and expand typesetting capacities. With the industrial applicability of the domestic system far from clear, it was tempting for publishing houses to import laser typesetting systems directly from abroad—which is what
happened with the British Monotype laser typesetting system.

Monotype, the first company in the world to invent laser typesetting, developed
a commercial system in 1976. Until Linotype came up with a similar product in
1985, Monotype's LaserCom was the only commercial laser typesetting system in the
world. The company had been working on adapting the system to Chinese-language
publishing. It planned to bring two sets of its laser typesetting systems to China for
exhibition in 1979.

There were controversies over importing the Monotype system. The government
agencies and research institutions that were directly involved in Project 748 insisted
on developing the system indigenously. More specifically, Office 748 was firmly
against any importation of systems from abroad. The same was true for the State
Planning Commission, the State Science and Technology Commission, and the
Ministry of Education. However, eager to upgrade the technology of the printing
industry, the State Bureau of Publishing Affairs Administration was pushing to
import the Monotype system.

To ward off the threat from Monotype, the development team of Project 748 intensified their efforts. A target was set to complete system prototyping and the printing of a sample newspaper page before the planned Monotype exhibition in
the autumn of 1979. The process was intense. The chief designer of the system,
Professor Wang Xuan, later recalled:

In the seventeen-year period from early 1976 to early 1993, I gave up almost all holidays,
including weekends, working day and night on the project. However, the most stressful period
was in 1979. At that time, we had advantages in system design. But our advantage in system
design had not yet been translated into an applicable industrial product. Only through hard

work and persistent innovation were we able to gain real market advantage. The process was perilous. Any slacking off could lead to failure.[13]

The team managed to complete the system prototyping and print out a sample newspaper page on 27 July 1979.

The success of the system prototyping boosted confidence among the members of the development team as well as the co-ordinators of Project 748 at MEI. As Wang argued: 'Using low-quality domestically made parts and components, we had come up with a system that had a superior performance in Chinese-font handling over the imported system. If we had used imported parts and components, we could definitely have come up with a superior product' (recollection, 1994).

Although Monotype's LaserCom was a mature product for alphabetic language publishing, it was not mature for Chinese-language publishing. The rate of its font information compressing technique was very limited. As a result, it had to use four 80-MB hard disk drives to store the required Chinese-font information. It took considerable time to access the hard drives, and hence the system was very slow.

Compared with the Monotype system, the system design idea of the indigenous technology was undoubtedly superior. In fact, the mathematical representation of Chinese fonts advanced by Professor Wang in early 1975 was a predecessor of the 'Hint' technique that became widely used in the West with alphabetic fonts ten years later (for example, the 'True Type' fonts that came with Microsoft Windows 3.1). However, because the prototype was made of domestic electronic parts and components, it did not function reliably. In fact, the system was so unstable that at the beginning it often took dozens of tries to come up with one correct layout. At this stage, industrial application was not a problem of the system design but the quality of the indigenous hardware.

Nevertheless, the success in prototyping was encouraging. It tipped the balance among various government ministries and bureaux in favour of developing the Chinese laser typesetting system domestically. After intense discussions among high-level government officials involving several deputy prime ministers, a consensus was reached, as summarized in a letter submitted to a deputy prime minister by the deputy commissioner of the State Import and Export Control Committee on 22 February 1980:

1. The Chinese-language laser typesetting technology developed by Beijing University and related institutions and enterprises has reached preliminary success. The technology is close to mature. Several performance criteria are on the cutting edge. The critical problem is that the domestically made computer systems as well as electronic parts and components are too heavy and not functionally reliable. We suggest supporting the project by providing a limited amount of hard currency (US $200,000) for importing a minicomputer system and some electronic parts and components for continuous experimentation, to turn it into an industrially applicable system, and even for export.

2. With the approval of Deputy Prime Ministers Yu and Fang, the British firm Monotype exhibited two sets of its system in Shanghai and Beijing last October. Deputy Prime

---

[13] From the transcript of Wang's personal recollections, 20 July 1994.

Ministers Wang and Fang have agreed to purchase the two systems. The State Bureau of Publishing Affairs Administration conducted a negotiation with Monotype subsequently, and signed an intent to purchase. The two systems are now still in Beijing. The bureau reports shortages of typesetting capacity. It is particularly severe in the Beijing area. Many manuscripts are waiting to be printed out. The laser typesetting system under development in Beijing University has not yet been made industrially applicable. It is suggested that the Bureau of Publishing Affairs be allowed to resume purchasing negotiations with Monotype, providing that we buy only the equipment, not the technology.

These policy suggestions were endorsed by five deputy prime ministers.[14]

With special permission to import a computer system and some IC components, the computer hardware problem was, to a large extent, alleviated. The team soon started to develop a second-generation system. The development efforts centred on two tasks. The first was to design a new Chinese font RIP with the newly available imported microprocessor and other LSIC components. The second was to transplant the system and applications software to the new computer system and to improve them subsequently. By the end 1982, the new system, Hua-Guang II, was complete and ready for industrial testing.

4.1.3. New government initiatives and the success of industrial testing

In 1982 a new large-scale government project designed to transform technologies and production facilities in a whole range of publishing- and printing-related industries brought new momentum to Project 748. The new initiative was crucial for the translation of the system prototype into an industrial product.

Besides the pre-press stage of typesetting, the printing industry involves a range of processing and material technologies that range from press machines to paper-and-ink technologies. Project 748 was conceived in the information technology industry, and was under the administrative jurisdiction of MEI, which had no jurisdiction over the printing and other related industries. Up until 1982, Project 748 was still far away from industrial application, while the general backwardness of the entire Chinese publishing industry was no longer bearable.

In June 1982 a retired senior official, Wang Yi, who worked in a high administrative post in the State Bureau of Publishing Affairs Administration, told a journalist from the Xinhua News Agency that the backwardness of the Chinese publishing industry could not continue. He called for a major overhaul of the industry. The talk was reported in the 7 August issue of the *Internal Reference of the Xinhua News Agency*—a newsletter that was instituted to inform the top party and government officials about the current affairs of the state that were not easily transmittable to the top through regular hierarchical channels. The report stimulated a chain reaction at the highest levels of the party and the government.

After reading the report, one of the members of the Politburo of the CCP (the highest governing body of the party), Hu Qiaomu, who was in charge of the propaganda function of the party, wrote a letter to the Chief of the Party Propaganda Department and the Commissioner of the State Economic Commission, urging the adoption of the suggestions of Mr Wang Yi.[15] The letter stated:

In order to solve the problem of the technological backwardness of our printing industry, it is necessary to have concerted actions among the government departments in charge of the machine industry, light industry and chemical industry. I hope the Propaganda Department and the State Economic Commission can co-ordinate that effort.[16]

On 26 August 1982, the Party Propaganda Department and the State Economic Commission jointly organized a meeting to discuss the issues of upgrading the Chinese publishing and printing industries.[17] Presiding over the meeting were the heads of the Party Propaganda Department, Deng Liqun, and the State Economic Commission, Zhang Jingfu. The participants were top bureaucrats from ministries and bureaus that were directly or indirectly related to the publishing and printing industries, including the Ministry of Culture, the Ministry of Machine Industry (formerly the First Ministry of Machine Industry), the Ministry of Electronics Industry (formerly the Fourth Ministry of Machine Industry), the Ministry of Chemical Industry, the Ministry of Light Industry, the Ministry of Finance, the State Planning Commission, the Ministry of Urban and Rural Development, the Ministry of Metallurgy, the Ministry of Transportation, and the Planning Commission of the Beijing Municipal Government. The conference authorized the State Economic Commission to assemble a Co-ordinating Committee for the Renewal of Publishing and Printing Industrial Technology and Equipment with members from all the relevant government agencies or party apparatuses. A senior official, Fan Muhan, who had long experience with the publishing and printing industries, was appointed the head of the committee. Similar to the case of Project 748, the Office for the Renewal of Publishing and Printing Industrial Technology and Equipment was set up to perform the secretarial work of the committee.

The committee started with a thorough investigation of the current status of the publishing and printing industries in order to draw up a comprehensive plan. They visited the printing shop of the nation's largest newspaper, the *People's Daily*, and one of the largest printing factories in China, the Xinhua Printing Factory. In the printing shop of the *People's Daily*, they saw an imported Japanese-made, third-generation phototypesetting system in operation. In the Xinhua Printing Factory, they saw the Monotype laser typesetting system, on which a team from the State Institute of Printing Science and Technology was working to adapt it to Chinese-language publishing.

---

[15] The State Economic Commission had the same rank as the State Planning Commission. They were the two most powerful departments in the State Council, ranking higher than the ministries. The major task of the State Planning Commission was to approve plans, while the major function of the State Economic Commission was to oversee the execution of those plans and the operation of the economy as a whole.

[16] Information about the new government initiative is drawn from the 'Chronicle of the Publishing Industry in the 1980s in China' in JNWJ.

[17] This is a typical case of overlapping functions between a Party organization and a government organization.

After the investigation, the team members formed a consensus on how to renovate the publishing and printing industries. They all agreed that the future lay in offset printing. The key to upgrading offset printing from lead-plate printing was electronic typesetting. The deputy director of Office 748 introduced the team to Project 748, and showed them the sample book that had been produced with the Hua-Guang I system. He announced that MEI recommended incorporating Project 748 into the state's new printing industry renovation plan. However, the system prototype of Project 748 had a long way to go before becoming an industrial product. Therefore, some government agencies continued to suggest adapting the Monotype system.

After listening to arguments made by Professor Wang Xuan, the chief system designer of Project 748, the team finally accepted the MEI's recommendation. They were convinced that the design principle of the system was solid. Although there were technological uncertainties, they felt that the development of a high-resolution Chinese-language electronic publishing system had to come from the Chinese themselves. They knew that the most difficult part would be developing the hardware, particularly the laser typesetter. As a hedge, they adopted two complementary measures. One was to continue adapting the Monotype system. The other was to allow the *People's Daily* to import one system from abroad as a back-up in case the Project 748 team could not come up with an industrially applicable system in the short run.

On 2 March 1983 a joint meeting between the State Planning Commission and the State Economic Commission, presided over by the then deputy prime minister and the commissioner of the State Planning Commission, Yao Yiling, approved the printing industry renovation plan prepared by the co-ordinating committee. It was agreed to set aside RMB 40 million each year for the remaining three years of the sixth five-year plan in 1981–5 to upgrade technologies and equipment in key enterprises in the publishing and printing industries.

The plan designated the Xinhua News Agency as the industrial testing site for the Hua-Guang II system. RMB 2.2 million was allocated to the Xinhua News Agency to set up a pilot printing shop (JNWJ 1994: 45). The Ministry of Personnel and Labour allocated funds to employ twenty personnel in the pilot shop (JNWJ 1994: 80–1).

The construction of the pilot plant started in 1983. By March 1984 the system installation was completed, and the test operation commenced. After nine months of preparation, the system started test publication of a weekly newspaper and a monthly newsletter in January 1985, in parallel with the lead-typesetting process in case of a system failure. In February 1985 the precautionary use of parallel lead typesetting was abandoned. From 1 February to 30 April, the system published eighty-eight issues of a weekly newspaper, twelve issues of a monthly newspaper, and some other journals and books, for a total of more than ten million words, or 2,000 pages, of typesetting. In May 1985 the system and the pilot plant were both approved by a panel of seventeen experts from sixteen state units organized by the State Economic Commission (JNWJ 1994: 79).

However, to completely prove the technological viability of the system, it had to pass the strictest test—publishing a daily newspaper, which has the shortest lead-time for publishing and demands a highly efficient and reliable system. At about the same time, the State Economic Commission made a new proposal to add RMB 10 million per year for five years to renovate the equipment of the major newspaper publishing houses (all major newspapers are state-run enterprises). It provided yet another reason to adapt the Hua-Guang II system to daily newspaper publishing.

In 1985 the *Economic Daily* had just resumed publishing after a decade-long disruption due to the Cultural Revolution. It inherited an old site along with old printing facilities from the *People's Daily*, and faced the task of renovating its printing equipment. The newspaper headquarters and its printing shop were located in the Wang Fu Jing area, the busiest shopping centre in central Beijing. Because of space constraints, there was no room for expansion with the old lead-typesetting system. The director of the print shop was actively seeking new types of technologies. He was enthusiastic about the new laser-typesetting system. With the sponsorship of the Office for the Renewal of Publishing and Printing Industrial Technology and Equipment, he managed to put the renovation of the printing shop of the *Economic Daily* into the state's newspaper renewal plan for the state's seventh five-year planning period in 1986–90. The development team installed the Hua-Guang III system, an improved version of the Hua-Guang II system, for testing. After an intensive test, the system was improved and stabilized to the degree that met the requirements for publishing daily newspapers by late 1987. The indigenous development of an industrially applicable laser-typesetting system was successful.

Table 4.1 is a summary of the participating institutions and enterprises and their roles in Project 748. Table 4.2 shows the evolution of the Hua-Guang systems in the development process.

The success in the development of the Hua-Guang system was the result of 'social-

TABLE 4.1. *Participants in Project 748*

Participants	Roles
Institute of Computer Science and Technology (ICST) of Beijing University	System design, development of the raster image processor (RIP), software development
Weifang Computer Company of the Ministry of Electronics Industry	Manufacture of minicomputer systems and the RIP; system integration
Telecommunication Equipment Factory of the Ministry of Post and Telecommunication	Laser typesetter (drum type)
Changchun Opti-Mechanics Institute of the Chinese Academy of Sciences	Laser typesetter (rotating mirror type)
Xinhua News Agency	Testing site, pilot plant
Economic Daily	Testing site

TABLE 4.2. *Development of the Hua-Guang systems*

Version	Sets	Price (RMB)	Time	Remarks
HG-I	1	n.a.	1979–81	Prototype
HG-II	~20	1,200,000	1982–5	Testing products
HG-III	43	460,000	1986–7	Pilot production
HG-IV	~1,700	400,000	1988–9	Commercial production

n.a. = not available.

Source: JNWJ Recollections 1994: 33, 135–6.

ist collaboration'. Most of the money was granted from state budgets. None of the participating institutes or enterprises had any independent financial interest in the project. The major motivation for these institutes and enterprises to develop the indigenous system was simply to stop the inroads being made by imported systems.

4.2. The Entry of Founder

Although Beijing University was the system designer, it was not the major financial beneficiary of the technology within the organizational framework of both Project 748 and the printing industry renewal project. The major beneficiary was the system manufacturer or integrator, Weifang, under MEI. Strictly speaking, in a centrally planned system, it does not matter who gets the profits from government R&D projects in the first place because almost all the profits made by enterprises are handed over to the state, which then redistributes them. However, starting in mid-1980, as the result of a series of reforms in the profit remittance regime, the proportion of profits retained by enterprises rose dramatically. Enterprises, as well as public institutions, developed independent financial interests. This financial independence also resulted in the rapid rise of extra-budgetary funds. As a manifestation of this trend Beijing University founded a new science and technology enterprise of its own in 1985, with its extra-budgetary funds, aiming to cash in by commercializing technologies developed in the university.

4.2.1. Founder's predecessor: The New Technology Development Company of Beijing University

By 1985 the appeal to reform the nation's science and technology system, of which the research university was a part, had been widely accepted. The central theme was to integrate science and technology into economic development. Under the science and technology system reforms, research universities were less pressed by grant cuts than the state research institutes because universities had their clear function as educational institutions. Like other research institutions, Beijing University started to act on the rationale that 'as the nation's leading research university with all of its high-quality science and technology resources, *Beida* (the nickname of the university) has to do something' (SYQB 16: 3).

In 1985 the university first set up an Office for Technology Development to transfer technology to industry. In the beginning, the major activity of the office was to sell those technologies developed in the labs of the university to enterprises. Although some technologies were sold in the arms-length market, the technology transfer was not as effective as was originally hoped due to the huge gap between the laboratory prototype and commercially viable products. To fill in missing organizational linkages for transforming laboratory prototypes into commercial products, the office decided to set up its own enterprise to be the vehicle for commercializing technologies. In addition, dozens of new high-technology firms were emerging in the area surrounding the campus.

Although Beijing University was the nation's top educational institution, with many talented people, it was still not easy to find people at the university to run a business. In the Confucian tradition merchants have low social status, a tradition remaining influential in all Chinese universities, and especially in the nation's top university. Nevertheless, the people in the Office for Technology Development did manage to persuade Luo Binglong, a professor in the physics department, to join and run the enterprise.

In an interview, Luo gave the reasons why he was chosen for the job and why he was willing to accept the position:

At the time, the research team I led had developed a night-viewing device for the Bureau of Public Security on a contractual basis. We used our knowledge in physics to develop the device for the Public Security Bureau for a fee. That was a kind of new horizontal technology transfer mechanism, and was different from the traditional way of doing research based on government budgetary grants via vertical administrative channels. Our project was the largest of its kind in terms of the income that we received from doing it. It caught the attention of the head of the Office for Technology Development, and he persuaded me to run the new enterprise. I accepted because I have different views about being a businessman. At the time, there were still a lot of negative views about the computer business in the so-called Electronics Alley.[18] Some thought that the people who ran computer businesses there were all speculators. They bought and sold computers without creating any value. I held a different view. In the past, if we needed parts and components that were not domestically available for scientific experimentation, we had to look through manuals and order them through bureaucratic channels. The state import and export corporation would collect all the orders annually to purchase them abroad. Often, it took years from the time an order was placed to the arrival of the parts and components. Once the parts and components finally arrived, the project was usually already finished. Now we could buy them directly from the market, thanks to these new computer shops. That made a big difference. It might also be because my father was a merchant, I had it in my blood to be a merchant.[19]

From an organizational perspective, the new enterprise was very similar to ICT Co. (the predecessor of Legend). The original name of the new enterprise was the

---

[18] Electronics Alley refers to the area surrounding Beijing University, where new computer companies have mushroomed since the 1980s.   [19] Personal interview in July 1996.

New Technology Development Company of Beijing University, or Beida New Tech. Its goal was the same as that of ICT Co.—to commercialize technologies developed in the university. The Office for Technology Development provided RMB 30,000 for initial office expenses. The university also planned to provide an additional RMB 300,000 for working capital, drawn from its extra-budgetary funds.[20]

Like most other new science and technology enterprises, Beida New Tech started with computer trading to accumulate capital. The RMB 300,000 that the university had made available provided Beida New Tech with the necessary financial backing that was required to register a subsidiary called the Beida Technology Development Company that specialized in computer trading. Trading was not considered a reputable business, however, and Beida New Tech was cautious not to actually spend the RMB 300,000 pledged by the university. Instead it sought alternative financial sources, and, like Stone, found a nearby rural township, Yuyuantan Township, that was willing to lend money to the company.

At the time, Luo had already managed to recruit several other professors from various departments, including one professor in the mathematics department whose son-in-law was responsible for Yuyuantan Township's industrial business. Like Evergreen Township, Yuyuantan Township was also a large economic concern with revenues of hundreds of millions of RMB from agricultural, industrial, and commercial activities. The Township accumulated significant amounts of money, and was seeking profitable investment opportunities. Through the mathematics professor, the company made contact with Yuyuantan Township.

A deal was cut between Beida New Tech and Yuyuantan Township. The township was to provide RMB 400,000 to be managed by Beida New Tech. The township and the company would share the profit on a 50–50 basis. The arrangement was called 'collaboration' (*hezhuo*), a peculiar arrangement at the time that had no clear legal underpinnings.

With the money, Beida New Tech purchased computers for resale. It ordered computers from southern China, where computer parts and components had been imported through Hong Kong and assembled at factories. Because of the huge difference in prices between an assembled computer, on the one hand, and its parts and components, on the other, the businesses of assembly and trading were very lucrative. Beida New Tech did not even need a storefront as most other computer shops did. Its only office space was a student dormitory on campus. The company distributed flyers to rooms in nearby hotels, the residents of which were likely to be people

[20] In 1986 universities in China had three financial sources. The first one was educational grants from the state budget via the administrative line of the State Educational Committee. The second one was grants for research projects from the State Planning Committee, the Science and Technology Committee, and various ministries. Such grants are budgetary funds. The third one was income that the university gets from various types of for-profit activities such as adult education programmes, the university press, guest hotels, and co-operative research projects. These sources of income were outside of the state budgetary channel, and hence were categorized as extra-budgetary funds. The grants from budgetary sources have to be used according to state directives, meaning that the university has no autonomy in spending the money. However, the university had a certain degree of autonomy in spending the extra-budgetary funds. From personal interviews with the former president of Beijing University in July 1996.

who had come to the Electronics Alley to buy computer-related products. Through computer trading, in just half a year, the company made a 100 per cent profit on the RMB 400,000 it had borrowed. According to the agreement, the township got RMB 200,000, a surprisingly high return. The township decided to invest RMB 3 million more. The company was accumulating money quickly.

But commodity trading was just a means to an end. With Beijing University in the company name, Beida New Tech had to become a real high-technology firm. Luo recalled, 'I knew that to be justifiable as a company run by Beijing University, I had to go for real high-tech products'.[21]

4.2.2. Moving into the electronic publishing systems business

The high-resolution Chinese electronic-publishing systems technology became Luo's prime target. In late 1987 and early 1988 the technology had already passed the daily newspaper publishing test at the print shop of the *Economic Daily*, and was ripe for large-scale industrial production and marketing. As already mentioned, from the very beginning of Project 748, the state-owned Weifang was designated by MEI as the sole producer or systems integrator. It had prototyped or made all the previous versions of the system, and started to produce the latest version of the product, Hua-Guang IV.

The Office for Technology Development of Beijing University signed a series of contracts with Weifang on behalf of the ICST (because the institute was not an independent legal entity at the time) as part of a technology transfer scheme begun in 1988. According to the contracts, for each system sold, Weifang had to pay RMB 10,000 (RMB 5,000 for a low-end system) in royalties to Beida. Beida Technology Development Co. started as a dealer for Weifang.

Owing to the high-technology content of the product, profit margins were very high. Compared with the high profits that Weifang received, the revenues from transferring the technology were insignificant. Many people at Beijing University thought that the university, as the leading institute in the development of the technology, was not getting a fair share. Therefore, Beida New Tech pressed for a licence to manufacture the system.

Incidentally, some serious quality problems were discovered in the system Weifang made. It malfunctioned when the control box heated up. Tensions arose between ICST of Beijing University and Weifang over who was responsible for the problem. The people at ICST thought it was a physical design problem, while the people at Weifang insisted that it was a software design problem for which ICST must be held accountable. It was difficult to prove who was really responsible.

Aiming to manufacture the RIP itself, Beida New Tech had been working on redesigning the system for a long time. They found that the real cause of the unsuitability of the system was indeed its physical design. Without any competitive pressure—now that all the foreign competition was being kept out—Weifang, as a

---

[21] Personal interview in Aug. 1996.

designated monopolist in the market, did not pay much attention to improving the product. Thus, when Luo approached Wang, the chief designer of the system, with the idea of selecting Beida New Tech as an additional site for manufacturing and marketing the product, Wang agreed.

On 8 January 1988, on the occasion of a visit to ICST by the head of the Office for the Renewal of Publishing and Printing Industrial Technology and Equipment, Shen Zhongkang, Wang raised the issue of granting the right to manufacture the system to Beida New Tech. Wang convinced Shen on two grounds. First, Weifang would not have any incentive to improve the product if there was no competition. Second, because of the monopoly it held, Weifang sold the product for much too high a price, thus slowing the diffusion of the new technology. As such, Weifang was not contributing to attaining the goal of the state's printing technology renewal project.

With Shen's oral permission, Beida New Tech began to organize production of the system based on its own design. It signed a contract with ICST based on a technology transfer scheme, which was, on paper, similar to the one ICST had created with Weifang. Starting in mid-1988, Beida New Tech marketed its own products. Thereafter, the two companies manufactured and marketed the same brand-name product—the Hua-Guang IV Electronic Publishing System—with different physical designs.

4.2.3. Rivalry with the state-owned computer electronics enterprise

Beida New Tech immediately engaged in a marketing war with Weifang. First, it replaced all the RIPs of the Weifang-made systems it sold with its own one for free, thus advertising the better quality of its product over Weifang's in industrial circles. The company then went on to target those provincial level newspapers that were most likely to adopt the new electronic systems at the time. Luo and his top managers started with Heilongjiang Province, in the north-eastern corner of the country. After extensive marketing efforts, Beida New Tech surpassed Weifang in terms of market share.

In 1988, when Beida New Tech got into the electronic publishing systems business, Weifang was already a well-established, state-owned computer electronics enterprise. It had been making general-purpose minicomputers for years. To prepare for industrial production of the electronic publishing system, Weifang had been undergoing a major renovation of its manufacturing facilities. The renovation project was incorporated into the central and local governments' seventh five-year plan in 1986–90. The actual spending on upgrading the production facilities exceeded RMB 10 million, including a more than RMB 3 million state budgetary grant, RMB 4 million preferential bank loans, and the remaining RMB 3 million financed with the enterprise's internal reserves.[22]

---

[22] Data from an internal report of Weifang Computer Co. Notice, this investment scheme already reflected the changes in financing technology and equipment renovation of state-owned enterprises. Before the economic reform, it was more likely that all the money required for the renovation plan would came from a state budgetary grant. For a general view on the reform of the investment system in China, see Yao 1994.

In contrast, Beida New Tech was a start-up company with very little initial capital and only several dozen employees. It did not have its own production facility. It out-sourced the production of the RIP to a state-owned electronic enterprise in Beijing, which had one of the most up-to-date wave-soldering production lines. The handful of personnel at the production department mainly focused on quality control (BDFZ 17: 4). One of the former presidents of Beida New Tech described how the company managed to come up with a very high-quality product:

We adopted higher quality standards. For example, there were two product standards, one was set for personal computers, one was for mini computers. We chose to adopt the standard for minicomputers for the production of the raster image processor. The production department controlled the purchasing of parts and components. It strictly followed the high standard for minicomputers. Although the production cost was higher using the higher standard, owing to the high value-added nature of the system, it was only a small portion of the value of the product.[23]

With superior product design and high-quality production, plus systematic mar-keting efforts, by the end of 1990, Beida New Tech had surpassed Weifang to become the leader in the Chinese electronics publishing market in less than two years. After a dispute regarding 'Hua-Guang', which was a registered trade mark of Weifang, in 1991 Beida New Tech registered its own trade mark 'Founder' for a new generation system. The company was reorganized and renamed the Founder Group Co. in Feb-ruary 1993.

By 1995, Founder had a 75 per cent share of the Chinese domestic electronic pub-lishing systems market, while Weifang had only 25 per cent. Weifang's client base was continuously shrinking, as their existing clients migrated to Founder's systems. Facing formidable competition from Founder, Weifang shifted to other electronic product markets—for example, telephone switches. The electronic publishing system now only accounts for 10–15 per cent of Weifang's revenues.

One of the major reasons for Weifang's loss of its market share was certainly the problem of product quality. According to a former president of Founder:

Weifang used a two-layered printing circuit board for the raster image processor. It was a very big one. It easily over-heated. When heated, it would get bent out of shape and that made the connection of the electronic components unreliable. What is more, the delicate ASIC [application-specific integrated circuit], the core of the raster image processor, would work abnormally in high temperatures. We happened to be their sales agent before our own product came out. Our clients told us that they often needed to hit the control box to make it work. When we designed the product, we used a four-layer printing circuit board, which was the most up-to-date. That greatly reduced the size of the board. Meanwhile, we put a heat dif-fuser on the ASIC chip—a technological secret that made our product more reliable. Indeed, the product design and production was so up-to-date, foreign visitors often asked us from which country we imported the product. The fact was, we had mastered world-class manu-facturing technology in only one year.[24]

---

[23] Personal interview in July 1996.
[24] From 1988 to 1990, a total of 1,700 sets of the Hua-Guang IV were sold. Among them, Weifang Computer Co. counted for 526, less than one-third (Wang, Twenty Decisions; Weifang, List of Products Sold, from company archives).

When Weifang finally realized that its system malfunctioned due to a product design problem, it tried to fix it. It took a substantial amount of time for Weifang to redesign the product, thus giving Beida New Tech the opportunity to increase its market share. Again to quote the former president of Founder: 'While Weifang spent time fixing its quality problem, our product became well entrenched in the market. We became the market leader in just one year.' A more fundamental problem was the organizational tie between ICST of Beijing University and Weifang. As a result of reform in the profit remittance regime, state-owned enterprises became more and more financially independent. Consequently, as both ICST and Weifang became more independent financially from the government, they each had greater ability and incentive to pursue their own self-interest. Tension arose because the two sides had different goals.

For the scientists in the institute, it was very important to maintain continuous technological improvement. Otherwise ICST ran the risk of losing its edge to foreign competitors. However, for Weifang, given its monopoly position in the market place, there was little imperative to improve process and product. Having mastered the technology through co-operation with ICST over a decade, the engineers at Weifang felt that they could proceed without the institute. In September 1990 Weifang unilaterally announced an upgraded version, Hua-Guang V, independent of ICST. This move effectively cut off the possibility of co-operation with ICST on future product development.

Unlike Weifang, Beida New Tech's close organizational tie with ICST provided it with ready access to new technologies, on which its own innovative efforts depended. With the end of direct grants from the state after completing Project 748, the institute relied more and more on the financial returns it got from Beida New Tech's sales. The two entities became symbiotic, with the result that ICST and Beida New Tech forged an organizational tie that ensured continuous technological innovation. On the one hand, the scientists in the institute were keenly aware of the most recent developments in science and technology, and developed innovative products accordingly. On the other hand, the company could turn lab results into commercial products with its development and marketing capabilities. Meanwhile, it could provide continuous feedback from the market to the scientists in ICST about new product design. Increasing integration between Beida New Tech and ICST resulted in an acceleration of technology development and shortened new product cycles.

4.3. Relations with the University

In continuously translating new technological breakthroughs from the institute into commercial successes, the fundamental organizational principles of Beida New Tech were akin to those of new non-governmental science and technology enterprises such as Stone, in the sense that its managers had full autonomy in making business decisions. This autonomy was due, to a large extent, to the open-mindedness of the leaders of Beijing University, to which both Beida New Tech and ICST belonged.

When asked about the university's policy toward Beida New Tech, the president of the university at that time said:

In terms of the university's relation with the enterprise, I have discussed this issue several times with vice-presidents and other high-level officials in the university. I had a notion that the enterprise should not be treated as if it were a sub-unit of the university, like an academic department. According to the rules of the university, many decisions regarding affairs at the department level had to be approved by the president. Sometimes, these decisions are not even within the mandate of the president. Often I had to call a president's meeting to make the decisions collectively. I was aware that lots of things in business dictate quick reactions. Problems would arise if the decision had to go through lengthy bureaucratic procedures. I remember that I had talked with Luo several times, and I joked with him that there are plenty of professors in the university but few businessmen. [I told him] I would like to throw you to the 'sea', to use a buzzword, that is, the 'business world'. You have to learn to swim by yourself. Please do not expect too much from the university. As you might know, we had a couple of university-run enterprises before. My treasurer told me, the profit of those enterprises was not real, for they were all appropriating the resources of the university without paying for them. For example, they were using the university's buildings, utilities, hospitals and other welfare facilities without paying for them. In other words, the enterprises were not independent from the university. I told Luo that we would do it for real this time. The university will not give free facilities to the enterprise. If he needed the facilities of the university, he would have to pay for them. In return, he had the right to recruit people from outside, and pay higher salaries to them. However, the university would not provide them in the health-care benefits, housing, etc., to which state employees are entitled. In return, the university would not interfere in the daily business operations of the enterprise.[25]

In the president's mind, the university was the boss, appointing the top management of the company. A vice-president of the university was appointed the chairman of the board of directors. In reality, the board of directors rarely exercised its power so that most people (including top managers of the company) were not even aware of its existence.

One of the former presidents of Beida New Tech put it this way:

Nominally, Beida New Tech is still a state-owned enterprise. However, it is different from the traditional state-owned enterprises, I mean, the ones under the jurisdiction of ministries of industries. It is actually owned by Beijing University. Yet it is operated as if it were a private enterprise. The university does not interfere with the daily business activities of the company. None of its wages, welfare benefits, or bonuses are constrained by the regulations set for state enterprises. We are completely autonomous for doing business. However, because it is not a state-owned enterprise in the traditional sense, its risk-bearing capability is also very low. If it fails, no one would bail it out. This is part of the reason why the enterprises in Electronics Alley rise and fall so quickly. It puts a lot of pressure on management.[26]

Nevertheless, as a supervisory body, Beijing University had close relations with Founder. The company was registered as a university-run enterprise, an institution-alized enterprise category that could be traced back to the late 1950s. It is natural

---

[25] Personal interviews in July 1996.   [26] Personal interviews in July 1996.

to think of Founder as a university-owned enterprise in legal terms. In fact, 'Beijing University' was never dropped from the name of the company. Besides, like Legend, the handful of co-founders of the company were and are still officially professors of the university. They get their base salary and all the welfare benefits including housing and health care, to which state employees are entitled, from the university.[27] As the company grew, the university continually gave the company its quota of state employees.[28] The commercial success of Founder relied on the continuous supply of new technologies from ICST.

In terms of its initial capital, source of technology, and key personnel, Founder had close connections with the university. As a result, the university had legitimate rights of control over the enterprise. Yet in practice, the university's controlling rights had been confined to appointing top management and deriving a certain amount of income from the enterprise. In other words, the university had restrained itself in exercising its rights.

There were good reasons for the university to exert only limited control over the company. First, the initial capital that the university had supplied was relatively insignificant. As the former president of the university frankly stated:

The RMB 300,000 was symbolic by business standards. I knew that. In other words, the university had invested very little. The company relied heavily on loans from outside in the beginning. I remember the president of the company told me that they had access to a relatively large fund from a local rural township.[29]

Second, although ICST was its source of technology, the company contributed decisively to the design of the product for manufacturing, organizing the actual production process, and marketing the product. It was a common understanding among the high-tech business community in the region that these processes could be even more difficult once the logical design of a technological product came out of the labs. In Founder's case, it was the in-house engineering team who redesigned the physical layout of the product that finally stabilized its performance and laid the foundation for the success of Founder over Weifang in the market place.

For the reasons mentioned above, Founder's management had a very high degree of autonomy in conducting business. Like the president of Legend, the president of Beida New Tech also attributed the success of the company to the laissez-faire attitude of the university towards the company. There was no written contract between the university and the company defining the allocation of controlling rights; in particular, the amount of returns the enterprises had to hand over to the university. The enterprise was managed so successfully, that, until 1993, management was left to determine how much to turn over to the university annually. The university under-

---

[27] The company started repayment of the salaries the university paid to the employees who were still attached to the university once it began making money. For Founder, it started in 1988. Legend also did the same.

[28] Since the company grew so fast, the university kept a cap on the number of the state-employees the company could have, which was 100. Generally, the company used that quota to recruit graduate students.   [29] Personal interview in July 1996.

stood the importance of retained earnings for the growth of a high-tech company, and in any case had only made a limited initial capital investment. The university's attitude was voiced by its president at the time:

To be honest, I had expected higher returns from the company in the beginning. However, I was convinced by company management that high-tech firms require very high capital inputs. The profit the company makes has to be reinvested, as long as we want to keep the company competitive and growing. That was imperative. There was no reason to squeeze the company to solve the financial problems of the university. Besides, I had other sources of extra-budgetary funds—the University Hotel and the University Press, to name a few. So I didn't have to rely exclusively on Founder.[30]

There had been an implicit agreement between the leadership of the university and company management. However, as the leadership of the university changed, and the company grew bigger and made more money, it was tempting for the university to seek more income from the enterprise. Yet from its own perspective, the management of the enterprise did not deem it justifiable to give up more revenues to the university than had hitherto been the norm. The tensions that arose between the university and the company over the allocation of returns contributed significantly to a leadership crisis in the company. In 1992 the university intervened to replace the first general manager of Beida New Tech, Luo Binglong.

The crisis reflected the control that the university could wield over the enterprise. However, the replacement of Luo created an outcry from the high-tech business community and media. For it was under Lou's leadership that the company had grown from a small start-up to a dominant enterprise in the professional publishing systems market. There was no apparent fault on his part that could be cited as a reason for him to step down. The incident also caused concern within the local district government and the State Education Commission, which was the supervisory body of the university. Although the replacement of Luo was not reversed, the strong reactions to it placed constraints on how far the leadership of the university could go in exercising its control. The issue was resolved by promoting an inside executive, an associate general manager, to the position of general manger, with his promise to increase by a fixed increment per year the profits that the company would turn over to the university.

Table 4.3 shows the financial performance of the company and the amounts of money it paid to the university over the years.

4.4. The Wellspring of Innovation: Indigenous Capability and New Organizational Structure

In 1985 the chief designer of the Hua-Guang Chinese electronic publishing system, Professor Wang Xuan, visited the leading international developers of electronic publishing systems in Germany, Japan, and the United States. Upon his return, he reported to the head of the Office for the Renewal of Publishing and Printing

---

[30] Personal interview in July 1996.

TABLE 4.3. *Founder's financial data and its remittances to Beijing University* (currency figures in millions RMB)

	1987	1988	1989	1990	1991	1992	1993	1994	1995
Employees (headquarters)	12	40	89	120	200	256	390	500	700
Revenue	n.a.	50	90	130	200	420	940	1,800	2,500
Profit		28	40	49	79	120	201	101	
R&D fee to ICST		0.7	1.2	2.0	3.5	6.5	8.0	11.0	9.0
Remittance to university		0.6	1.2	1.8	4.0	8.0	12.0	16.0	20.0

n.a. = not available.

Sources: Personal interview with the former president of Founder Group in July 1996; Yearbook of Electronics Industry 1995.

TABLE 4.4. *Founder's competition with major international producers in China*

Company	Country	Founder's replacement
Monotype	UK	Sold typesetting publishing systems in China before 1988, but was replaced by Founder later
Wang	US	Used by *Guangmin Daily* and *Shanxi Daily* before Founder replacement in 1990
HTS	US	Used by *People's Daily* before Founder replacement in 1990
Nihon Shaken	Japan	Used by Shanghai's *Liberation Daily*, *People's Daily* (overseas version), and *Hong Kong Daily News* before Founder replacement
Nihon Morisawa	Japan	Used by *Ming Pao*, *Commercial Daily* (both Hong Kong newspapers), and *Taiwan Independent News* before Founder replacement

Source: Crédit Lyonnais Securities Asia: China Research, Feb. 1996.

Industrial Technology and Equipment that the technological lead the Hua-Guang systems had should prevent all the foreign systems from competing in the Chinese market over the next three to five years. By 1988 Wang's prediction was shown to be correct. The Hua-Guang systems and the subsequently developed Founder systems replaced all existing imported newspaper publishing systems (Table 4.4), and kept foreign systems from entering into the Chinese market thereafter. What is more, the Hua-Guang systems came to dominate the Chinese-language electronic publishing systems' overseas markets, including Hong Kong, Taiwan, Singapore, Malaysia, the United States, and Europe.

4.4.1. Indigenous innovation and market competitiveness

Wang's confidence sprang from his direct observations of the systems that were under development in the labs of Founder's major international competitors. As he recalled:

In 1979, when I started designing the raster image processor for the Hua-Guang II system, I decided to use a newly available microprocessor AM2900. In the summer of 1985, when I visited Germany, Japan, and the US, I saw that Germany's Hell was using the AM2900 for a new system under development. I saw that Japan's NEC also used the AM2900 for its Japanese-language publishing system. In September 1984, when I started designing the RIP for the Hua-Guang IV system, I decided to use a combination of the AM2916 with an application specific integrated circuit [ASIC] as an accelerator. Given the IC fabrication technology of the time, a combination of a microprocessor with a small-scale ASIC was probably the most efficient solution for the Chinese-font RIP. Because of this design, Hua-Guang IV reached an unprecedented speed of 710 Chinese characters per second for 100×100 resolution fonts. This made the TC86 the fastest RIP in the world. When I was visiting those companies, the design of the TC86 RIP for Hua-Guang IV had already been completed. I felt that Hell's LS210, and other raster image processors that were under development in the labs of other companies would be no match for our TC86 because they only used the AM2900 without an ASIC.

Following Hua-Guang IV, Founder developed two consecutive systems—Founder 91 and Founder 93. If the superior design ideas of the Hua-Guang IV system were the technological basis for Founder to keep all the foreign systems at bay in China's domestic electronic publishing market, then a breakthrough innovation in adapting the PostScript Level 2 standard in the Founder 93 RIP laid the foundation for Founder's dominance in the markets for Chinese-language publishing systems overseas.

PostScript was a page-description language designed for a professional publishing system. It had been invented by the US company, Adobe, in 1983. Along with Apple and Linotype, Adobe developed the PostScript Level 1 standard. However, the standard was not popularized until the late 1980s due to its high requirements for computing speed and other system resources. In 1990 Adobe announced the PostScript Level 2, which greatly enhanced the standard. It soon became the de facto industrial standard for professional publishing systems. Any publishing system that did not support the PostScript Level 2 was no longer marketable internationally.

Beida New Tech had been using its own page-description language—BDPDL—for the Hua-Guang system for years, and it had sold more than 20,000 copies in China. However, in 1990 it faced the issue of adapting PostScript Level 2 in order to keep current with the industrial trend.

One approach to adapting PostScript Level 2 to Chinese electronic publishing systems was simply to add Chinese fonts to an existing system developed for alphabetic language publishing. This approach was adaptive in the sense that it did not change the functionality of the original system. However, as was always the case, due to the inherently large information content of Chinese fonts, any design that was efficient for an alphabetic system would not be efficient for a Chinese-language system. Font information was represented by general third-order curve mathematical expressions under PostScript Level 2. The advantage of this representation was that it ensured very high-quality font printouts. One of the fundamental operations in the PostScript was converting the contour of fonts represented in the general third-order curve into a dot matrix for controlling laser output devices. For an alphabetic system, with only several dozen characters, all the conversions could be done at once. The dot-matrix information of the characters then could be stored in the computer internal memory for repetitive use. However, a high-end Chinese electronic publishing system requires more than 20,000 characters (including both the simple and complex character sets) and has more than 50 font types. It was extremely inefficient, if not impossible, to convert all the font information of the Chinese characters up-front, and store them in the computer's internal memory for repetitive use. Font information had to be converted each and every time a character was chosen. Thus, a system designed for alphabetic font processing would run considerably more slowly when processing Chinese fonts. The key was to raise the speed of the conversion operation so that the performance of a Chinese-language publishing system could match that of an alphabetic system.

Once the problem was clear, Wang decided to develop an ASIC chip to accelerate the conversion operation. The process entailed developing an algorithm, and subsequently designing an ASIC chip to implement the algorithm. One of Wang's graduate students came up with an efficient algorithm that was capable of executing one curve-to-dot operation in one computer clock cycle. It was implemented with a design of an ASIC chip that was capable of conducting large amounts of parallel operations. The chip was given the name 'PostScript co-processor' in the spring of 1991.

In autumn 1991, when the design and simulation of the Chinese PostScript co-processor was completed, Wang saw a report that Adobe had developed the Type I co-processor, a product that resembled the Founder co-processor. Wang realized that ICST was not the first one to come up with the idea of developing a co-processor. Nevertheless, the fact that ICST had done so indicated that Beida had independently chosen a viable technological approach. It was estimated that the speed advantage of the co-processors would last at least for three years. 'In this regard, both Founder and Adobe were the world's leaders', said Wang (BDFZ 24: 3).

The Adobe chip was designed for pictographic language publishing systems. It sold very well in Japan. The Founder chip surpassed the Adobe chip in at least two ways. First, the Founder chip integrated image processing with font processing. This made it faster than the Adobe chip in processing mixed text and image materials. Second, manufactured with 0.7 nm technology, the Founder chip had a higher integration density than the Adobe chip, which was manufactured with 1 nm technology. As Wang put it:

You know, the Intel 60 MHz Pentium was based on 0.8 nm technology. We used an even narrower manufacturing technique for our co-processor. Such a 120 leg large ASIC chip with 160 pieces of blueprint (compared with six pieces of blueprint for the TC86 RIP) could not be fabricated in China. We outsourced to one of the world's leading semiconductor manufacturers. Thus, we used the world's most advanced semiconductor manufacturing technology with our own design capability, coming up with a world-class chip that raised the Chinese Post-Script technology to a very high level.[31]

The technological advantage of the chip was attested to by the fact that Adobe as an industrial leader never challenged Founder's position in the Chinese-language publishing systems market. In contrast, after realizing its technological strength, Founder made plans to enter the Japanese- and Korean-language publishing systems markets, strongholds of the Adobe chip.[32]

The successful development of the Chinese PostScript Level 2 system created an avenue for Founder to dominate overseas Chinese-language publishing systems markets. Until 1992 Founder's presence in the overseas market was mainly confined to several newspapers in Hong Kong and Macao. After the development of the Chinese PostScript Level 2, Founder's overseas markets expanded rapidly. It started with a call for tenders from one of the largest newspaper and magazine publishing groups in Hong Kong—the *Ming Pao* Group—for a publishing system upgrade worth US $14 million. In 1993 *Ming Pao* planned to buy systems from the world's best publishing systems makers. The criteria were that it had to be a Post-Script system, have high-quality colour capability, be fast, and run under a Windows environment. Tests were very strict. If one item failed, the system would not be considered. The finalists were Founder and two companies from Taiwan and Hong Kong respectively. Only the Founder system passed all the tests, and was chosen by *Ming Pao* (BDFZ 14: 1).

Founder's success in bidding for the *Ming Pao* project produced a ripple effect. Large newspaper groups in Hong Kong, Taiwan, and Malaysia started buying the Founder system. Within less than half a year, Founder's overseas sales had soared. The three largest Taiwan newspapers, *Central Daily*, *United Daily*, and *China Times*, all sent people to the site at *Ming Pao* to examine the Founder system. They were all surprised by Founder's achievement in electronic publishing technology. At the time, the *Central Daily*, a major Taiwan newspaper, was using the British Monotype system. It took twelve minutes for the system to come up with one 1000-DPI resolution film. In contrast, the Founder system could produce four 1200-DPI colour films in less than ten minutes (BDFZ 14: 1; 24: 3). All three Taiwanese newspapers migrated to the Founder system thereafter.

There is an anecdote that illustrates the extent of the technological advantage of the Founder system. The *Central Daily* was the official newspaper of KMT (the Nationalist Party) in Taiwan. The editor-in-chief of the newspaper joked by saying that even if they used a 'communist technology', they would not come up with a communist newspaper. Nevertheless, Founder's success in Taiwan's electronic publishing systems market was remarkable, given the leading position of Taiwan in the global IT industry and the contentious political relations between the two sides of the Taiwan Strait.

---

[31] From transcripts of Wang's lecture at Yunnan University in Apr. 1994 (BDFZ 24: 3).
[32] The plan was to take 1% of the US $10 billion Japanese market in 1997 and 5% by 2000; see 'New Issue Prospectus, of Founder (Hong Kong), Ltd., Dec. 1995.

The chief designer of the Founder system summarized its technology development strategy as 'catching up and leaping forward'. As he put it:

In high-tech areas, there are big lags between our country and advanced countries. Many new ideas and methods originate abroad. . . . However, we should not be satisfied with merely catching up because this would not come up with competitive products. It was inevitable that we would catch up for quite a long time. However, it was possible to leap forward based on our indigenous innovative capabilities (BDFZ 29: 1).

Both the development of the TC86 of the Hua-Guang IV system and the PostScript co-processor of the Founder 93 system were illustrative of this strategy of 'catching up and leaping forward'.

It has to be pointed out, however, that there were clusters of indigenous technological breakthroughs underpinning both the Hua-Guang systems and the subsequent Founder systems. The RIP technology was but one—albeit an important one. The chief systems designer, Wang Xuan, identified a total of twenty major technological breakthroughs over the twenty-year period of developing the Chinese electronic publishing systems (see Fig. 4.1). All of them were developed under the same spirit of 'catching up and leaping forward'.

It was understood that indigenous innovation was imperative, as IT systems became more and more open, and market competition became more and more severe (BDFZ 25: 3). Under the new circumstances, 'if a system was not competitive in the international market, it would not be competitive in the domestic market either'.

4.4.2. The significance of integrating postgraduate education into research and development

Although both the Hua-Guang systems and the Founder systems had been developed in a similar spirit of 'catching up and leaping forward', the organizational foundations of the strategy had changed fundamentally. One of the most important organizational characteristics of the development of the Founder systems was the integration of postgraduate education into the technology development process. Among one dozen or so key technological breakthroughs underpinning the Founder systems, the majority were developed by graduate students (MS or Ph.D. candidates) of ICST.

The Founder systems made advances over the previous Hua-Guang systems on three technological fronts: PostScript, the Windows environment, and colour publishing. As previously indicated, Wang made the decision to develop the Chinese PostScript co-processor in 1990. The key was to find an efficient curve-to-dot conversion algorithm. The algorithm was found by one of Wang's doctoral students. As Wang recalled:

I know when it comes to algorithms, I am no longer doing better than my graduate students. So I chose one of my best graduate students, Yang Zhengkun. He graduated with a mathematics degree from Beijing University. He finished the four-year college programme in three years. He then got his Masters in mathematics under the guidance of the famous mathematician, Professor Zhang Gongqing. Later he became my doctoral student. He liked to read and

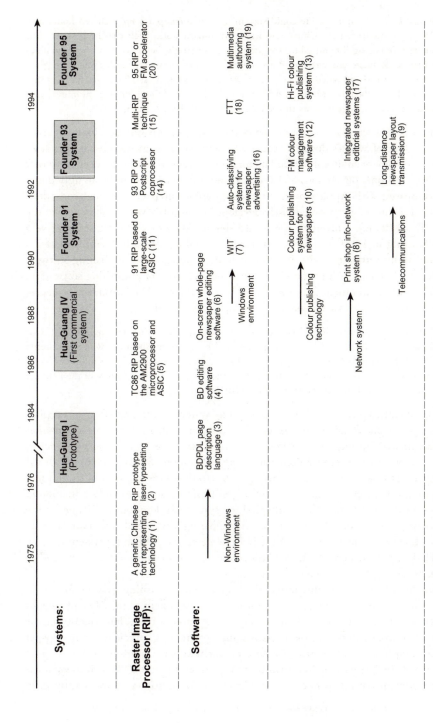

Fig. 4.1. Technological breakthroughs in developing Founder's electronic publishing systems

was obsessed with computers. He could stay in front of a computer for eighteen hours each day. Plus, he came from rural China, and was used to hard work. I felt that he possessed the kind of creative potential required for the job. Not surprisingly, he did come up with an algorithm that could make one curve-to-dot conversion in one computer clock cycle. The speed of the ASIC that had embodied this algorithm was extraordinarily fast. That was the chip that was comparable to the most advanced Adobe chip. It laid one of the technological foundations for the success of Founder systems in the overseas market (BDFZ 12: 3; 24: 3).

The same was true for the adaptation of the Windows software development environment. One of Wang's doctoral students, Zheng Ming, suggested using Windows as the development environment for Founder systems as early as 1988, when Microsoft Windows was only on versions of 1.0 to 2.0 and was considered to be an ugly duckling compared with Apple's more advanced graphic interface. Personal computer-based publishing systems were mostly developed for Apple's Macintosh system at the time. Thus, Beijing University started developing Windows Chinese software very early. Starting in 1990, Windows 3.0 started overtaking Macintosh as the platform for publishing software in the West. Two leading professional publishing software developers, Coral and Aldus, developed their new versions of publishing software in the Windows environment first, then transplanting them to Macintosh, the reverse of what was usually the case for software developers. Wang said:

It was fortunate that we developed Founder systems software in a Windows environment. Our WITS was the first Windows Chinese-language publishing systems software. WITS was highly regarded in the overseas Chinese-language publishing systems market. It was another reason, in addition to the speed of our PostScript RIP, for the *Ming Pao* Group's choice of the Founder system for its US $14 million system upgrade (BDFZ 9: 4; 25: 3).

Traditionally, a professional colour publishing system was separate from a text publishing system and required very expensive and sophisticated equipment. The market was dominated by four international makers. They were Hell (Germany), Scitex (United States), Crossfield (United States), and Dainippon Screen (Japan). With the emergence of PostScript Level 2, it was possible to integrate colour publishing functions into a desktop computer's electronic publishing system. At only a fraction of the cost of the traditional system, the desktop system was a serious challenger to the traditional colour publishing systems. Anticipating this trend, the two German firms—Linotype, which was one of the leading electronic publishing system makers, and Hell, which was one of the leading colour system makers—actually merged in 1990, becoming Linotype-Hell.[33]

Founder developed an integrated desktop colour publishing system for newspapers in late 1991. It replaced the traditional colour system at the *Macao Daily* for publishing the colour pages of the newspaper. Although the colour quality of the printout from the desktop colour publishing system was sufficient for newspaper publication, it was still far from being on a par with the traditional colour system in terms of the quality of colour printouts. The colour texture of the printouts of the desktop system was not as fine as the traditional colour separator. However, by 1993

[33] From Linotype-Hell's home page on the Internet, created on 30 Apr. 1996.

a new colour texture modulation technique appeared which raised the quality of desktop publishing to a level that was comparable with that of the traditional system. The new system had the advantage of costing much less as well as offering text and image integration.

The people at ICST had been following the trend since late 1991. They saw a news report about the almost simultaneous announcement of the release of new technology by Linotype-Hell and AGFA in March 1993. Upon learning about the new development, ICST decided to develop their own frequency-modulation techniques.

Again, it was one of the graduate students at the institute who made the breakthrough—coming up with a frequency-modulation technique that was comparable to those of the leading international developers. But because of its very high demand for computing capacity, the technique was very slow when implemented in the form of pure software. With its experience in ASIC-chips acceleration, ICST decided to develop an ASIC to accelerate the frequency-modulation process. The chip was designed by a 26-year-old former graduate student, currently an associate professor of ICST, in early 1995. It was the first such chip in the world, demonstrating that Founder was at the forefront of in the new generation of colour publishing technology. As had happened when the development of the Hua-Guang IV system had displaced international producers from the Chinese-language electronic publishing market, the emergence of the Founder professional desktop colour system ended the dominance of the Chinese market by the world's largest professional colour systems equipment manufacturers, Hell, Dainippon Screen, Scitex, and Crossfield.

In a paper published in Founder's internal newsletter regarding software development strategies in China, Wang explained the importance of the younger generation of scientists and engineers working in the research labs for continuous innovation:

IT is a fast-changing industry. Successful innovators are seldom over the age of 45. Twenty years ago when I was designing the Hua-Guang system, I was also just a little over 30. Now my creative period has passed. It is very difficult for me to come up with new breakthrough ideas again (BDFZ 27: 3).

Elsewhere, Wang gave an example from his personal experience of how he was convinced by the capabilities of young people.

Over the holidays of 1993 Spring Festival, I was working to improve the design of the ASIC chip for ten days non-stop. It slightly increased the speed of the chip. One of my Masters' students looked at it, saying that all of it was unnecessary. He knew of an existing function in the Windows operating systems that was more effective. I was furious at first, blaming him for not having told me earlier. Nevertheless, this episode further convinced me that young people were doing better than me. I had been working in the forefront of technology development for more than two decades at the time. After that, I began retiring from direct involvement in the actual development process and instead focused more on R&D strategy (BDFZ 24: 3).

Wang's role, then, was to ensure that talented young graduate students had the opportunity and incentives to contribute to the research and development process. By 1995 most of the ICST labs were headed by former graduate students of ICST.

4.4.3. The changing role of the state in industrial R&D

To a large extent, the integration of postgraduate education into research and development was possible because of the close organizational tie between ICST and Founder. This organizational tie led to close coupling between the R&D activities of ICST and the commercial activities of Founder. On the one hand, Founder, through its marketing activities, provided ICST with financial resources and product-feedback information. On the other hand, ICST with its postgraduate educational function attracted talented young graduates and became a wellspring of continuous innovation.

What is more, as a public institution, ICST also integrated a set of new organizational devices being developed in the process of China's science and technology system reform. This role made ICST an even more important resource for innovation. Among these new organizational devices were the National Key Laboratory and the National Engineering Centre.

The concept of the National Key Laboratory was conceived in the late 1980s by technocrats in the State Planning Commission, the State Science and Technology Commission, the State Educational Commission, and the Chinese Academy of Sciences. It was proposed that, by the year 2000, China would build some 100 national key laboratories in selected fields where China has an advantage. The World Bank agreed to provide a thirty-year interest-free loan of US $130 million.[34]

ICST was designated as a site for establishing a National Key Laboratory in the field of computer information-processing technology in 1989. The mission of the laboratory was to extend ICST's existing research activities. According to the director of ICST, Wang Xuan, 'Although the Hua-Guang system has been a great success, we need to conduct more in-depth research in key science and technology areas in order to maintain the technological lead' (BDFZ 1: 1). The World Bank loan of about US $1 million to this particular National Key Laboratory was mainly used to equip the lab with up-to-date computing facilities.

The National Engineering Centre was initiated by the State Planning Commission as an experiment in new organizational forms for accelerating the process of translating lab results into commercial products.[35] In April 1994 the State Planning Commission and the State Educational Commission jointly provided a RMB 12 million preferential loan to ICST to establish the National Engineering Research Centre for Electronic Publishing Systems. The mission of the centre was the development of high-end professional colour publishing systems, as well as integrated news reporting, transmission, editing and publishing systems (BDFZ 19: 1).

In addition to the above two organizational devices, in an effort to move industrial R&D from state research institutions to enterprises, the State Economics and Trade Commission (formerly the State Economics Commission), the State Tax

---

[34] Interview with a former staff member of the Office of the World Bank Loan Administration under the State Educational Commission in Apr. 1997.

[35] In fact, the National Engineering Research Centre was inspired by the US's National Science Foundation Engineering Centre in the early 1990s. From interviews with a former high-ranking official at the Chinese Academy of Sciences in Aug. 1996.

Bureau, and the State Bureau of Customs jointly initiated a plan for sponsoring 100 enterprise R&D centres in 1994.[36] The sponsored enterprise R&D centres would get tax breaks on R&D expenditures and exemption from import duties for R&D-related materials and equipment (BDFZ 25: 1). ICST, as Founder's R&D centre, was selected as one of them.

The director of ICST, Professor Wang, described the multifaceted organizational structure of ICST as a 'dragon'. With its multiple organizational devices, such as the National Key Laboratory, the National Engineering Research Centre, and the Enterprise R&D Centre, ICST was like a dragon surging forward at the cutting edge of research and development. It was continuously bringing technological breakthroughs to the products of the Founder Group, enabling it to compete effectively in the increasingly competitive IT market.

This new organizational structure implied a fundamental change in the role of the government in organizing scientific research, particularly industrial R&D—a change from direct involvement in the decision-making, financing, and co-ordinating of scientific research to building institutional infrastructures to facilitate scientific research. One of the notable changes in this regard was the alteration of the government's planning mechanism in allocating financial resources to industrial R&D—a shift from grants to loans.

For example, ICST had been receiving research funds from Project 748 and the State Publishing and Printing Technology Renewal Plan. In the sixth five-year planning period in 1981–5, ICST received several millions of RMB in government grants. Entering the seventh five-year planning period in 1986–90, ICST spent a total of RMB 5.38 million on R&D, of which government grants accounted for RMB 2.86 million and ICST's own retained earnings for RMB 2.52 million (BDFZ 4: 1). In the eighth five-year planning period in 1991–5, all government funding was distributed through loans, albeit low-interest preferential loans (BDFZ 7: 1). ICST's earnings were composed of royalties from both Weifang and Beida New Tech between 1988 and 1990, and later solely from Beida New Tech or Founder from technology transfer schemes. As the market for the electronic publishing systems expanded, ICST's income also increased (Table 4.3), thus enabling it to sustain and expand its R&D activities over time.

As it became obvious that ICST was the de facto R&D centre for the Founder Group, it was only natural for ICST to become part of Founder. The process of integration was gradual, however. In 1993 the group set up a technology committee, chaired by the director of ICST, to co-ordinate R&D activities across ICST and the group. In late 1995, as part of a corporate reorganization for public listing, ICST was formally integrated into the Founder Group as its R&D centre.

Summarizing the changing funding mechanisms of ICST, Wang wrote:

In more than a decade from the mid-1970s to the late 1980s, ICST received a total of RMB 10 million in government grants for research and development of the electronic publishing

---

[36] The enterprise R&D lab initiative was inspired by the central R&D labs of large enterprises in the West, particularly the US. Ironically, at the time large US corporations were eliminating their central R&D labs (cf. Rosenbloom and Spencer 1996).

system. Today, we spend more than RMB 15 million per year on R&D (not including industrial testing), all derived from the sales of our products in the market.[37]

4.5. The Road to Big Business

The constant flow of innovations out of the labs of ICST was the foundation for Beida New Tech, and then Founder, to ensure high returns from manufacturing and marketing activities. With Beijing University refraining from taking money out of the company, Founder accumulated a sizeable capital. By 1992 Beida New Tech had consolidated its dominant position in the electronic publishing systems market in China and was expanding into Chinese electronic-publishing systems markets overseas.

In 1993 the company was reorganized into an enterprise group to accommodate further expansion. Beida New Tech was renamed Founder Group Co. At the ceremony celebrating its establishment, government and party leaders of the Beijing Municipality voiced the expectation that Founder would be a RMB 10 billion business by the year 2000. Thereafter, '10 Billion RMB by the Year 2000' became the group's corporate goal (BDFZ, Special Issue, 30 June 1995). Like Stone and Legend, Founder took three complementary approaches for further growth: industrialization (backward integration into manufacturing), diversification (expansion into new businesses), and corporatization (going public on the Hong Kong Stock Exchange).

4.5.1. Industrialization

The electronic publishing system was an integration of computer hardware and software, including input and output devices. What ICST had developed were the core technologies of the system—RIP (which was equivalent to a special-purpose microprocessor)—and the systems application software. RIP entailed manufacturing, but, when at most only several thousand systems were sold each year, the potential economies of scale did not justify in-house production of RIP. Founder, therefore, had been outsourcing the production of RIP to a state-owned electronics enterprise, which was equipped with imported state-of-the-art production facilities. Other system components, mainly computers and peripherals (such as scanners, laser printers, laser-image recorders), were mostly available on the open market.

By 1993, however, Founder had built a client base of more than 10,000 newspaper, magazine, and book publishers in addition to printing shops. It had built a nationwide sales and service network with more than twenty branch companies and subsidiaries,[38] and close to 100 dealers (BDFZ 12: 1). The electronic publishing systems had long been shifted from minicomputers to personal computers. With an extensive sales and after-sales service network and a sufficient back-up market in its

---

[37] From Wang's manuscript entitled 'Promoting the Close Connection between Technology and Market'.

[38] In 1992 alone, Founder established nine wholly owned branch companies and three associate companies (joint ownership) (BDFZ 10: 1).

existing electronic publishing systems business, Founder decided to diversify into the personal computer business, exploring the opportunity of backward integration into manufacturing.

The company started with a strategic alliance with the world's second largest computer company, Digital Equipment Corporation (DEC). It signed a joint-venture agreement with DEC in November 1993. DEC was to provide US $1.5 millions' worth of computer products to Founder for setting up a DEC product demonstration centre that would introduce into the Chinese market DEC's 64-bit Alpha-chip-based computer systems, including PCs, workstations, servers, and network systems.[39] DEC planned to send experts to China to give seminars, and to invite Chinese computer scientists to DEC's facilities in the United States for technological exchanges.

According to the joint-venture agreement, Founder and DEC would jointly invest US $30 million to develop computer products according to local market needs, and manufacture them according to DEC's quality standards. Earlier, in August, Founder had been granted the general dealership of DEC computer products in China and Hong Kong. Founder planned to distribute 50,000 units of DEC PCs in the Chinese market in 1994 (BDFZ 15: 1, 18: 1).

Founder's extensive nationwide sales and after-sales service network and effective marketing activities gave the distribution of the DEC personal computers a jump start; sales reached RMB 150 million (about US $20 million) in the remaining five months of 1993. The figure more than doubled in 1994. Within two years, Founder had turned DEC from a virtual nonentity in the Chinese market into the fifth largest PC brand in China. Meanwhile, distribution of computer products provided Founder with another substantial revenue-generating business, alongside electronic publishing systems (Table 4.5).[40]

The plan for a DEC–Founder joint venture to develop and manufacture personal computers in China, however, never materialized because of a lack of commitment from DEC. However, Founder had accumulated substantial PC-specific marketing capabilities after two years of successfully distributing DEC PCs in China. It decided to launch its own brand-name computers independently.

In November 1995 Founder started testing production of its Founder brand-name personal computers. The first 3,000 units were manufactured through an OEM arrangement with a state-owned computer manufacturing plant in Shenzhen. Meanwhile, the company was building its own in-house manufacturing facilities in Shenzhen. These first 3,000 Founder brand-name PCs sold out in just one month. The expectation was that the volume of sales for 1996 would be 20,000 to 30,000 units, making Founder one of the top ten brand-name PCs in China.[41] In fact, in 1996,

[39] The Alpha was at the time, and remains, the most advanced microprocessor in the world. See 'Why the Fastest Chip Didn't Win', *Business Week*, 28 Apr. 1997: 58–60.

[40] It should be pointed out that although the sales revenue from computer distribution was a little more than that of the electronic publishing system in 1995, the net profit of the former was only a little over one-third of the latter, reflecting the high value-added of the indigenous proprietary technologies embodied in the electronic publishing systems (1995 Annual Report of Founder (Hong Kong), Ltd.: 7–8).

[41] See *China Infoworld*, 18 Mar. 1996; 1995 Annual Report of Founder (Hong Kong), Ltd.: 10.

TABLE 4.5. *Founder Group's information technology business, 1992–1995* (currency in millions of HK $)

Business	1992	1993	1994	1995
1. Systems integration				
Electronic publishing	401 (84.7%)	361 (61.3%)	359 (42.4%)	443 (40.4%)
Other (banking, retailing, etc.)	—	2 (0.3%)	27 (3.2%)	158 (14.4%)
2. Distribution of computer products	45 (9.4%)	165 (28.1%)	404 (47.7%)	473 (43.2%)
3. Chinese word-processing cards	23 (4.9%)	49 (8.4%)	47 (5.6%)	18 (1.6%)
4. Others	5 (1.0%)	11 (1.9%)	10 (1.1%)	4 (0.4%)
Total	473 (100%)	589 (100%)	846 (100%)	1,096 (100%)

Sources: 1992–4 figures are from the 'New Issue Prospectus' of Founder (Hong Kong), Ltd., 1995: 38, 57; 1995 figures are from the 1995 Annual Report of Founder (Hong Kong), Ltd.: 7–8.

Founder became China's fourth largest indigenous PC maker, after Legend, Great Wall, and another new computer manufacturer, Tongru.[42]

4.5.2. Diversification

Until 1995 customers of computer products in China were mostly government agencies, corporations, and other public institutions. It was often the case that computers were part of an integrated information system. The development of such integrated systems was given a further boost starting in 1994 when the government initiated the 'Three Golden Projects', which aimed to computerize banking (Golden Card), foreign trade (Golden Gate), and telecommunications (Golden Bridge).[43]

Computer systems integration induced computer sales, but to take advantage of this upsurge in demand a company had to have strong technological capabilities. Founder's strengths in systems integration were evident in its dominance of the Chinese electronic publishing systems market. Therefore, with the establishment of its computer sales business, it made sense for Founder to apply its expertise and experience in systems integration to other industrial sectors.

In 1994 the group assembled, through internal transfer and outside recruitment, a technical team to form a new subsidiary company called the Founder Information Systems Engineering Company to specialize in systems integration for commercial/industrial sectors other than electronic publishing. The new subsidiary company utilized the group's experience in electronic publishing systems integration, and successfully developed application software for systems integration projects related to banking, retailing, and office automation. With its strong technological capabilities, the new subsidiary company soon captured sizeable shares of those systems integration markets. In one year, revenues from systems integration other than the electronic

---

[42] *People's Daily*, 24 Apr. 1997.
[43] 'Three Golden Projects' was inspired by the Information Super Highway project of the US. For an overview of China's golden projects, see Simon 1996.

publishing systems increased more than fourfold, from RMB 27 million in 1994 to RMB 158 million in 1995 (Table 4.5), making this area the third largest business of the group.

As can be seen from Table 4.5, the sales of the group's electronic publishing system peaked in 1992, and flattened out in 1993 and 1994. After four years of rapid expansion, the domestic Chinese-language electronic publishing systems market was saturated. New sales revenues came from either upgrading the installed systems or from sales of the high-end colour publishing system. The price of the latter was much higher than that of the text electronic publishing system because high-end colour publishing entailed more dedicated and sophisticated system technologies and equipment. To facilitate the sales of high-end colour publishing systems, the group decided to establish a financial leasing company. It hoped that by providing financing to prospective buyers who were not able to pay in advance, the company could sell more of its core products. In early 1994 Founder, allying with three other enterprises, jointly established the Sichuan Finance Leasing Co., Ltd. The initial capital was RMB 50 million. Founder took a controlling 50 per cent interest. The financial leasing company started operating in May 1994.[44]

To reach the goal of '10 Billion RMB by the Year 2000', the group also diversified into other industrial sectors that were not directly related to information technology, such as the chemical industry. The diversification into chemicals took place through a merger. Besides Founder, Beijing University had set up several dozen high-tech companies. Like Founder, they were set up to commercialize technologies developed in the labs of the university. Most of them had not grown as big. The leadership of the university decided to let some of them merge into Founder so that it might provide them with committed finance.

By 1995 Founder had formed a group structure, with subsidiaries in information technology and other commercial/industrial sectors, and two dozen branch companies as the backbone of a nationwide sales and service network (see Fig. 4.2).

4.5.3. *Going public on the Hong Kong Stock Exchange*

It was clear from early on that the company's internal financial resources were not sufficient to meet the kind of investment that was needed for reaching the ambitious goal of '10 Billion RMB by the Year 2000'. With the government no longer providing free investment funds, the stock market became an attractive source of financing. Like Stone and Legend, Founder decided to go public on the Hong Kong Stock Exchange for two reasons: first, to raise capital, and second, to raise the status of the company in the international market place. From 1992 a public offering on the Hong Kong Stock Exchange had been a priority of the Founder Group's management.

In June 1992 Beida New Tech established a branch company in Hong Kong as the company's overseas operations centre, assisted by local Hong Kong businessman Cheung Shuen Lung and his family. The branch was incorporated in Hong Kong as

---

[44] See *Shing Tao Daily*, 21 Feb. 1994.

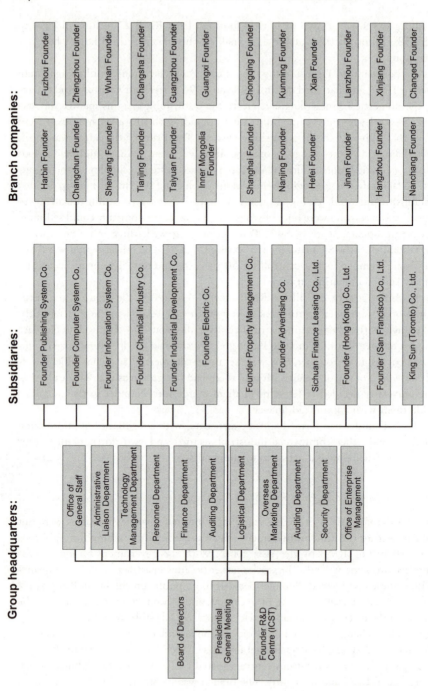

Fig. 4.2. Organizational structure of Founder Group Co.

Source: 1996 company brochure.

a private limited company with an authorized share capital of HK $10,000, divided into 10,000 shares of HK $1 each. These shares were registered in the names of members of the Cheung family (as holders of 50 per cent of the shares) and representatives of Beida New Tech (as holders of the remaining 50 per cent). It was always understood, however, that all these shares were held on behalf of Beida New Tech and that the branch company was in fact a wholly owned subsidiary of Beida New Tech. Upon the reorganization of Beida New Tech into the Founder Group Company in 1993, the Hong Kong Company was renamed Founder (Hong Kong), Ltd.

Cheung and his family had been running a small computer business, called King Sun, in Hong Kong since 1980. Like Lui Tam Ping and his associates, the owners of Daw, who had been induced to help set up Hong Kong Legend by the rich technological capabilities at ICT Co.,[45] Cheung was also attracted by the technological potential of Beida New Tech. He recalled:

Why I came to Founder had a lot to do with Professor Wang Xuan. I had attended EXPO '85 in Japan. At that time, the majority of exhibits in the China Hall were traditional crafts. Only one stand displayed a computer. It was Professor Wang's and his associates' research product. I was deeply impressed with that, because King Sun also specialized in computers and Chinese-language word processing.[46]

Around that time, King Sun recruited a young computer engineer, Qiu Bojun, from China, and Qiu developed a DOS-based Chinese word-processing add-on card for the company. The product later became the dominant Chinese word-processing add-on card in Hong Kong, and also one of the most popular add-on cards in China (after Legend had shifted its focus from the Legend Chinese word-processing add-on cards to personal computers).[47]

Cheung was appointed the general manager of Founder (Hong Kong), Ltd. It was understood, as a matter of faith, that the Cheung family would actively assist Beida New Tech (later Founder Group Co.) in expanding its businesses outside China. In fact, Founder (Hong Kong) led the major marketing effort to expand the sales of the group's electronic publishing systems from Hong Kong/Macao to Taiwan, Malaysia, Singapore, and other overseas markets. It also acted as the purchasing arm for the group's computer products distribution businesses in China. The Cheung family gradually directed its computer-related business to Founder (Hong Kong), Ltd. For example, sales of Chinese word-processing cards became part of the business of Founder (Hong Kong), Ltd. (Table 4.5). By late 1995 the Cheung family ceased their own computer-related business altogether in anticipation of the public listing of Founder (Hong Kong) on the Hong Kong Stock Exchange.

In turning Founder (Hong Kong), Ltd. from a privately held into a publicly held company, the Founder Group transferred all its information-related business to

---

[45] See Ch. 3.

[46] From transcript of Cheung's talk at a company meeting (cf. BDFZ, Special Issue, June 1995: 3).

[47] King Sun's Chinese word-processing add-on card seems to have had some technology linkages with Stone's MS-2401 integrated Chinese word processor. Before transferring to King Sun, Qiu had a temporary stint in Stone's R&D team under Wang Jizhi, the chief designer of the MS-series Chinese word processors. Personal interview with a former member of Stone's R&D team in May 1996.

Founder (Hong Kong), Ltd. On 7 December 1995, the authorized shares of Founder (Hong Kong), Ltd. were increased from 10,000 shares of HK $1 each to 700,000,000 shares of HK $0.10 each. The same day, Founder (Hong Kong), Ltd. set up a wholly owned subsidiary, Beijing Founder Electronics, in China. The Founder Group Company then transferred to Beijing Founder Electronics the businesses of electronic publishing, systems integration, and the trading of computers and related products. More specifically, the Founder Group moved its three subsidiaries—the Publishing System Engineering Company, the Computer System Engineering Company, and the Information System Engineering Company, together with its twenty-four branch companies, into Beijing Founder Electronics. In exchange, the Founder Group received a total of 303,124,000 shares in Founder (Hong Kong), Ltd.

Meanwhile, as a step forward to formalize the partnership relations between Founder Group Co. and the Cheung family, Founder (Hong Kong), Ltd. entered into agreements with Swan-City International Group, Ltd., Pacific Star Overseas, Ltd., and World Conquest, Ltd., companies that were owned by two Cheung brothers and their wives. According to the agreements, Founder (Hong Kong) allotted and issued 20,000,000 shares to Swan-City (subscription price, HK $10,575,690), 19,375,000 shares to World Conquest (subscription price, HK $10,245,200), and 15,000,000 shares to Pacific Star (subscription price, HK $7,931,780). In addition, Founder (Hong Kong), Ltd. also allotted and issued 5,000,000 shares to Scriven Trading, Ltd. for a subscription price of HK $2,643,330. Scriven was registered in Hong Kong and owned by the Beijing Municipal Government, on behalf of which Scriven held a number of other investments.

After this corporate reorganization and share placement, Founder (Hong Kong), Ltd. went public on the Hong Kong Stock Exchange on 21 December 1995. It issued to the public 137,500,000 shares (par value, HK $0.10 per share) at a price of HK $1.98 per share. As a result of the initial public offering, a total of 500,000,000 out of 700,000,000 authorized shares were issued. The resultant share structure is shown in Table 4.6.

As the majority shareholder, the Founder Group had firm control over Founder (Hong Kong), Ltd. after it went public. Among five executive directors on the board of Founder (Hong Kong), Ltd., four were from the Founder Group, with Professor Wang Xuan as chairman of the board of directors. The other executive director was Cheung Shuen Lung, the elder brother in the Cheung Family, who became the president of Founder (Hong Kong), Ltd. The two non-executive directors were the president and first vice-president of Beijing University. Of the eleven additional senior managers, ten were from the Founder Group and only one from the Cheung family— the brother-in-law of Cheung Shuen Lung.

The company raised a total of HK $277,346,000 in cash (HK $303,646,000 net of HK $26,300,000 listing expenses) through the initial public offering. The plans for using the proceeds were:

• HK $22,000,000 toward the further development and expansion of colour publishing systems and an integrated newspaper management network;

TABLE 4.6. *The initial public offering of Founder (Hong Kong), Ltd., December 1995*

Shareholders	Shares	Percentage of issued shares	Cash received (HK $)
Founder Group Co.	278,125,000	55.6	—
Swan-City International Group, Ltd.*	20,000,000	4.0	10,575,690
World Conquest, Ltd.*	19,375,000	3.9	10,245,200
Pacific Star Overseas, Ltd.*	15,000,000	3.0	7,931,780
Scriven Trading, Ltd.	5,000,000	1.0	2,643,330
New issues to the public	137,500,000	27.5	272,250,000
Total shares in issue	500,000,000	100.0	303,646,000
Total authorized shares	700,000,000		

* Cheung family concerns. Cheung family interests as a whole totalled 10.9%.

Sources: 'New Issue Prospectus' of Founder (Hong Kong), Ltd., 1995: 19, 35–6, 131–2; 1995 Annual Report: 26–7, 32, 34, 53.

- HK $25,000,000 toward the establishment of a colour publishing centre and thirty colour output centres in Beijing;
- HK $22,000,000 toward the further development and expansion of systems integration relating to banking, retailing, and office automation;
- HK $60,000,000 for working capital for the distribution of computers and related products;
- HK $50,000,000 toward the assembly and sales of personal computers and monitors under the Founder brand name;
- HK $12,000,000 toward the research and development of Japanese and Korean publishing systems;
- HK $20,000,000 toward the establishment of thirteen new branches or subsidiaries in China and one subsidiary in Japan;
- the remaining balance for additional working capital.

The resultant corporate structure of Founder (Hong Kong), Ltd. after the initial public offering is shown in Fig. 4.3.

4.6. Concluding Remarks

Founder is a genuinely internationally competitive Chinese firm that is based on leading technology, not cheap labour.[48] Underpinning the market competitiveness of the company is a new organizational structure of innovation. The transition from the Hua-Guang systems to Founder systems saw a transformation of the organization of innovation from government-centred activities to enterprise-based activities. The

[48] Founder has served as a showcase for the success of the Chinese government's economic reforms. More than a dozen presidents or prime ministers from developing countries and Eastern European countries have visited Founder on their official trips to China.

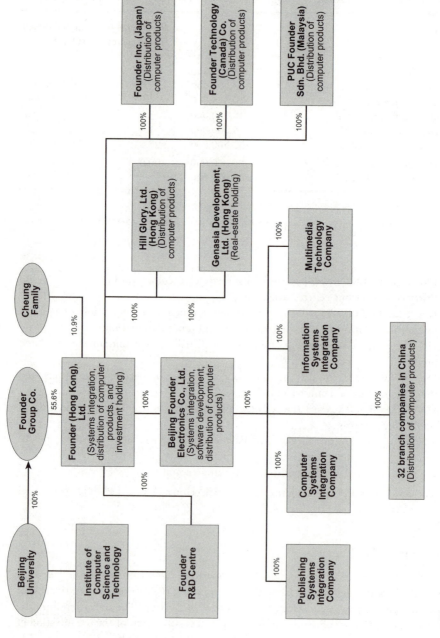

Fig. 4.3. Organizational chart of Founder (Hong Kong), Ltd.
Source: 'New Issue Prospectus' of Founder (Hong Kong), Ltd., 1996.

development of the Hua-Guang systems occurred under the umbrellas of two large-scale government-led industrial R&D projects—Project 748 and the State Publishing and Printing Industrial Technology and Equipment Renewal Project. Both can be seen as civilian versions of the projects of 'two bullets, one star' (the atomic and hydrogen bomb projects and the satellite project) that were typical of central planning. The success of these civilian projects depended on unfailing financial support from the state, direct government involvement in organization and co-ordination, and willing co-operation between research institutions, enterprises, and industrial users across organizational boundaries.

Nevertheless, the development of the Hua-Guang systems from prototype to industrial release was a prolonged and sluggish process. The reasons were partly technological and partly organizational. Wang's ideas on Chinese-font processing technology were ahead of their time,[49] and the decision to develop the fourth-generation technology indigenously was made at a time when the technology had just appeared in the West and the widespread diffusion of the technology was still ten years away. Wang and his team had sufficient time to turn out a commercial product, even though they faced severe technological and organizational constraints.

There were times when the continuation of the project was challenged, especially in the mid-1980s, when state newspaper publishing houses started to import systems from abroad. The inherent difficulty of Chinese-font processing, however, meant that these threats did not materialize. The biggest threat was from Monotype, the inventor of the fourth-generation technology. However, because Monotype did not innovate in compressing and then regenerating high-resolution Chinese fonts, their system was not workable until the late 1980s, when the Hua-Guang system was already a mature industrial product. The case of a US firm called HTS is also illustrative in this regard. In 1986 the largest official newspaper in China, the *People's Daily*, signed a contract with HTS to buy a Chinese newspaper publishing system for US $4 million under the state printing industrial renewal plan. HTS did provide an advanced computer hardware system. However, the technicians at HTS just could not make their way through the labyrinth of Chinese-font processing techniques, and were unable to deliver a workable system. HTS finally gave up, claiming bankruptcy to avoid the financial consequences of their breach of contract. In general, pictographic font processing was a formidable technological challenge, even for leading international computer companies.[50]

Thus, the deficiencies of the old organizational form did not prove fatal, given the circumstances. The traditional structure worked when the technological ideas were outstanding (the result of China's highly effective system for educating large numbers of scientists and engineers) and when, in terms of international technological development, a project was ahead of its time.

Still, the financial success of the Hua-Guang IV system in the market place was

[49] Again, the 'hint' technique, which was the fundamental principle for treating Chinese fonts in Wang's idea, appeared in the West for representing high-resolution alphabetic fonts at least ten years later.

[50] IBM failed in its effort to develop a computer model that was targeted for pictographic language markets. Personal interview with a senior manager of Great Wall Computer Co. in Sep. 1996.

made possible by the involvement of Beida New Tech, the predecessor of Founder. It was Beida New Tech that replaced all the imported Chinese electronic systems by designing first the Hua-Guang IV system and then the Founder systems. The entrance of Founder into the industry marked the formation of a new organizational structure of innovation.

The prime difference in the new organizational structure was that top government officials (deputy prime ministers, for example) were no longer directly involved in making decisions concerning the purchase of equipment and the provision of funding, or the co-ordination of research activities across administrative boundaries.[51] Instead of direct funding from the state to industrial R&D, indirect subsidies were now provided in such forms as tax breaks and preferential loans. Henceforth, the state's direct role was confined to the provision of resources for building organizational infrastructure, such as the National Key Laboratory and National Engineering Centre schemes. The actual funding for industrial R&D now came directly from revenues that companies secured by selling innovative products. Entrepreneurs at the research institutes and the enterprises were the ones who made the decisions about the direction of R&D, according to their understanding of trends in technological development and market needs.

The new organization of innovation proved more suitable for the new competitive environment. Entering the 1990s, the technological peculiarity of Chinese-font processing was no longer an obstacle for foreign companies wanting to break into the Chinese-language information technology market. Given that the computing power of current personal computers of the 1990s were equivalent to that of super computers of the 1970s, the storage of large amounts of Chinese-font information no longer represented a technological problem. In addition, the pictographic font-processing technique has become an international standard that is equally accessible to foreign companies. Meanwhile, Founder moved into the professional desktop colour-publishing systems market, in which the ability to deal with the Chinese language no longer gives it a competitive advantage.

During the 1990s, both domestically and overseas, competition in electronic publishing systems markets became more and more international. Adobe planned to get into the Chinese market. Aldus developed PageMaker 5.0 with a Chinese word-processing function. Linotype-Hell announced its Chinese-language colour-publishing system (JNWJ 1994: 100). According to the general manager of the Founder Publishing Systems Company in mid-1995: 'There are more and more rival companies in the market now. In the high-end colour systems market, our major competitors were none other than the ones that had been squeezed out by us in the Chinese-language publishing systems market. They were now back'.[52]

Under the new open-systems environment with increasingly integrated global information technologies, a company can 'only become competitive in the international market if it is able to stand out in the domestic market', to quote Wang Xuan

---

[51] Nowadays, top government officials still frequently visit Founder due to its high profile, but they come as visitors rather than decision-makers.
[52] From transcripts of a conference address on 30 June 1995 (BDFZ, Special Issue).

(BDFZ 25: 3). Market performance has become more and more reliant on genuine technological capabilities. The integration of investment strategy and organizational structure to develop and use technologies has become the key to staying alive and forging ahead.

So far, Founder has remained on the cutting edge of the technological frontier. Its dominant position in Chinese-language electronic publishing systems markets, both domestically and overseas, shows no sign of weakening. With its financial resources, newly acquired from the Hong Kong Stock Exchange, Founder has been venturing into the Japanese and Korean markets. Its performance in these ventures will be a further test of the soundness of this new organizational structure of innovation in China.

5

The China Great Wall Computer Company: Transforming the State-Run Computer Industry

> The computer industry is a newly established industry attracting worldwide attention. It would have been a great pity for the Chinese people if they could not have a share in this area or could not have one or more of their own famous brand-name products.
>
> From the company's brochure.

China Great Wall Computer Company (CGC) is the result of exploring and experimenting with new forms of organizing the Chinese state-run computer industry in the mid-1980s by the technocrats at the Ministry of Electronics Industry (MEI). It was a spin-off of the Bureau of Computer Industry Administration (hereafter Computer Bureau) under MEI, which oversaw dozens of state-run computer enterprises and research institutes. Realizing that the traditional way of organizing was insufficient for an industry undergoing rapid technological change, the technocrats at the Computer Bureau, started exploring new organizational forms. Like the three non-government-run enterprises presented in the previous chapters, CGC started with a successful product innovation based on its privileged access to indigenous science and technology resources. More specifically, it started by organizing the manufacturing and marketing of a PC that was developed specifically to suit the specific needs of Chinese-language word processing. In the process, CGC experimented with new organizational forms that were common in Western market economies. Its huge success established CGC's leading position in the Chinese PC market throughout the last half of the 1980s. Having lost its monopoly position as a result of the entry of multinational companies into the Chinese market coupled with the rise of new non-governmental science and technology enterprises in the early 1990s, CGC tried out various strategies. In particular, it formed strategic alliances with world IT leaders and secured its position among the top domestic PC makers.

The company has now grown into a large-scale, fully integrated high-tech enterprise group engaging in a wide range of IT related businesses, including R&D, manufacturing, distribution, services, systems integration, foreign trade and finance. It has production and service enterprises in more than ten Chinese provinces as well as branches in Hong Kong and the United States. It has also formed an impressive array of strategic alliances with the industry's biggest names, such as IBM, Intel, and Microsoft.

The CGC case demonstrates how China's state-run computer industry was transformed over time as a result of exploring new organizational forms and adapting to a new business environment at the highest level of the industrial administrative hierarchy.

5.1. Mandarins Becoming Entrepreneurs: A New Approach to Organizing the State-Run Computer Industry

5.1.1. The IBM revelation

As mentioned in the first chapter, China's traditional state-run computer industry followed an import-substitution strategy in the early 1980s. It started by assembling imported kits of parts and components in semi-knocked-down (SKD) or completely knocked-down (CKD) conditions, aiming to localize the production of parts and components, and move up the technological ladder in the process. Dozens of state-owned electronic enterprises were licensed as manufacturing sites, with each enterprise importing production lines. They were given foreign currency quotas for importing the kits. The plant would then assemble the kits into the final products and sell them in the domestic market. Given the huge differences in import duties between the final products and kits, which were intended to protect the infant industry, the profit rate was artificially high. However, due to the structural segmentation between research institutions and production enterprises, the strategy did not use indigenous technological capabilities accumulated in state research institutions. Without indigenous technology inputs, there was very little value-added in the production process. The intended localization process was very slow, creating a dependence on hard currency to import the kits, which was not sustainable in the long run.

By 1984 the industry faced an over-capacity crisis. This high artificial profit rate lured more and more enterprises into assembling computers from imported kits, even without the permission of government authorities. On the other hand, the lack of mature Chinese-language processing technologies limited market size, leading to a rapid pile-up of stock. By the end of 1984, nine major computer enterprises had accumulated more than 15,000 PCs, 37,000 peripherals, which tied up more than RMB 410 million in capital, including RMB 310 million in bank loans. Many production lines remained idle. Wang Zhi, the then deputy bureau chief of the Computer Industry Administration, who later became president of CGC, recalled:

By 1984, we realized that the existing way of organizing the industry had reached a dead end. We had to find new ways, but none of us had any experience in this. Since there was no existing model to follow in the country, we had to explore (Xu and Zhan 1990: 13).

One thing was clear to the technocrats at the Computer Bureau, that is, the development of the Chinese computer industry had to take advantage of the international division of labour, using advanced technologies, equipment, and components from abroad. Complete self-reliance was not realistic.

At the time, IBM was interested in setting up joint ventures in China. The technocrats at the Computer Bureau were also interested. So the two sides started negotiating, but soon ran into major obstacles. First of all, the two sides had different goals: the Chinese technocrats were mainly interested in gleaning advanced technologies from IBM, while IBM had no intention of giving up its technologies. The company was mainly interested in China's huge potential market. Due to these differences, the negotiations eventually failed. However, the Chinese technocrats learned a new way of organizing business in the negotiation process. As Wang recalled:

The negotiation was a detailed and painstaking process. At the centre was how to divide the profits. You had to go step by step though each of the stages of the value chain to see each partner's contributions. So we went through each and every aspect of the business process, including R&D, purchasing, production and marketing. This way we learned how IBM organized its business. It was the first time we learned first-hand that there were different ways of organizing a business.

As a technocrat, Wang had always felt that China was able to develop and produce PCs independently. The problem was on the organizational side. Again to quote Wang:

We went to Japan. We learned that IBM (Japan) conducted business differently. Product development was done in-house. Production was outsourced to several Japanese companies. The company only controlled marketing and distribution. Such a model could still be successful.[1] It was quite revealing. We thought that we could certainly copy this model.

Wang and his colleagues at the Computer Bureau knew that the computer industry differed from traditional industries in that both R&D and application services played a very important role. Among computers, the PC differed from mainframes in that it had very short product cycles. To develop a viable PC industry, there must be a flexible organizational structure that integrates R&D, manufacturing, distribution, and service in such a way that enterprises could rapidly respond to changing technologies as well as market conditions. They decided to follow the IBM model. The idea was to develop a product with its own proprietary technologies that were targeted to Chinese-language processing. With this product as a lead, the bureau would organize production and marketing as in IBM (Japan), so as to transform the organization of the industry. The bureau would assume a leading role in the process.

5.1.2. Great Wall 0520CH: The model that bested IBM

The first thing Wang did was to organize a product development team. He called upon Lu Ming, a young deputy chief engineer from a computer service company, to

---

[1] This was a typical OEM arrangement—a business practice that was widely adopted in Taiwan between Taiwanese electronics firms and US multinational companies, see Johnstone 1989: 50–1; Hobday 1995: 49.

head the team. He asked him to choose team members from research institutes and enterprises under the jurisdiction of the Computer Bureau. The team would directly report to the bureau, which allocated RMB 300,000 from its R&D budget. In this way, the bureau effectively centralized the product development process. This was in itself a break from the traditional way of organizing research and development.

To start a new research project at that time, research institutes or enterprises had to try to have it listed in governmental plans, a process that often took months. The government would then allocate funds through several layers of budgetary authorities. Even after the funds were in place, however, it would often take years from the time a project was initiated until it was actually completed. This procedure was obviously not suited to a fast-changing market environment. As a result, what the market often needed most was not getting developed, and completed research projects were often not in market demand. The new centralized organization was able to shorten the product development cycle and allow quick response to market needs.

The product development team consisted of a dozen or so young engineers or technicians, with an average age of 24. Most of them were new graduates from elite Chinese universities. The purpose of developing the new product was to occupy the Chinese market. It aimed to surpass the IBM PC/XT in handling Chinese fonts. The design target was to break the structural limits of the IBM PC/XT, developing a high-speed high-resolution system for displaying Chinese fonts so as to make a PC practical in Chinese-language word processing. At the time, the IBM PC/XT was already the leading brand-name product in the Chinese market. However, like all imported models that were originally designed for processing information in alphabetical languages, it was weak in handling Chinese fonts, which need much higher display resolutions. Although NEC had developed systems that would display the Chinese fonts in high resolution, they were not compatible with IBM's PCs. At the time, China was already locked into the IBM PC standard. Therefore, the technological target was to develop a model that had a Chinese font display resolution equivalent to the NEC models and also compatible with the IBM PC standard.

The team spent two months coming up with design specifications and approaches. It decided to use a separate Chinese font generator for generating high-resolution Chinese fonts. This approach was technologically more advanced but fundamentally different from the approach NEC had used, that is, the graphic display method. The team also decided to use the newest gate-array technology in developing the font generator.

At the time, China lacked up-to-date product development tools, especially for the cutting-edge gate-array technology. For this reason, the Computer Bureau made an unprecedented decision to move the development process abroad. The team was split into two: one went to Hong Kong, working on the high-resolution Chinese font display technology, and the other went to Tokyo, to co-operate with IBM (Japan) on developing Chinese word-processing software.

It took only three months for both teams to come up with results. By February 1985, all the necessary designs and corresponding test data for the new model were completed. The two teams came back to Beijing and put together their designs. They came up with the prototype in March. The test-run results exceeded expectations. The resulting product was the first computer that incorporated a built-in Chinese font generator add-on card. It had the same speed as the IBM PC/XT but with a display resolution five times higher.

Eager to see the market's reaction, the team moved to launch the product at the forthcoming national computer show in June. In preparing for the product launch, the Computer Bureau decided to turn the development team into a company—the Great Wall Microcomputer Development Co. The head of the development team was designated as the general manager. The company mission was to develop and market the new Great Wall brand-name computer, the GW0520CH. The price was set at a very competitive level: RMB 32,000, in comparison with competing RMB 40,000 for other domestic models and RMB 50,000 for the IBM PC/XT.

With its superior performance and lower price, the product was an instant hit at the computer show. It became the best-selling model almost immediately with 2,200 being sold in the first two months alone. Orders topped 10,000 in the first quarter of the following year—the first domestic model to ever reach that level. In fact, this product was so successful that IBM abandoned its model (the 5550) that was specifically designed for the Chinese market, as did Japan's NEC.[2]

5.1.3. New organizational arrangements in production and marketing

The high demand for the GW0520CH laid the foundation for the Computer Bureau to adopt new organizational forms in production and marketing. On the production side, it seemed natural for them to adopt the OEM method they had learned from IBM. The bureau set up another company, Longxing Electronics Co., alongside Great Wall Microcomputer Development Co. to organize production. Longxing would centralize purchases of parts and components, and distribute them to carefully selected state-run computer manufacturing enterprises as OEM sites. On the marketing side, Longxing would organize a dealer system that was also copied from IBM.

At the time, microcomputers were already among the first capital goods in China that were distributed through the market rather than central-planning mechanisms—even though the production side was still somewhat under a centrally planned mechanism due to its heavy reliance on hard currencies, which was centrally controlled, for importing parts and components. Under previous import-substitution arrangements, the enterprises would import parts and components with allocated or self-obtained hard currencies, assemble them into final products, and sell them on the market. Each enterprise acted by itself in the market place. As a result, the computer market was close to a spot market.

If the computer had been an ordinary commodity, then a very decentralized system would have been fine, perhaps even ideal. In reality, the computer industry was trapped in over-capacity, and the market was somewhat chaotic. The problem was that computers needed after-sales servicing, which not only included maintenance and

---

[2] Or to put it another way, the models developed by IBM and NEC were not as successful as Great Wall 0520CH in handling Chinese fonts.

repairs, but also training, technical support, and software applications development. Recognizing that all these required substantial organizational resources, the enterprise realized that a well-organized dealership system and proper profit-sharing between manufacturers and dealers would provide the necessary organizational structure and resources. Longxing set up a nationwide dealer system, which was among the first to distribute capital goods in China. At the time, the commission for the dealers was set higher than for the manufacturers. This was an incredible change in thinking for those who had grown up under central planning and who used to think that only manufacturing could add value. Nevertheless, it was understood that for computers, the industry had to learn to sell on the markets to ensure their survival. And markets eventually lead to production. Increasing dealers' profitability would increase the sales volume, which in turn would increase the production volume. This strategy apparently worked. By 1987 the number of first-tier dealerships had reached twenty-six. Including their branches and second-tier dealerships, the total surpassed one hundred.

The new strategy and structure of organizing the industry injected new life into state-owned computer enterprises. For example, the Beijing Number Three Computer Manufacturing Factory, which was a large state-owned enterprise (SOE) under MEI, invested in automating its production line under the sixth five-year state plan between 1981 and 1985. It had been operating under capacity. After accepting the OEM order from Longxing, annual production doubled in just one year. The Tianjing Computer Factory, another state-owned computer enterprise, had just installed one of the most advanced computer assembly lines, but it would only work efficiently with large-batch production. It received an OEM order of 5,000 units from Longxing in 1987. As the factory director put it, 'this way, we did not have to worry about purchasing parts and components, or about marketing. We were able to focus on improving process technology and product quality' (Xu and Zhan 1990: 29).

The OEM arrangement not only revived the assembly plants, but also dozens of second-tier suppliers. The product's indigenous design made it easier to localize parts and components. The surplus of domestically made disk drivers, keyboards, electric suppliers, print circuit boards, printers, monitors was then mostly absorbed. The localization rate of parts and components increased from zero in 1984 to 40 per cent in 1986, and more than 70 per cent in 1987. Thirteen computer manufacturing plants were involved in the OEM arrangements for assembling the GW0520CH, and another ten in the supply chain.

This new organizational model came to be known as the Great Wall Model. It had four basic ingredients: market orientation, independent product development, OEM production arrangements, and a dealer distribution system. The model's essence was to bring up manufacturing technologies by focusing on R&D and marketing.

5.1.4. The formation of the China Computer Development Corporation (CCDC)

This experimentation with new organizational form was not only important for the rejuvenation of the state-run computer industry but also had far-reaching consequences on the transformation of the industrial administration.

Certainly, the existing industrial administration was geared to the needs of central planning. But now that the economic system was changing to a market-oriented one, the industrial ministries also needed to change. In fact, decentralization caused MEI to lose most of its power over enterprises at the time. The ministry had previously had several dozen state-owned electronics enterprises under its direct jurisdiction. By 1986 only two remained. The rest were decentralized and were put under the jurisdiction of the provincial governments where they were located. The ministry, of which the Computer Bureau was a part, was faced with redundancy. Restructuring was long overdue.

The organizational experiment around GW0520CH became a stepping stone for the restructuring of the administration of the computer industries. By 1986, the bureau had been organizing the development, production, and marketing of the GW0520CH for two years, and it was done in such a way that the bureau resembled a corporate headquarters. Time was ripe for a sweeping change from the traditional industrial administrative structure to a new corporate one.

Led by deputy bureau chief, Wang Zhi, the technocrats who were involved in bringing the GW0520CH to market, requested that MEI form a corporation. In October 1986 MEI officially approved the establishment of the China Computer Development Corporation, or CCDC. Wang was assigned as its general manager. More than 140 staff, including twenty high-ranking bureaucrats, from the Computer Bureau were transferred to the new company, making the CCDC a spin-off of the Computer Bureau.[3]

CCDC took over the Great Wall Microcomputer Development Company and Longxing and tried to build upon their well-established businesses of developing, manufacturing, and marketing the Great Wall brand of computers.

The formation of CCDC marked a turning point in the organization of China's state-run computer industry. The idea was to restructure the computer industry into a multi-tier industrial group, something akin to the Japanese *keiretsu*. In November 1987, after a series of asset realignments under the direction of MEI, the CCDC's structure was clarified. Centred around CCDC headquarters were five CCDC branch companies located in five provinces. CCDC had wholly owned subsidiaries including Shenzhen Aihua Electronics Co., Ltd., Great Wall Microcomputer Development Co., Longxing Corporation, Kunlun Electronic Publishing Equipment Co., Northern CAD Co., Computer Exhibition and Advertisement Co., Guiling Training Centre, and the China Great Wall Finance Co. It also had subsidiaries with controlling shares including China Computer Leasing Co., Ltd., Huabei Computer Terminal Equipment Co., Huaming Electronic Industrial Real-Estate Co., Southern Information Enterprises Co., Ltd., and Yantai Training Centre. It also had a number of associated companies through holding minority stakes, including Baxian Plastic Centre, Kaifa Keji Co., Ltd., China HP Co., Ltd. As a result, CCDC itself became a

---

[3] In fact, the Computer Bureau was split into three parts. A small portion remained as the Bureau of Computer Industry Administration. The second part spun off to become CCDC. The third part became the Centre for Computer and Microelectronics Industry Development Research (CCID), an information service company.

conglomerate with comprehensive capabilities in R&D, manufacturing, distribution, marketing, systems integration, import and export, and finance. Meanwhile, MEI was also working with relevant provincial or municipal governments to form the Great Wall Computer Industry Group that would tie together the CCDC, the China Computer System Engineering Corporation, the China Computer Service Corporation, the Beijing Number Three Computer Manufacturing Factory, and the Hunan Huaihua Jiannan Machinery Factory.[4]

5.2. Building Integrated Organizational Capabilities

5.2.1. *The strategy of 'upgrading the domestic computer industry through exports'*

With the establishment of CCDC, the 'mandarin'-turned-management team started considering long-term development strategies for the company. They realized at the time that the computer industry's technologies, parts and components, and major markets were all outside China. Therefore it was imperative to participate in the international division of labour. The management formed a new strategy, encapsulated by the motto 'upgrading the domestic computer industry through exports'. The idea was first, to preserve the technological advances in the company's products by subjecting the products to the discipline of international market competition and, second, to seek economy of scale by tapping into the international market. The company sought to make breakthroughs in new product development, large-scale production, and high-tech product exports. By exporting the low end of the high-tech product spectrum, it could gradually climb the product ladder.

The new strategy was also dictated by the imperative of balancing hard currency. Although due to the indigenous design, the localization rate of GW0520CH had increased considerably over the previous CKD- and SKD-based approach, the product still required a substantial amount of hard currency for importing key components. Since the government had substantially reduced the hard currency quota to the PC industry, the company had to find new sources of hard currency to sustain and increase the scale of production. Only through exports was the company able to balance hard currency in the long run.

At the same time, opportunities also existed for China to get a foot in the international computer electronics market. As Wang put it,

The industrial leaders had long been large American and Japanese corporations. It was once thought that it would be very difficult to compete with them. However, in the past several years, Taiwan and South Korea had caught up, having become major exporters in the industry.[5]

The management saw no reason why China could not follow suit. In fact, China had several advantages over both Taiwan and South Korea. First of all, labour costs were considerably lower. Second, the quality of Chinese computer engineers and

---

[4] Wang, 'Retrospect and Prospect', CJB, No. 7, 10 Dec. 1988: 1, 4.
[5] Wang's interview with a journalist in 1990, see Xu and Zhan 1990: 56.

technicians was high, and they could be found in relatively high numbers. More importantly, China had a domestic market with enormous potential. As Wang explained: 'Export-orientation does not mean 100 per cent exports. Chinese companies could start in the domestic market and could always use it as a back-up. Few countries in the world had such favourable conditions.'[6]

5.2.2. Building integrated product development and manufacturing capabilities

The first concrete step in implementing the new strategy was to build an export-oriented product development and manufacturing base in Shenzhen, the city across the border from Hong Kong, in early 1987.

This major investment undertook the building of a product development centre and five manufacturing plants, including manufacturing plants for computer assembly, computer monitors, computer cases, and computer motherboards and add-on cards. The total investment was RMB 20 million, and the project was funded from the retained earnings of the GW0520CH. It was projected that, under the market conditions at that time, the investment could be recouped within one year of operation.

The construction of the integrated product development and manufacturing base was completed in less than one year. By early 1988 three of the plants were up and running, and production capacities were for 30,000 PCs, 100,000 monitors, and 150,000 computer cases, respectively. The structure of production capacity reflected the export strategy of starting with the low end of the high-tech product spectrum in the export market.

Parallel to the construction of the new product development centre and manufacturing facilities, the company launched a new product development campaign in June 1987. The design target was to move from a single product, the GW0520CH, to a product series that would fit different market segments, both domestic and international.

The two dozen or so young product developers in the original GW0520CH development team had accumulated sufficient experience for them to be able to carry out new product development projects independently. Besides their outstanding technological skills, these young engineers were also highly motivated and were devoted to the idea of building a viable domestic computer company. To quote one developer:

I was assigned to the GW0520EM and CMGA display card, two projects! That year, I was only 23 years old and had only graduated a year before. To be honest, the pressure was very high. However, in comparing myself with my college classmates, I never heard of any of them getting the chance to do such important work. I was very proud of myself. The experience was unforgettable. I had never worked so hard, but at the same time, I had never felt so fulfilled. We worked day and night, often working through until morning. Everyone was like that.[7]

---

[6] Ibid.   [7] Quoted in Xu and Zhan 1990: 77.

Relying on the skills and sacrifices of the young developers, CCDC came up with a series of new products, including five new models of computers and two monitors in less than one year.

On 20 April 1988 CCDC launched its new series of Great Wall brand-name computers. The new products were characterized by multiple models that fitted different market segments centred around high speed and performance, new Chinese word-processing standards, and lower prices. This event marked a large step forward for CCDC in forming integrated capabilities in new product development and manufacturing. Since then, CCDC has closely followed the pace of rapid product upgrades in the industry and taken a leading role in the domestic PC market.

Although CCDC's main target was the domestic market, its new capabilities also laid the foundation for developing products that would be competitive in the international market. The upgrading of CCDC's product development capabilities in computer monitors was a case in point.

The monitor development team consisted of four members: two young engineers originally from the Beijing Television Manufacturing Factory, and two recent college graduates. They were assigned tasks to develop two new models of computer monitors—the GW100 and GW300—for the new product series. Since the computer monitor was new in China, few people had design experience with it. To compensate for their lack of experience, they worked very hard. The new product designs came out just as the new monitor production line was completed. After a test run in production, the product was put into full production. It soon became a mainstream product in China's domestic market. After the successful launch of these two products in the domestic market, the team was soon assigned the tasks of developing two new models that were specifically targeted to the international market. To ensure the highest possible design quality, the team moved to Hong Kong to do the work. The two new models were put into production in June 1989 and were exported in quantity right away. By 1990 the team had developed yet another two models, the GW400A and GW500. The GW500 was their high-end product, marking the company's closing of the gap in the development of computer monitors.

The export-oriented strategy gradually paid off. The company's exports grew over time, easing the balance of payments problem. Table 5.1 shows CCDC's export performance from 1987 to 1991.

With the new production facilities up and running, the company gradually internalized the production of its PC product, moving away from OEM or contract manufacturing arrangements. By the end of 1990 more then 80 per cent of Great Wall PCs were produced at its Shenzhen manufacturing plants.

In late 1988 CCDC was renamed the China Great Wall Computer Company or CGC, after the brand name. It became China's largest domestic computer company.

5.2.3. The new regulatory regime

It is noteworthy that CCDC made the new investment decision on its own and financed the project with internally accumulated retained earnings. This reflected a

TABLE 5.1. *CCDC's export performance, 1987–1991*

	1987	1988	1989	1990	1991	Total
PCs (units)	200	1,090	5,261	5,185	5,500	17,236
Monitors (units)			4,727	11,713	10,800	27,240
Add-on cards (units)			11,300	9,580	10,000	30,880
Export Value (US $1,000)	218	1,871	10,210	14,920	10,000	37,223
Import Value (US $1,000)			21,450	14,520	15,000	50,970

Source: Company Archives, 1991 Company Report, Nov. 1991: 18.

big change in government–enterprise relations, the most fundamental of which was the financial independence of CCDC from the government. Besides an initial RMB 300,000 research grant for developing the GW0520CH, CCDC did not receive any investment funds from the government. Due to innovations in both products and organization, CCDC was able to profit under the market mechanism and accumulate capital for new investments. This was a notable departure from the central-planning mechanism, under which layers of authorities made investment decisions and allocated investment funds on behalf of the enterprises. It was now the enterprise's management that came up with its major investment decisions, exercising its newly acquired financial independence.

The change was gradual. CCDC continued to benefit from government favouritism, due to its special status as a spin-off from a government industrial bureau. For example, one important benefit was foreign currency quotas; however, these privileges were diminishing over time as the government reduced these quotas to the computer industry. This gradually levelled off the playing field and made it possible for other enterprises such as Legend and Founder to rise.

In place of government favouritism, a regulatory regime that aimed at promoting high-tech industries in general, and the computer industry in particular, was instituted. Two industrial policies were particularly important: one allowing enterprises to take a pre-tax charge equivalent to 10 per cent of sales revenue for R&D expenditures for high-tech products, including computer, software, semi-conductors, and programmed telephone switchboards. This policy allowed CCDC to pursue a so-called 'saturated funding policy' in new product development. In other words, the company was able to fully fund all its R&D and new product development projects. Table 5.2 describes the funding situation for R&D and product development projects between 1986 and 1990.

The policy of fully funding R&D became the financial underpinning of CCDC's continuous product upgrades that were so essential for computer enterprises. It ensured CCDC's dominant position in China's domestic PC industry. Table 5.3 shows the results of CCDC's new product development activities.

The other important industrial policy was the tax concessions the government made to high-tech firms. CCDC was matched with other new high-tech firms in the

TABLE 5.2. *Funding of R&D and product development projects, Great Wall Computer, 1986–1990*

	No. of R&D projects	Planned funding (RMB millions)	Actual spending (RMB millions)
Headquarters	56	17	15.4
Shenzhen Base	76	38	24.1
Others	17	8.6	7.7
Total	149	63.6	47.2

Source: Company Archives, 1991 Company Report, Nov. 1991: 10.

TABLE 5.3. *Results of CCDC's new product development activities, 1985–1990*

	Computers	Monitors	Display cards	Software	Others
1985–6	GW0520				
1987	GW286, Multi-User System			CWART Desktop Publishing System, CAD System	
1988	GW0520EM, 0520DH, 286B, 286EX, 386	GW100, 300	CEGA, CMGA		
1989	GW286BH, 386SX, Workstation	GW240, 400		Three Systems Integration Software Packages	
1990	GW0520HM, 0520DH/10, 286/12, 286/16/20, 386sx, 386/25c, 386/33c, 386sx/lp, 486/25	GW400b, 500	CVGA, HGAI	GW Spreadsheet, Database, Big Chinese, Eight Application Software Packages	GW1000 Printer, Network System

Sources: Xu and Zhan 1990; Company Archives, 1991 Company Report, Nov. 1991.

Beijing High Tech Developmental Zone in this regard. Like Stone, Legend, and Founder, CCDC got an income-tax break for three years. As a result, from 1987 to 1989 CCDC saved RMB 33.87 million in value-added taxes and RMB 36.9 million in income taxes. Taking into account certain adjustment taxes, CCDC collected a net

TABLE 5.4. *Domestic production of personal computers and imports in China* (in units)

	1985	1986	1987	1988	1989	1990	1991
Total domestic output	35,700	39,200	47,500	53,300	69,700	80,100	93,400
CGC output			20,456	13,594	20,544	15,606	18,000
CGC sales (domestic)			16,366	15,209	15,877	15,216	15,500
Total imports	18,700	20,400	22,500	26,700	20,300	24,900	111,300
Total (domestic output+imports)	54,400	59,600	70,000	80,000	90,000	105,000	204,700

Note: CCDC, the predecessor of Great Wall Co., was formed in 1987.

Sources: CCID; see also 'New Issue of Stone'; 21–2. Great Wall: 1991 Company Report: 16.

of RMB 57.5 million that was available for investment (Xu and Zhan 1990: 103). This amount was more than enough to fund the construction of its Shenzhen product development centre and manufacturing base. The latter cost only RMB 20 million in total.

5.3. Corporate Renewal through Strategic Alliances

5.3.1. Problems of the old organizational structure in the new market environment

CGC had dominated the Chinese PC market in the early years. However, its market share was declining over time. As seen from CGC's market performance data in Table 5.4, although the company had an established production capacity of more than 30,000 PCs per year, its domestic sales had been stagnating at around 15,000, only half of its production capacity. The size of China's domestic market was certainly a constraint; the market was still underdeveloped. Even taking that into account, CGC's performance was less than satisfactory, as indicated by the fact that its sales did not even keep pace with the slow growth of the overall market.

The problem was the quality of their products. In 1989 the National Product Quality Inspection Centre conducted a product inspection and ranked the Great Wall PC the lowest among major domestically made PCs. Testing on Great Wall's PC sample revealed 17 hard-drive errors and three floppy-drive errors. 'Unthinkable', recalled one of the former marketing directors, 'It was obvious that the manufacturing quality problems were coming from the suppliers of the hard drive and floppy drives. But Great Wall as the system integrator got all the blame.'[8]

A careful examination of the problem showed that it was as much organizational as technological. There was a mismatch between the organizational structure of pro-

---

[8] Personal interview with a former marketing director of CGC in Apr. 1998.

duction and the new competitive market environment. The organization, especially, in the area of supplier relations, was still very much influenced by the central-planning mechanism. Due to the emphasis on localization, Great Wall relied heavily on local suppliers for parts and components. Localization required importing production lines and, sometimes, CKD kits to start with. Due to hard currency constraints, the central ministry, in this case MEI, only licensed a handful of state-owned enterprises to engage in the localization process. Consequently, these enterprises were virtually monopolies in their respective product markets. As a result, the quality of local parts and components was often questionable. Yet Great Wall had no choice but to take in their supplies. That made it very difficult for Great Wall to control the quality of its final product.

What happened in the case of hard and floppy drives was that local parts and components suppliers provided Great Wall with their least reliable products. They exported the higher quality products made from CKD kits in return for hard currency, or sold them to PC makers in the market place for higher prices. The lower quality local duplicates delivered to Great Wall were sold at prices set by MEI, often lower than the market prices. Other local PC makers, however, were less constrained by the burden of localization and were more flexible in purchasing parts and components.

That incident came as a big blow to Great Wall's already shaky market image. Management sought to overcome the problem through expansion of its in-house manufacturing capacity. Long preoccupied by economy of scale in production, they knew that Great Wall's production scale was too small compared with international standards. A World Bank report recommended 200,000 PCs per year as the optimal scale of production. The company submitted a proposal for a major investment project to be listed in the government's eighth five-year plan in 1991–5 for policy loans. The loan was for building new production facilities with production capacity of 200,000 PCs and 50,000 high-resolution monitors per annum.[9] Meanwhile, it also sought to add the design capacity of application specific integrated circuit (ASIC) chips onto its R&D facilities—an investment projected at RMB 150 million. Construction of the new facilities started in the second half of 1992.

However, this major expansion project coincided with an unprecedented intensification of competition in the Chinese PC market. By the early 1990s CGC had already lost its monopolistic position in Chinese-language processing technologies. New science and technology enterprises such as Stone, Legend, and Founder had developed Chinese word-processing add-on cards that could be inserted into general-purpose PCs to make systems that would handle Chinese language information equally well. These firms also acted as agencies for multinational companies to distribute PCs and related products in China. For example, Legend developed a Chinese word-processing add-on card and bundled it with import models such as AST's. The combination of domestic-made Chinese-language add-on cards with imported brand-name computers were tough competition for Great Wall computer models. As the

---

[9] Electronics Yearbook of China 1991: VII-5.

Chinese market became increasingly integrated into the global market and the Chinese-language processing was no longer a barrier, the level of foreign competition intensified substantially in the Chinese market. The volume of imported PCs increased more than threefold, from 24,900 to 111,300 in 1991 alone. Cheap imports squeezed the market shares of Chinese domestic makers, preventing Great Wall from further expanding its sales volume in the domestic market.

Given the situation, it became apparent by 1992 that the company would not have a market for its much enlarged production capacity that was scheduled to operate by 1995. Major action was called for to avoid the serious consequences of over-capacity.

So far, the company had mainly worked independently in developing its organizational capabilities. Given the new competitive market environment, it was imperative to seek strategic alliances with major international players to narrow the competitive gap. As Wang, the company's president remarked in a company planning meeting in October 1992:

In the past, we thought we could rely on ourselves to conquer the world given our products and capabilities. Five years have now passed and how have we fared? We thought we could at least make it in the lower end of the high-tech product spectrum. We have not even made breakthroughs in that area. Now, we should consider opening part of our company up to international co-operation. From now on, we should seek to shorten the gaps in product development, production management and marketing through strategic alliances with foreign companies.[10]

5.3.2. *The joint venture with IBM*

Inspired by the concept of corporate re-engineering overseas, the company launched a campaign for corporate renewal, meant to be a 'recreation' of the company.

A strategic alliance with a foreign company seemed to be the best choice because it could solve several problems at once. First of all, it was an effective learning device. Management had to learn how to manage large-scale production. 'We probably know how to make 20,000 PCs per year with consistent quality, but not 200,000. That is something we have to learn.'[11] Second, it could shift the burden of sales in the international market to foreign partners, thereby solving its over-capacity problem.

CGC management identified IBM as the top candidate. At the time, IBM was also interested in finding a local partner. Though IBM was among the first foreign computer companies that entered China, its business there had never really taken off. IBM's high expectations for the Chinese market were shattered by the extremely difficult business environment.[12] As a result, IBM was very cautious in pursuing its strategy in China. That did not pose a big problem for IBM in the 1980s, given the tiny size of the Chinese PC market. Things changed dramatically in the early 1990s when the huge potential of the Chinese PC market was finally turning into reality. Yet IBM had already trailed far behind other PC makers such as AST and Compaq

---

[10] Transcript of Wang's remark in a strategic planning meeting in Oct. 1992, from company archives.
[11] Personal interview with the former general manager of CGC Beijing Market Division, June 1996.
[12] Personal interviews with former IBM employees in Sept. 1994.

in terms of market share. One of its biggest problems was local distribution channels. Without a local partner, it would be extremely difficult for IBM to expand in China. CGC, as China's number one PC maker, was an ideal partner for IBM.

In a sense the CGC–IBM negotiation picked up where the joint-venture negotiation between IBM and the Computer Bureau had left off some ten years previously. There was no question about the need for setting up a joint venture this time—the only potential barrier was the terms. CGC wanted a 50–50 equity joint venture. IBM, on the other hand, feared a loss of control in a less familiar environment and insisted on a majority share. CGC eventually gave up on the equity side. The resulting share of equity was 49 to 51, with IBM in a majority position. 'We spent six months just on this one percentage point', the chairman of CGC recalled.[13]

The CGC–IBM joint venture was officially launched in February 1994. Its English name was International Information Process Co. or IIPC. The Chinese name was more straightforward as GW–IBM. The joint venture was to assemble both IBM and Great Wall PCs and sell them in both the Chinese and international markets.

5.3.3. Product renewal: The Golden Great Wall Campaign[14]

The company sought to overhaul its product image by leveraging its strategic alliance with IBM. The market for local brand PCs was in a critical situation. Local brands were squeezed in between high-priced, high-quality, imported brand-name PCs and low-priced, generic, locally made PCs. The generic models were often smuggled into China in assembled or SKD forms. Local brands were losing their market identities. It was very important to redefine the market niche for local brand-name PCs. In October 1993, with the negotiation of a PC joint venture with IBM well under way, Great Wall's management decided to create a high-end locally made PC brand. The product would have a quality that would equal the likes of IBM but would be sold at a lower price. The new model was named Golden Great Wall, signalling both the product's quality and the company's identity.

The product development took a holistic approach that integrated market positioning, product design, and manufacturing. The deputy general manager and chief engineer led the development effort. They formed a new product development team, and a gifted young engineer was assigned as the chief product designer. To ensure the integration of product development with market needs, the company had previously moved one of its key R&D directors to the post of marketing director. The new marketing director worked closely with the chief product designer in supplying product specifications based on stringent marketing requirements. In fact, the product specifications were set against one of IBM's. The marketing director had also provided product development procedure that was said to be a copy of IBM's.

---

[13] Personal interview with CGC's president in Apr. 1998.
[14] Data for the following two sections are drawn from: 'The Story of "Golden Great Wall" ', *Computer Business Information* (in Chinese), 24 April 1995: 21; 'The Gold Content of "Golden Great Wall" ', *China InfoWorld* (in Chinese), 2 May 1995: 38, 41–2; and personal interviews with the chief designer of the 'Golden Great Wall' and the former director of the Business Planning Unit of CGC in Apr. 1998.

The new product was envisioned to be high in functionality, quality, and taste but low in cost. The design process followed four principles: embedding quality control in the design process; using a system optimizing the design approach; pursuing IBM's level of product quality; and incorporating special features to meet local needs. The team bought IBM, Compaq, and other top computer models and conducted thorough analyses of their inner workings. They also incorporated the most advanced technologies, such as Surface Mounting Technology (SMT) in the design of circuit boards, ergonomic structure, proprietary Chinese-language processing technologies, etc.

Golden Great Wall went into scale production in October 1994, and was produced side by side with IBM PCs in the same production lines at IIPC. It met with huge success in the market.

5.3.4. Strategic alliance as a learning device

CGC once again opened up a new avenue in developing and upgrading the Chinese indigenous computer industry through a combination of indigenous design capabilities and learning from strategic alliances. The strength of CGC was in its design capabilities, accumulated from the design experiences of products over the years. Yet mere in-house design capabilities were not enough to generate market success in the increasingly competitive Chinese PC market. The weakness of CGC was its lack of experience in large-scale production and marketing. The joint venture became a platform for CGC to learn product development, production, and marketing techniques from IBM. The speed and effectiveness of learning through strategic alliances was much faster than other means such as technology licensing and importation of turnkey production lines. CGC learned from IBM at each stage of the new product development cycle.

At the product design and manufacturing stages, CGC's engineers were introduced to sophisticated production techniques and strict quality control measures by IBM engineers at IIPC. IBM engineers also worked closely with CGC's design engineers in the diagnosis of problems associated with the transfer of blueprints to manufacturing.

For example, Chinese engineers used to use yield as a measure of production quality. They learned that IBM used throughput instead. Throughput rate measures 100 per cent of input minus any reworking in the production process, while yield measures the percentage of output against input. The former not only indicates material productivity but also product quality because a high-quality product requires little reworking in the production process. Higher yield does not mean high throughput. Only if throughput and yield were both high, would the quality of the product be high. The new quality control concept led CGC's design engineers to improve the product design to meet the stringent requirement of high throughput rate. As a result, the throughput rate of Golden Great Wall reached 95 per cent, which was only 1 to 2 percentage points below IBM PCs.

Besides the final products, the joint venture also helped to improve the quality of local parts and components. The local sourcing from the joint venture not only provided a ready market for local parts and component manufacturers, but also forced the local suppliers to improve their product quality. With a wide range of parts and components manufacturing plants in operation, CGC was a major beneficiary of local sourcing.

The company made a quantum leap in both product quality and corporate image by leveraging its strategic alliance with IBM. CGC's independent product design, using the most advanced design techniques, and the manufacturing of the product by CGC–IBM joint venture with world-class processing technologies made Golden Great Wall an unequivocal first-class product. Meanwhile, CGC could still offer a price that was much lower than equivalent international brand-name products due to the economies of scale of its production of parts and components.

It was a win-win situation, with IBM benefiting just as much from the alliance. Since IBM received favourable media exposure due to the high-profile joint venture, its market share started taking off. It jumped into the top rank in market share in less than two years, from number 5 in 1994 to number 2 in 1996.

The high demand for both Golden Great Wall and IBM PCs created a need for a larger production capacity. The large-scale expansion of production facilities started two years previously by CGC was completed just in time; IIPC moved to the new facility in 1995. Of five production lines, two were allocated to produce Golden Great Wall PCs, and three to IBM PCs. Production picked up rapidly: the number of PCs produced by IIPC reached more than 100,000 in 1995, and 200,000 in 1996.

One manager at CGC proudly summarized in retrospect: 'We acquired the technical know-how, established our own brand name, and didn't give up our market.'[15]

5.4. Corporatization

5.4.1. The formation of a large industrial conglomerate

As an integral part of the corporate rejuvenation campaign, the company had also expanded into an array of IT-related businesses, besides its core PC business.

In 1992, as a result of a realignment of state-owned productive assets, CGC merged with two large state-owned computer electronics factories, the Hunan Computer Factory and the Jiannan Machinery Factory. The two factories were previously members of the Great Wall Computer Industry Group. Hunan Computer Factory was one of the largest manufacturers of computer terminals in China. Jiannan Machinery Factory was formerly designated by MEI as a major manufacturer of computer storage devices. CGC accelerated the pace of product development and expanded the production of the Hunan Computer Factory after the merger. It developed a series of new Chinese–English font and graphic display terminals, making it another core business of the group.

CGC's own parts and components manufacturing plants that were originally designed to supply in-house PC productions were encouraged to become

---

[15] Personal interview in Apr. 1998.

independent OEM suppliers in their respective markets. As a result, the group made a major breakthrough in expanding the production of parts, components, and peripherals. Production volumes increased dramatically: monitor production increased to 90,000 units, UPS to 50,000 units, electric power units to 200,000, computer motherboards and add-on cards to one million pieces, hard drives to 300,000 units, and floppy drives to 340,000 units in 1993. By 1995 CGC had become the largest OEM supplier of computer parts and components to both domestic and overseas PC makers in China.

In June 1993, in response to the explosive growth of the information systems integration market, CGC formed Great Wall Software and Systems Inc. The company was an extension of CGC's existing systems integration division. CGC had been active in large systems integration projects, particularly systems integration projects for nationwide bank network systems since 1989. From 1994 on, the Great Wall Software and Systems Inc. became a major participant in the government's 'Golden Projects', the Chinese equivalent of the Information Super Highway.[16] It was the major contractor working on the national VAT systems integration project or the Golden Tax Project. In 1994 alone, the company had won the contracts for sixteen projects with total revenue of RMB 197 million, becoming the largest systems integrator in China.

The company continued to extend its strategic alliances with leading international players. The success of IIPC led to a second joint venture with IBM in September 1995, which was in the circuit-card assembly business. It was a three-way joint venture between Great Wall, Kaifa Keji (a listed company in Shenzhen of which CGC was a major shareholder), and IBM, named as GKI Electronics Co., Ltd. The production capacity was 20 million motherboards or add-on cards per year. That made GKI one of the major suppliers of computer cards to both IBM and the international market. In March 1997 CGC formed yet another joint venture with IBM, Hailiang Storage Products Co., Ltd., manufacturing the latest version of magnetic resonance heads for computer storage devices (see Table 5.5).

Besides the joint ventures with IBM, CGC formed a wide array of technological alliances with other leading international players (Table 5.6).

As a result of these expansions, CGC became one of the largest conglomerates in the Chinese IT industry, providing a wide array of IT products and services (Table 5.7). By 1996 it had evolved into a complex organization with branch companies, wholly owned subsidiaries, subsidiaries with controlling shares, and associate companies (Fig. 5.1). The company's sales started picking up in 1993. By 1996, after the new production facilities went into full operation, sales jumped again (Table 5.8).

5.4.2. Corporatization and the changing investment regime

One of the major imperatives for the corporate renewal campaign was to utilize the large investments initiated in the beginning of the eighth five-year planning period

---

[16] For an illustration of China's Golden Projects, see Simon 1996: 10.

TABLE 5.5. *CGC's strategic alliances with IBM*

Name	Date	Investment (US $ millions)	CGC share (%)	IBM share (%)	Product	Staff
International Information Product Co., Ltd. (IIPC)	Feb. 1994	10	49	51	PCs	300
Shenzhen GKI Electronics Co., Ltd.	Sept. 1995	13	20	80	Motherboards and add-on cards	350
Shenzhen Hailiang Storage Products Co., Ltd.	March 1997	43	10	80	MR head gimbals assemblies	1,000

TABLE 5.6. *CGC's other international alliances*

	Partners	Product	Date
Beijing Gaoteng Business Computer System Co., Ltd.	Omron, Stone, Qindao TV	VAT cash register development	May 1994
Sino-Italian International Business Machine Equipment Co., Ltd.	STREMA (Italy)	VAT cash register manufacturing	June 1995
Technology co-operation	DEC	High-end computer terminal product development	Dec. 1994
Co-development	Microsoft	Windows 3.2, Chinese version	Apr. 1995

Source: *Chinese Computer News*, special issue, 4 Mar. 1996.

in 1991–5. These investment projects required enormous sums of funding. The company's internal funds were no longer sufficient for two reasons. The first was erosion of the retained earnings due to the intensification of market competition. The second was the sheer scale of the investments. Given that CGC, like most other state-owned enterprises, no longer received budgetary funds from the government for capital investment projects because of the changes in investment regimes, the major

TABLE 5.7. *CGC's major products*

Product	Factory	Location	Ownership
PCs	IIPC	Shenzhen	Joint venture
Printers	Great Wall Group Shenzhen Co.	Shenzhen	Wholly owned
Monitors	Great Wall Group Shenzhen Co.	Shenzhen	Wholly owned
Terminals	Hunan Computer Factory	Hunan	Wholly owned
Motherboards	GKI Electronic Co., Ltd.	Shenzhen	Joint venture
Cases	Great Wall Group Shenzhen Co.	Shenzhen	Wholly owned
FDDs	Jiannan Machinery Factory	Hunan	Wholly owned
Power units	Great Wall Group Shenzhen Co.	Shenzhen	Wholly owned
CD-ROMs	Wearers Peripherals Co.	Shenzhen	Joint venture
Storage	Hailiang Storage Products Co.	Shenzhen	Joint venture

TABLE 5.8. *CGC's sales data over the years*

	1987	1988	1989	1990	1991	1992	1993	1994	1995	1996
Output (computer units)	20,456	13,594	21,271	16,757	18,000	15,000	25,000	42,347	120,000	208,000
Total sales (RMB millions)	380	499	579	541	511	1,130	1,646	1,814	1,898	3,638

Sources: Company Archives, 1991 Company Report, Nov. 1991; China Electronics Yearbook 1992–8; 'CGC (Shenzhen) Initial Public Offering Prospectus'; The New Century Group 1997c.

sources of funding shifted to policy loans from state-owned banks. Table 5.9 estimates the company's capital requirements from 1992 to 1996.

Even though these investments were fully utilized, as were the results of the successful campaign of corporate renewal, the group still operated at high debt–equity ratios. According to an account report, the debt–equity ratio in the PC-related businesses for 1994, 1995, and 1996 were 6:4; 6:4, and 7:3 respectively, which did not include the bulk of debt incurred for any major investment projects.

It was stipulated in the beginning of the corporate renewal campaign that the company should explore the possibility of corporatization (restructuring into a joint-stock company) as a way of raising capital and improving management. In fact, corporatization had been a major policy initiative for revitalizing SOEs. The policy goal of corporatization was much broader than merely raising capital. By restructuring state-owned enterprises and subjecting them to the discipline of stock markets, it was hoped to change SOEs' behaviour, weaken government intervention, enhance managerial responsibility, and reinforce employee incentives.[17]

---

[17] These rationales were expressed in a remark by CGC's president in a company strategic planning meeting on 22 Sept. 1992—information from the transcripts in the company archives.

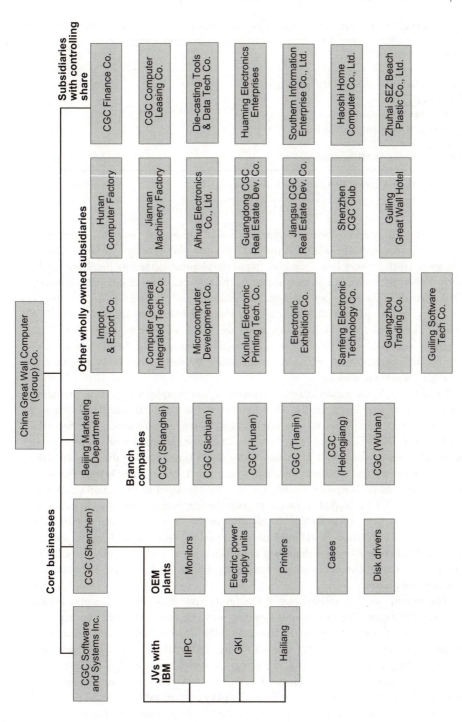

Fig. 5.1. CGC's group structure

TABLE 5.9. *Estimated capital demand for CGC's major investment projects 1992–1996*

Item	1992–6
Fixed capital investment (RMB millions)	300
Including:	
Shenzhen Expansion Project	150
Beijing R&D Centre Project	50
Others	100
Working capital (RMB millions)	160–240 per year

Source: Company Archives, 1991 Company Report, Nov. 1991.

Two conditions had to be met before this would happen: one was the development of the stock markets, the other was the attractiveness of the company's assets. China's domestic stock market had undergone rapid development since its inception in the early 1990s. By 1996, in less than six years, the number of listed companies, mostly state-owned, in the two stock markets, the Shanghai and Shenzhen Stock Exchanges, had risen from zero to 530, with a market capitalization of more than one trillion RMB. Meanwhile, due to the success of the corporate renewal campaign, both revenues and profits of CGC's core IT-related businesses had been growing very rapidly and become very attractive to investors. By early 1997 both internal and external conditions were ripe.

In early 1997 the group started restructuring its productive assets in preparing an initial public offering on the Shenzhen Stock Exchange. It was decided to list two joint-stock companies for the group's core IT-related businesses. The first, the China Great Wall Computer Shenzhen Co., Ltd., was created out of the productive assets of China Great Wall Shenzhen Computer Company, bundling it with the group's Software and Systems, Inc. and the group's Beijing Marketing Division. China Great Wall Computer Shenzhen Company consisted of the group's core productive assets. It included a product development centre and a wide range of manufacturing facilities as well as the holdings of the three joint ventures with IBM. After integrating Great Wall Software and Systems, Inc., as well as the group's Beijing Marketing Division, the newly established joint-stock company included all the group's major computer-related businesses, including hardware, software, and systems integration.

The second one was formed out of the productive assets of the Group's Hunan Computer Factory. The factory was brought into the group in 1992 as a result of realignment of state-owned productive assets. By 1996 it had already became the largest enterprise in developing, manufacturing, and marketing computer terminals in China. In preparing the listing, the group transferred one-third of the ownership rights to the newly established Hunan Electronics Information Industrial Group Co., Ltd. The latter was an asset management company authorized by Hunan's provincial government to manage the state-owned assets under its jurisdiction. The two groups together with two other state-owned companies jointly set up the Hunan Computer Co., Ltd. for a listing on the Shenzhen Stock Exchange.

The two joint-stock companies went public almost simultaneously on the Shenzhen Stock Exchange in June 1997. The resulting corporate structure is shown in Fig. 5.2, where it can be seen that CGC as a holding company held controlling shares in both joint-stock companies. By offering the public minority shares in both companies, the group raised net capitals of RMB 364 million and RMB 285 million respectively.

As seen previously, CGC had a very high debt–equity ratio because of its investment-driven strategy. The substantial amount of new capital raised through the two initial public offerings in the stock market had a profound impact on the company's capital structure and the way it financed its new investments.

The net proceeds from the IPOs were used to retire debt as well as fund new investments. According to the 'Initial Public Offering Prospectus', the net proceeds of RMB 364 million raised for CGC Shenzhen Co., Ltd., were to be used as follows:[18]

1. Acquiring the new production facilities for the expansion project of the CGC Shenzhen Company. The project was approved in 1992 by the State Planning Committee as one of the largest investment projects in the Chinese computer industry in the state's eighth five-year planning period. Construction started in early 1993, and was completed in late 1995. Total investment, including both factory space and equipment, was RMB 278 million. It was funded mostly on bank loans. The facilities occupied a site of 47,000 square metres and had more than 50,000 square metres of factory space. It was capable of producing 400,000 PCs, one million monitors, two million electric power units, and three million motherboards and add-on cards. The joint-stock company would pay RMB 230 million to buy these assets from its holding company. The money would be used to retire the holding company's debts to the banks.

2. Investing RMB 150 million to expand the above-mentioned production facilities by adding development and manufacturing capabilities for 150,000 multimedia computers and 500,000 multimedia software packages.

3. Investing RMB 29 million to build a software development and information service centre with a capacity of 2,000 software development and systems integration projects.[19]

The RMB 285 million raised through the IPO of Hunan Computer Co., Ltd., was used as follows:[20]

1. Investing RMB 154.5 million in constructing computer terminal product development, manufacturing, and servicing facilities. The projected capacity was 300,000 computer terminals per year. The project started in December 1995 and

---

[18] See 'CGC (Shenzhen) IPO Prospectus': 16–18.

[19] There was still a 44.7 million shortfall in funds for the three projects. The company planned to seek loans to make it up. See 'CGC (Shenzhen) IPO Prospectus': 18.

[20] See the 'IPO Prospectus' of Hunan Computer Co., Ltd.: 12–13.

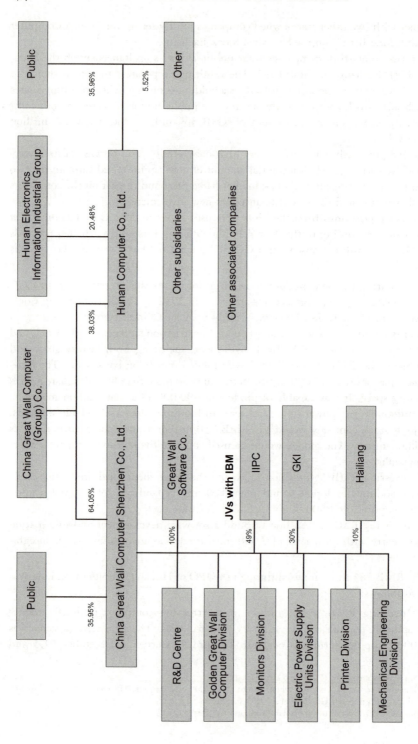

Fig. 5.2. CGC's corporate structure after restructuring

had already spent RMB 31 million in bank loans. It was planned to be completed in early 1998.

2. Investing RMB 48.4 million in network computer terminal production facilities. The project started in October 1996 and RMB 9 million in bank loans had already been spent. It was projected to have a production capacity of 60,000 network computer terminals per annum.

3. Investing RMB 52 million in VAT cash registers, started in May 1996. This was an integral part of the government's Golden Tax Project. An additional RMB 52 million investment was planned to create a production capacity of 250,000 VAT tax registers in 1997–8.

4. Investing RMB 28.6 million in the development and production of a new type of battery. The project was to form a production capacity of 24 million Ah, equivalent to 24 million AA batteries per year, by the end of 1998.

Clearly, corporatization through IPOs brought a windfall of cash into the group that allowed it to expand its capabilities in its core businesses aggressively without incurring high financial costs. It marked a fundamental change in the investment regime of the state-owned enterprises.

5.5. Concluding Remarks

CGC was a success story in the transformation of the Chinese state-owned computer industry. It demonstrated that all-out privatization was not a necessary condition for a successful transformation of state owned industries. What laid the foundation for the success of CGC was the indigenous product innovations that met specific local needs from the very beginning and the corresponding adoption of a market-oriented organizational structure. The so-called Great Wall Model, with its four basic ingredients—market orientation, independent product development, OEM production arrangement, and dealership distribution system—proved that it was possible to build a competitive enterprise without relinquishing state ownership altogether.

What changed in the process was the structure of enterprise governance. Indigenous product innovations coupled with the adoption of a market-oriented organizational structure allowed CGC to accumulate capital through the market, independent from the state. This financial independence resulted in significant managerial autonomy in its decision-making.

What we have also seen was a process of building up organizational capabilities over time through a combination of indigenous development and strategic alliances with foreign multinationals. The result was the accumulation and enlargement of state-owned assets as embodied in the enterprises. That allowed the enterprise to privatize part of its assets through the stock market while keeping both the assets and its control over them intact. And the low-cost financing from the stock market allowed a further build-up in organizational capabilities.

CGC's success in fending off fierce competition from foreign multinationals became a model for other state-owned computer enterprises. It was the inspiration behind the recent recovery of several large state-owned computer enterprises such as

Changjiang, Langchao, and Tongru, which had almost been wiped out by the competition. Together with other newly established state-owned science and technology enterprises such as Legend and Founder, they have re-emerged as market leaders in the world's fastest growing PC market.

Great Wall, as well as a handful of other state-owned computer enterprises, will face more challenges ahead as competition further intensifies. However, given its accumulated organizational and technological capabilities, the indigenous computer industry will, most probably, continue to forge ahead, as long as the entrepreneurial spirit of 'mandarin- or scientist-turned-manager' remains alive.

6

A New Mode of
Technology Learning

We can find a consistent pattern with regard to the trajectories of technology learning or capability acquisition among the four enterprises from the case studies.

All four of them started directly with certain kinds of indigenous innovation at the levels of product redesign or product design. Stone started with redesigning (forward engineering) a Japanese dot-matrix printer, making it capable of handling Chinese characters. Legend started with the commercialization of a Chinese word-processing add-on card for imported computer systems. Founder built on the fruit of a large-scale government-sponsored R&D project, starting directly with a product for the Chinese-language electronic publishing system. Great Wall started with the design of the first IBM-compatible PC that has integrated Chinese-language word-processing capabilities. A distinctive feature at this stage of learning was the close coupling of the innovative products with market demand. With virtually no in-house manufacturing capabilities in the beginning, all four enterprises resorted to external production capabilities through contractual arrangements. In the case of Stone, it was the manufacturing capabilities of Japanese companies. The other three used the manufacturing capabilities of existing state-owned electronics manufacturing enterprises in one way or another. The advantage of this strategy was that it could secure market acceptance of the new products before committing to investing in in-house manufacturing capabilities. Meanwhile, the strategy also served for the accumulation of much needed capital for further investment in R&D and manufacturing.

Having secured market acceptance for their new and innovative products, all four enterprises moved on to upgrade their technological capabilities, either by moving from product redesign to product design in the cases of Stone and Legend, or by continuous product upgrades in the cases of Founder and Great Wall. The continuous innovations in product design reinforced market acceptance of these products until the market was large enough to allow the exploitation of economies of scale in production. The enterprises then started investing in building up manufacturing capabilities. At this stage, technology transfer from abroad became significant. The indigenous manufacturing capabilities of the existing state-owned electronics enterprises were no longer sufficient, particularly when the enterprises moved into general-purpose computer systems competing directly with multinational companies, as in the cases of Legend and Great Wall. The most commonly used organizational form of technology transfer was the joint venture. Both Stone and Great Wall used joint ventures extensively as a scheme for technology transfer. In the case of Legend, the manufacturing capabilities were mostly developed in-house after the initial acquisition of a small Hong Kong manufacturing company. As for Founder, its core technology was in systems integration, meaning that its limited volume made it less imperative for it to internalize manufacturing capabilities.[1]

Their resulting successes in the market place based on their integrated capabilities in R&D, marketing, and manufacturing made it possible for the enterprises to pass the stringent listing requirements of the stock exchanges, particularly the Hong Kong Stock Exchange. All four enterprises were capitalized substantially through the initial public offerings (IPOs), enabling them to invest in a further build-up of their integrated capabilities in R&D, marketing, and manufacturing.

Thus, we saw the evolution of a unique top-down mode of technology learning. This was in sharp contrast to the conventional mode of technology learning among developing countries, including the East Asian newly industrialized economies (NIEs), whereby technology learning starts with labour-intensive assembly, and reaches the level of indigenous product design only at a much later stage.

Clearly, these enterprises' ready access to the science and technology resources that had been accumulated in the state sector was indispensable in permitting them to start directly with product innovation. In some cases, notably Legend and Founder, their first products were the result of commercializing technologies already developed in the state S&T sectors. Stone and Great Wall, in contrast, relied on scientists and engineers from state S&T institutions in developing their first products. Another important factor was specific local needs. In all four cases, indigenous technological innovations stemmed from the need to process Chinese-language information. However, it was the organizational innovation in the institutional structure of enterprise governance that enabled these enterprises to bring the technological capabilities to meet the market needs. There was a coupling between the institutional structure of enterprise governance and the trajectories of technology learning. Fig. 6.1 is a schematic representation of this organizational mechanism. I shall elaborate on it in the following sections.

6.1. Coupling between Technology Commercialization and Non-Governmentalization

The commercialization of technological resources accumulated in the state science and technology sector set the four enterprises along the unique path of a top-down mode of technology learning. This technology commercialization, or indigenous innovation, was possible because of the emergence of a set of new organizational structures of enterprise governance that was characterized by managerial autonomy from the government. In other words, coupled with the commercialization of technology

---

[1] Founder leveraged its existing technology and marketing capabilities and ventured into PC manufacturing at a late stage. By that time, it had already acquired the capability to manufacture PCs on its own.

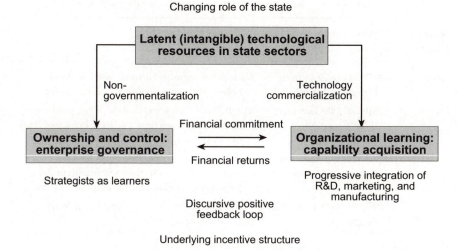

Fig. 6.1. Sources of dynamism among the Chinese science and technology enterprises

was the process of non-governmentalization of enterprise governance. The latter stemmed from the extra-budgetary nature of enterprise finance.

Unlike the traditional state-owned enterprises, whose start-up funds were usually granted from state capital construction budgets, the start-up funds of these enterprises were raised independently. They came from various sources other than central or local government budgets. These sources included bank loans and individual borrowing and the extra-budgetary funds of various public institutions. For example, Stone had borrowed its start-up capital (RMB 20,000) from a rural township. Legend's initial capital was a loan from the Institution of Computing Technology of the Chinese Academy of Sciences. And Founder's start-up fund came from surplus funds at Beijing University. The start-up fund for Great Wall was allocated from the state R&D budget.

Note that the start-up funds were usually for the purpose of enterprise registration. The fund was often very small and insignificant in business terms. The real financial resources, crucial to the rapid development of the enterprises, were loans as well as their retained earnings. For instance, Stone's working capital was originally from local urban credit co-operatives. Legend's working capital that funded its launching of the associative Chinese word add-on card was earned from its early computer service businesses. It has used commercial loans from the local branch of the Bank of China since 1987. Founder initially used money from a local township as working capital for its computer trading business. It used a bank loan to launch its own high-resolution Chinese electronic publishing system in 1988. The loan was secured by Beijing University from the local branch of the State Industrial and Commercial Bank. Great Wall's initial working capital came from advance payments for

TABLE 6.1. *Financial sources of the four enterprises in their early years*

Name of company	Sources of company registration capital	Sources of working capital
Stone	RMB 20,000 loan from Evergreen Township	Short-term commercial loans from the local urban credit co-operative; retained earnings
Legend	RMB 200,000 loan from ICT	The ICT loan, plus retained earnings; short-term commercial loans from the local branch of Bank of China since 1987
Founder	RMB 300,000 loan from Beijing University	Loans from Yuyuantan Township; retained earnings; loans from the local branch of State Industrial and Commercial Bank since 1988
Great Wall	RMB 300,000 R&D budget	Pre-payments for the innovative Great Wall 0520 model of computers

Source: Summary of information from Chapters 2, 3, 4, 5.

its innovative computer product, the Great Wall 0520. Table 6.1 summarizes the financial sources of the four enterprises in their early years.

Although these enterprises did not get their financing directly from the state, all of them had direct access to the rich technological resources in the state sector, often for free. On the one hand, the extra-budgetary nature of indirect finance ensured the autonomy crucial to the enterprise managers' incentives and performance. On the other hand, easy access to the rich technological resources provided the enterprises with resource positioning advantages that enabled them to launch high-value-added products in a short period of time with relatively small capital expenditures.

In fact, the mission of these enterprises was to turn the state's accumulated—but commercially underdeveloped—technological resources into competitive industrial products. As a matter of fact, China had a relatively higher level of science and technology capabilities than most of the countries at a comparable level of economic development. That was, to a large extent, a legacy of central planning.[2] The technologies that later constituted the core competencies of these respective enterprises all had their roots in the state S&T sectors. In the case of Stone, the technological skills of its R&D team in developing the integrated Chinese word processor had been fully developed when they were all employees in various state institutions while the Great Wall 0520 PC was developed by a team of computer scientists and engineers from research institutions under MEI.

As for Legend, its associative Chinese word-processing technology was originally a fruit of ICT's research under CAS, first developed without any commercial consideration. That was due, in large part, to a lack of horizontal commercialization chan-

---

[2] By the same token, the former Soviet Union had a much higher level of science and technology than China. Yet the fact that contemporary Russia has not developed commercially viable high-tech industrial sectors as compared with China, is something worth pondering.

nels under the central-planning mechanism. The technology behind the high-resolution Chinese electronic publishing systems that Founder later worked on had its origin in a large-scale, state-led industrial R&D project. However, the slow progress of the projects under the central-planning mechanism was proof of the old system's weakness in turning out commercially viable products.

Comparing the associative Chinese word-processing technology being developed at ICT with the high-resolution Chinese electronic publishing systems technology under the state's industrial R&D project, it was clear that innovation or technology commercialization under the centrally planned system was more a function of the government than one of enterprise. What the new enterprises had done was create new institutional frameworks or organizational arrangements that bridged the gap between scientific research and industrial activities. Thus, they transformed the innovation from governmental behaviour under central planning to enterprise endeavour in a new market environment.

The ease of access of these enterprises to the rich science and technology resources in the state sector was indispensable to their rapid success in commercializing the technology. In fact, the technological resources represented substantial hidden subsidies from the state, although it was difficult to evaluate them in monetary terms.[3]

6.2. The New Institutional Structure of Enterprise Governance

The significance of the extra-budgetary sources of finance was that it set the tune for the relationship between the enterprises and the government. It provided a basis for a new institutional framework of enterprise governance that featured autonomous management with the incentives as well as the resources to pursue innovative strategies, and a governmental regulatory regime that focused on development-oriented industrial policies.

If we define enterprise governance as an institutional framework that determines who makes the investment decisions, what types of investments they make, and how returns are distributed (Lazonick and O'Sullivan 1996; O'Sullivan 1996), then the new S&T enterprises were distinctive in all three dimensions in comparison with the traditional state-owned enterprises.

Using this definition under China's centrally planned economy, enterprise governance was the function of government agencies rather than enterprise management. As described in Chapter 2, under the traditional central-planning system, enterprise management was only a passive agent that executed the directives from government agencies. It was the planning authorities at various levels of the government that made the investment decisions on behalf of the enterprises. Correspondingly, the type of investment was often extensive, that is, mere expansion of the scale of production, rather than intensive, that is, innovations in products and processes. And the returns

---

[3] This access to public sector resources is akin to the access of the high-tech firms in Silicon Valley or Route 128 (Massachusetts) to the rich technological resources of Stanford University and MIT respectively. The latter two are obviously some of the most important factors for the clusters of the high-tech firms in the two regions in the US (Saxenian 1994).

from investments constituted a major part of the government's revenue, with which the planning authorities made new investment decisions. Obviously, the basis of this institutional framework was the fact that government budgets were the sole sources of finance for almost all investment activities.

The extra-budgetary financing of the new S&T enterprises laid a foundation for the separation of the state's regulatory role from its ownership role over the new enterprises. Since the government no longer directly owns and runs the enterprises, it can no longer exercise the right to extract excess revenues beyond taxes from the enterprises and cannot intervene directly in their daily operations.

Under this new institutional framework, management must have sufficient financial resources to give them discretion in pursuing innovative strategies. On the one hand, although managers had discretionary rights over the productive resources of the enterprises, they were not entitled to the capital gains from the productive assets because the enterprises were not legally their private property. On the other hand, there were no clear outside owners demanding maximum returns from the assets. Although public institutions, such as Evergreen Township, ICT of CAS, and Beijing University, to which the new-tech firms were attached administratively, normally collected a limited fee from the enterprises, the money was more like a rent for the 'titles of attachment' rather than the rent for capital assets. Most of the after-tax profits were held as retained earnings. They were split between the enterprise development fund (50 per cent), the employees' welfare fund (30 per cent), and the employees' bonus fund (20 per cent). Under these arrangements, the assets of all of these companies were the products of sheer accumulations of retained earnings. As a result, the government could not claim ownership rights over these enterprises in the same sense as it did for the state-owned enterprises.

For the same reason, the public institutions to which the enterprises were nominally attached could not readily claim ownership rights over these enterprises either. In the case of Stone, its initial supervisory body, the Evergreen Township, had relinquished all of their claims over the enterprise except for a fixed annual fee of about half a million Chinese RMB after only one year. Thus, Stone actually became a stand-alone enterprise with the maximum autonomy that a collectively owned enterprise could possibly have had under the Chinese system at the time. The role of the township was basically to provide the organizational framework—a rural township enterprise—for Stone to start with. Stone actually depended very little on the township. It derived its initial technological resources from other sources. In the case of Legend, the exclusive ties in both human and technological resources to the Institute of Computing Technology under the Chinese Academy of Sciences might have led to less autonomy for the enterprise. Yet the dynamism of Stone sufficiently demonstrated the importance of managerial autonomy in developing a viable enterprise to the decision-makers at CAS. It prompted them to adopt the organizational rules and practices from enterprises like Stone. The same thing was true for Founder, and Great Wall. To a certain extent, the closer links of Legend, Founder, and Great Wall to their respective supervisory governmental bodies rendered them less autonomous than Stone. Yet their closer links to the technologically rich resource base made them even more competitive technologically.

With the state's retreat from controlling the internal financial resources of the enterprises, management assumed the right to allocate these financial resources. In other words, management could make investment decisions with the funds under its discretion without necessarily going through lengthy procedures to obtain approval from various government agencies, as was the case for the traditional state-owned enterprises. This was significant in at least two senses. First, managerial autonomy from burdensome bureaucratic procedures was essential for quick responses to changing market conditions. Second, investment decisions made by insiders who had intimate knowledge of the market and technology were crucial for the learning process within firms.[4] In fact, in all four cases, strategic decision-makers consisted of entrepreneurial managers who were former scientists or engineers and product development champions who were keen on business opportunities—a combination of what was called 'scientifically minded entrepreneurs' with 'entrepreneurially minded scientists'.

The withdrawal of the government from directly managing the enterprises did not prevent it from indirectly influencing the direction of their investments. The state could shape the incentive and resource structures of the enterprises by manipulating institutional structures of property rights (Campbell and Lindberg 1990; Campbell et al. 1991), as well as by allocating resources indirectly through taxation and loan schemes.

Perhaps the most conspicuous practice regarding this role of the government is the establishment of special economic or enterprise zones.[5] This practice is a deliberate industrial policy and is typical of the approaches used by the governments of East Asian economies (Vogel 1979, 1991; Johnson 1982; Glasmeier 1988a,b; Best 1990; Wade 1990; World Bank 1993). In the case of the Chinese IT industry, the government established the Beijing New-Tech Industries Developmental Zone in the Haidian District where the new S&T enterprises flourished.

In the enterprise zone, the government adopted institutional devices nested in the taxation process and investment process that redistributed resources to strategic sectors. In the taxation process, sophisticated tax-concession schemes were devised to promote innovations in products and processes for enterprises in targeted industries. In the investment process, the devices included setting aside special venture loans in state banks with interest rates no higher, and sometimes even lower, than the ones of normal commercial loans for investments in innovative products, lower equity-to-debt ratio requirements for bank loans, pre-tax loan repayment, etc.

What is unique with respect to these redistributive devices is the regulatory regime imposed upon them. In granting S&T enterprises a special legal status, the government obliged them to meet certain requirements. These requirements

---

[4] For a theoretical treatment of the importance of integration of the strategic decision-makers into the collective learning process, see O'Sullivan 1996.

[5] For a general description of special economic zones and their roles in the economic reforms of China, see Vogel 1989: 125–60.

included specifying the number of technology personnel, the percentage of sales contributed by new products, the percentage of products exported, the allocation of retained earnings, etc. The institutional devices and the corresponding regulatory regimes were designed to create incentives and provide resources to induce enterprises to pursue ongoing improvements in products and processes.

6.3. The Trajectory of Learning: Progressive Integration of R&D, Marketing, and Manufacturing Capabilities

The small and limited start-up funds from extra-budgetary sources forced the new enterprises to rely on the market to raise capital. A commonly used strategy was to engage in high-tech commodity trading as well as technology services to accumulate the necessary capital to support product development. For instance, Legend accumulated much needed capital in its first year of operation through high-tech product services to finance R&D on its first-generation Chinese word-processing add-on cards. The direct access to the rich and high-quality technological resources in the state sector allowed the new S&T enterprises to adapt imported high-tech commodities to fit local conditions—a strategy that was called 'forward or second engineering'. This approach greatly reduced the uncertainties in the process of technology commercialization.

The initial successes in technology commercialization through integration of new product development with high-tech commodity trading provided a base for further innovations in the same or related products.[6] For example, Stone evolved from developing Chinese-language printers to integrated Chinese word processors. Legend advanced from developing Chinese word-processing add-on cards to computer motherboards and other add-on cards, and finally to personal computer systems. Founder evolved from developing high-resolution Chinese-language publishing systems to high-resolution colour publishing systems. Great Wall extended its product line from one model to a series of models that fitted different market demands. The result was the top-down approach in capability building, that is, starting with product redesign or system design before acquiring manufacturing capabilities. The high-value-added nature associated with product redesign and system design, as opposed to pure commodity trading, had the effect of accelerating the rate of capital accumulation among these enterprises. It laid the financial basis for the subsequent strategy of 'industrialization', that is, backward integration into manufacturing.

Meanwhile, the close coupling between new product development and high-tech commodity trading helped build extensive marketing capabilities among these enterprises. All four enterprises had built nationwide distribution channels or sales networks. The extensive market capabilities reduced the risk of investment in in-house manufacturing capabilities. For the latter was only meaningful when the size of the market allowed economies of scale in production. The size of the market would help

---

[6] This is in line with other studies that show the importance of user–producer interfaces or what was called 'the effect of advanced domestic users'; see Fagerberg 1998; Lundvall 1988.

to turn high-fixed costs of investing in manufacturing facilities into low unit costs of products, increasing the market competitiveness of their products.

It should be pointed out, however, that it was the enterprise governance regime and the corresponding governmental policy pertaining to the allocation of retained earnings that influenced the resources for, and the direction of, the investment. In other words, the collective or public nature of their ownership and control ensured that the money was to be invested in building organizational capabilities, rather than distributed more or less into private hands. The public nature of the enterprises stemmed from the fact that the initial technological resources were transferred from state sectors in the form of intangible assets through various organizational arrangements.

The implementation of the strategy of 'industrialization', or backward integration into manufacturing, posed a great challenge to the enterprises due to the general backwardness of high-tech product manufacturing in China. The four enterprises adopted various organizational vehicles to acquire manufacturing capabilities from abroad. One of the most common approaches was through various strategic alliance arrangements. For instance, Stone set up several joint ventures with large Japanese industrial corporations through Mitsui & Co. to produce the integrated Chinese word processors. Legend got its initial manufacturing facility through acquiring a troubled Hong Kong computer manufacturing company, Quantum Design, Inc., or QDI, and used it as a basis for acquiring manufacturing capabilities and further industrialization. Founder co-operated with DEC in an attempt to produce high-end computers for its high-resolution Chinese-language publishing systems. Great Wall teamed up with IBM to set up several manufacturing joint ventures.

The learning from foreign companies went well beyond narrowly defined technological transfers. The Chinese not only picked up manufacturing and managerial know-how from the multinationals, as in the cases of several joint-ventures between Stone and Japanese companies; but also marketing know-how from big US companies as in the cases of strategic alliances between Legend and HP, between Founder and DEC, and between Great Wall and IBM; and the international business experiences of Hong Kong companies as in the cases of Legend with DAW and QDI, and Founder with Kingsun. Table 6.2 is a summary of the organizational arrangements of learning from foreign firms among the four Chinese computer enterprises.

6.4. The Evolving Structure of Corporate Governance

The fast accumulation of capital and the corresponding build-up of R&D, manufacturing, and marketing capabilities through various organizational arrangements laid a solid foundation for the enterprises to expand further. As new opportunities opened up from the continuous evolution of the government's reform and open-door policies, the enterprises were able to exploit new avenues in obtaining financial resources. The most significant step in this direction was going public on stock exchanges. In the case of Stone, Legend, and Founder, it was the Hong Kong Stock Exchange. In the case of Great Wall, it was the Shenzhen Stock Exchange. By issuing stock

TABLE 6.2. *Organizational arrangements of learning from foreign firms*

Organizational arrangements	Content of learning
Stone–Mitsui equity joint venture	Product and process technologies and production management
Stone–Mitsui–Fujitsu equity joint venture	Product and process technologies and production management
Stone–Mitsui–Matsushita equity joint venture	Product and process technologies and production management
Stone–Mitsui–Mitsubishi equity joint venture	Product and process technologies and production management
Legend–DAW–China Technology equity joint venture	International marketing know-how
Legend's acquisition of Hong Kong QDI	Organization of manufacturing businesses in Hong Kong
Legend's acquisition of Hong Kong Valence	Business know-how in semiconductor product design, manufacturing, and marketing
Legend–AST marketing partnership	Large-scale marketing know-how
Founder's partnership with Hong Kong Kingsun	International marketing know-how
Founder–DEC marketing partnership	Large-scale marketing know-how
Great Wall–IBM PC manufacturing joint venture	Large-scale PC manufacturing know-how, marketing know-how
Great Wall–IBM card assembly joint venture	Large-scale card manufacturing know-how
Great Wall–IBM magnetic head joint venture	High-tech manufacturing knowledge

Source: Summary of information from Chapters 2, 3, 4, 5.

through initial public offerings on the stock exchange, these companies were able to raise substantial amounts of capital.

The initial public offering provided substantial financial resources for the companies to consolidate their existing capabilities and build new capabilities in R&D, marketing, and manufacturing. To a large extent, the reorganization into public corporations—a process that was called 'corporatization' in China—coincided with the process of industrialization, that is, backward integration into manufacturing. It indicates a strategic transition from an early stage, which centred around technology commercialization with emphasis on R&D and marketing, to a later stage emphasizing the build-up of manufacturing capabilities.

It is interesting to notice that a common corporate structure emerged after the

TABLE 6.3. *Summary of the share structure of the four listed companies* (in %)

Name of the listed companies	Shares of the group	Other stable shares	Shares issued to public
Stone Electronic Technology, Ltd.	58	15	27
Legend Holdings, Ltd.	38.8	36.2	25
Founder (Hong Kong), Ltd.	55.6	16.9	27.5
Great Wall Computer (Shenzhen), Ltd.	64.05		35.95

Source: Summary of information from Chapters 2, 3, 4, 5.

corporate reorganization of all four enterprises. All had adopted a group structure with only part of their businesses, albeit the core businesses, being listed on the stock exchange. In all four cases, the groups kept controlling shares in the listed companies (see Table 6.3). As a result, they raised a substantial amount of capital from the stock market without losing control over their core businesses.

The organizational arrangements combined collective or state ownership—the legacy of central planning—with the requirements of the stock market, the foremost institutional innovation of the capitalist market economy. Although the arrangement reflected the persistence of socialist institutions and ideology in China, its consequences were not all negative. In fact, it reflected a collective rationality of building strong organizational capabilities with the strong financial commitment within the institutional framework. The incentive issue is of course still present with respect to the collectively accumulated productive assets, especially with the gap of wealth widening between individual Hong Kong partners and the Chinese founding members as the enterprises grew. This was an issue that was increasingly voiced by the top Chinese managers. This challenging issue has been put onto the agenda of government policy-makers: how can they strike a balance between preserving the collective rationality of capability building while maintaining incentives among the members of the companies? However, like all the other institutional imperfections, it could create another opportunity for an institutional breakthrough. For that, the experiment of Legend with regard to its collectively accumulated assets is something worth following closely (see Section 3.6).

To summarize, through continuous technological innovation and organizational adaptation, the four enterprises were able to weather uncertainties inherent in market competition and to grow into viable large business concerns in only one decade. They have become indigenous Chinese high-tech success stories.

6.5. Concluding Remarks

Two major conclusions can be drawn from the case studies of the learning experiences of the Chinese computer enterprises. One is related to the role that indigenous innovation plays in the ability of late developers to catch up. The other has to do with the issue of organizational underpinnings of technology innovation in the context of economic transition.

An often-overlooked fact in dealing with the issue of the transition from centrally planned economies to market-oriented ones is that many former centrally planned economies are late developers.[7] This is particularly true for China, which could be considered a late late developer before the start of its current economic reform in 1978.[8] China wanted not only to make the transition to a market-oriented economy but also to develop economically.

According to Schumpeter, the essence of economic development is innovation, that is, commercial or industrial applications of new technology and new organization of production (Schumpeter 1934, 1950). In the context of late development, innovation involves learning and imitation, including borrowing and copying technologies from advanced nations.

Amsden, taking South Korea as an example, argues that the mode of late industrialization in the twentieth century is learning, which is different from the situation in the nineteenth century, when innovation was the mode, as in the cases of the United States and Germany. She defines learning as copying or borrowing technologies. As she notes: 'all late industrializers have in common industrialization on the basis of learning, . . . These countries industrialized by borrowing foreign technology rather than by generating new products and processes, the hallmark of earlier industrializing nations' (1989: preface). Her assertion is based on the observation that all the late developers have a so-called 'late development advantage', that is, they could borrow technologies directly from the advanced nations.

But the thesis 'industrialization through mere copying or borrowing' leaves no room for indigenous innovation. This makes it look incomplete against empirical evidence that some late developers of the twentieth century such as Japan and South Korea caught up in a wide range of industrial sectors. A classic case is the development of automatic loom technologies at Toyoda, the predecessor of Toyota, in the 1920s and 1930s (Mass and Miyajima 1992; Mass and Robertson 1996). Another case is the jump by Korean firms into the world's leading position in DRAM manufacturing technology (Kim *et al.* 1987; Langlois and Steinmueller 1998). In both cases there were not only technologies borrowed from abroad, but also genuine indigenous innovations in products and processes. These genuine indigenous innovation efforts assured not only the ability of these firms to catch up but also to leapfrog older technologies to arrive at the cutting edge of the latest technology. This indicates the importance of combining learning in the strict sense of imitation with indigenous innovation. The latter 'builds on knowledge acquired abroad to develop unique productive capabilities at home' (Lazonick and Mass 1995: 2)—a process I would call innovative learning. These Chinese cases demonstrate once again the importance of innovative learning.

It has to be pointed out that the opportunities provided by the so-called microelectronics revolution may also have helped to shape the unique pattern of

---

[7] For the notion of late development, see Gerschenkron 1952.
[8] For the concept of late late developer, see Dore 1987, 1990 [1973].

technology-learning in the Chinese computer enterprises. Soete (1985) pointed out that the new technology paradigm of microelectronics provided a unique window of opportunity for late developers to catch up, even to leapfrog. As he put it:

Electronics technology differs fundamentally from technical change in both the process industries (materials, chemicals) and the mechanical and electrical industries in terms of its closer reliance on scientific knowledge and technical/educational learning. In both the process and mechanical production, technical change is in the first instance based on productive 'learning by doing' and 'learning by using', such as setting up of a process plant, or designing of new machine tools. Again, to the extent that scientific and technical education is not as much the critical bottleneck in semi- or newly industrializing countries as productive learning and experience, electronics might well diffuse more rapidly in industrializing countries than expected.

The fact that the Chinese computer enterprises started with product redesign and product design, which rely more on scientific knowledge and higher education than shop-floor technical skills, supports this view. This reliance shows how relevant the science and technology capabilities accumulated during the central-planning era were.

It is worth pointing out that China was not the only former centrally planned economy that had developed science and technology capabilities before its transition. The fact is, however, that of these transitional economies only China seized the window of opportunity created by the microelectronics revolution and developed a viable indigenous computer electronics industry. That underscores the significance of the unique institutional and organizational arrangements embodied in these Chinese enterprises. This leads us to the second major conclusion.

As previously pointed out, the focus on allocative efficiency led mainstream economists to come up with policy recommendations centred around privatization and price liberalization.[9] My case studies have shown that the leading Chinese computer enterprises that contributed the most to the rise of a viable Chinese domestic computer industry were not at all privately owned in the sense of Western market economics. They were all, and still are, under some sort of state ownership (such as Legend, Founder, and Great Wall), or collective ownership (such as Stone). Why is that the case? How are such structures ever viable?

One important factor is that a large part of the science and technology resources developed in the state sector were intangible prior to their being developed into commercial products. It is very difficult to define property rights over these resources. Sudden and complete privatization, as prescribed by 'shock therapists', runs the risk of destroying the intangible productive resources before they had a chance to be developed fully into valuable products.

Furthermore, developing these technological resources into commercially viable products, that is, technology commercialization, or innovation, is a complicated organizational process. The market by itself would not do the trick. Certain kinds of shared ownership structures in the organization of technology commercialization seemed unavoidable.

---

[9] For the shock-therapist policy prescription for the transition from a centrally planned economy to a market economy, see Blanchard *et al.* 1991, 1993; and Sachs 1994.

What we have seen is a process of non-governmentalization, which was different from privatization. The crux of the former was financial independence and managerial autonomy. Financial independence assured managerial autonomy in business decision-making, while the shared-ownership arrangement provided both incentives and financial resources for management to make innovative decisions. It seems that it is more fruitful to look at the issue from the perspective of enterprise governance rather than the dichotomy of private versus public ownership.[10] In fact, private ownership over productive assets has long been weakened in the wake of the rise of large corporations in major capitalist market economies, wherein ownership and control have mostly been separated (Berle and Means 1991 [1932]). What is fundamental is having an institutional structure of corporate governance that is conducive to learning and innovation.

Joseph Stiglitz, a prominent mainstream economist, who has travelled to China several times, recognized this:

The success during the past twelve years of China, and particularly the southern provinces, suggests both that ownership (private property) is less important, and that there are other governance structures that may be effective, at least in the short run. Growth has been based on enterprises that are owned by villages, townships, other government enterprises, a variety of state agencies, and so on. There is shared governance. Managers are given wide latitude, and oversight is provided by various stakeholders, not only the nominal 'owners' (who themselves are mostly public organizations) but by industry ministries and local finance bureaux who depend on the success of these enterprises for their revenues (1994: 78).

The case studies in this book have shown the reasons why shared governance might be viable for technological development in the context of economic transition, by demonstrating the causal linkages between the structure of enterprise governance and the mode of technological learning and innovation. It is in this sense that the Chinese experience in the computer industry has its appeal in theory, as well as in policy.

---

[10] In substance, as we know from the case studies, the ownership structures of the new S&T enterprises were different from both traditional collectively owned and state-owned enterprises, even though they were, and still are, categorized as collectively owned or state-owned. It would only cause confusion to use the concept of ownership in this context. For a discussion of the relevance and irrelevance of ownership in Chinese economic reform from a macroeconomic perspective, see Lo 1994, 1995, 1997. For a discussion of the problems of corporate governance after privatization in Eastern European countries and republics of the former Soviet Union, see Frydman et al. 1993.

References

AMSDEN, A. (1989), *Asia's Next Giant: South Korea and Late Industrialization* (Oxford: Oxford University Press).

ARROW, K. J. (1962), 'Economic Welfare and Allocation of Resources for Invention', in National Bureau of Economic Research, *The Rate and Direction of Inventive Activity* (Princeton: Princeton University Press).

BERLE, A., and MEANS, G. C. (1991 [1932]), *The Modern Corporation and Private Property* (New Brunswick: Transaction).

BERLINER, J. S. (1976), *The Innovation Decision in Soviet Industry* (Cambridge, Mass.: MIT Press).

BEST, M. (1990), *The New Competition: Institutions of Industrial Restructuring* (Cambridge, Mass.: Harvard University Press).

BLANCHARD, O. J., KRUGMAN, P., DORNBUSCH, R., and SUMMERS, L. (1991), *Reform in Eastern Europe* (Cambridge, Mass.: MIT Press).

————————(1993), *Post-Communist Reform: Pain and Progress* (Cambridge, Mass.: MIT Press).

CAMPBELL, J. L., and LINDBERG, L. N. (1990), 'Property Rights and the Organization of Economic Activity by State', *American Sociological Review*, 55: 634–47.

——HOLLINGSWORTH, J. R., and LINDBERG, L. N. (1991), *Economic Governance of the American Economy* (New York: Cambridge University Press).

CCP DOCUMENT RESEARCH OFFICE (1982), *Since the Third Plenum* (Beijing: People's Press).

DAHLMAN, C. J., ROSS-LARSON, B., and WESTPHAL, L. E. (1985), 'Managing Technological Development: Lessons from the Newly Industrializing Countries' (Washington, DC: World Bank).

DEBREU, G. (1959), *Theory of Value* (New Haven: Yale University Press).

DEMSETZ, H. (1991), 'The Theory of the Firm Revisited', in O. E. Williamson and S. G. Winter (eds.), *The Nature of the Firm* (Oxford: Oxford University Press).

DIERICKX, I., and COOL, K. (1989), 'Asset Stock Accumulation and Sustainability of Competitive Advantage', *Management Science*, 35/12: 1504–14.

DORE, R. (1987), *Taking Japan Seriously: A Confucian Perspective on Leading Economic Issues* (Stanford: Stanford University Press).

——(1990 [1973]), *British Factory—Japanese Factory: The Origins of National Diversity in Industrial Relations* (Berkeley: University of California Press).

FAGERBERG, J. (1998), 'User–Producer Interaction, Learning and Comparative Advantage', in D. Archibugi and J. Michie (eds.), *Trade, Growth and Technical Change* (Cambridge: Cambridge University Press).

FAMA, E., and JENSEN, M. (1983), 'Separation of Ownership and Control', *Journal of Law and Economics*, 26: 301–26.

FEINSTEIN, C., and HOWE, C. (eds.) (1997), *Chinese Technology Transfer in 1990s* (Cheltenham: Elgar).

FORREST, J. E. (1991), 'Models of the Process of Technological Innovation', *Technology Analysis and Strategic Management*, 3/4: 439–53.

FRYDMAN, R., PHELPS, E., RAPACZYNSKI, A., and SCHLEIFER, A. (1993), 'Needed Mechanisms of Corporate Governance and Finance in East Europe', *Economics of Transition*, 1/2: 171–207.

FURST, A. (1988), 'High-Tech in China: The New Private Sector', *Electronic Business* (15 Aug.).

GERSCHENKRON, A. (1952), 'Economic Backwardness in Historical Perspective', in B. Hoselitz (ed.), *The Progress of Underdeveloped Countries* (Chicago: Chicago University Press).

GLASMEIER, A. (1988*a*), 'Factors Governing the Development of High-Tech Agglomerations: A Tale of Three Cities', *Regional Studies*, 22/4: 287–301.

——(1988*b*), 'The Japanese Technopolis Programme: High-Tech Development Strategies or Industrial Policy in Disguise?', *International Journal of Urban and Regional Research*, 12/2: 268–84.

GOLDMAN, M. I. (1983), *USSR in Crisis: The Failure of an Economic System* (New York: Norton).

HARPER, D. (1992), 'Small N's and Community Case Studies', in Ragin and Becker (eds.) (1992).

HOBDAY, M. (1995), *Innovation in East Asia: The Challenge to Japan* (Cheltenham: Elgar).

HOWE, C. (1997), 'Introduction', in Feinstein and Howe (eds.) (1997).

JENSEN, M. (1989), 'Eclipse of the Public Corporation', *Harvard Business Review*, 5: 61–74.

——and MECKLING, W. (1976), 'Theory of the Firm: Managerial Behavior, Agency Costs and Ownership Structure', *Journal of Financial Economics*, 3: 305–60.

JOHNSON, C. (1982), *MITI and the Japanese Miracle: The Growth of Industrial Policy, 1925–1975* (Stanford: Stanford University Press).

JOHNSTONE, B. (1989), 'Taiwan Holds its Lead, Local Makers Move into New Systems', *Far Eastern Economic Review* (Aug.), 50–1.

KENNEDY, SCOTT (1995), 'Reaching into All Corners: From Word Processors to Candy, the Stone Group is Making it All', *China Business Review*, Jan.–Feb.

KIM, L., LEE, J., and LEE, J. (1987), 'Korea's Entry into the Computer Industry and its Aquisition of Technological Capabilities', *Technovation*, 6: 277–93.

KLOCHKO, M. K. (1963), *Soviet Scientists in China* (London: Hillis & Carter).

KONRAD, G., and SZELENYI, I. (1979), *The Intellectuals on the Road to Class Power* (New York: Harcourt Brace Jovanovich).

LALL, S. (1982), *Developing Countries as Exporters of Technology* (London: Macmillan).

LANGLOIS, R., and STEINMUELLER, W. (1998), 'The Evolution of Competitive Advantage in the Worldwide Semiconductor Industry, 1947–1996', in D. Mowery and R. Nelson (eds.), *The Sources of Industrial Leadership* (New York: Cambridge University Press).

LAZONICK, W. (1990), *Competitive Advantage on the Shop Floor* (Cambridge, Mass.: Harvard University Press).

——(1991), *Business Organization and the Myth of the Market Economy* (New York: Cambridge University Press).

——(1992), 'Controlling Market for Corporate Control: The Historical Significance of Managerial Capitalism', *Industrial and Corporate Change*, 1.

——and MASS, W. (1995), 'Indigenous Innovation and Industrialization: Foundations of Japanese Development and Advantage', The MIT Japan Program (MITJP 95-03).

——and O'SULLIVAN, M. (1996), 'Organization, Finance and International Competition', *Industrial and Corporate Change*, 5/1.

LEE, C. K. (1995), 'Engendering the Worlds of Labor: Women Workers, Labor Markets, and Production Politics in the South China Economic Miracle', *American Sociological Review*, 60: 378–97.

LEONARD-BARTON, D. (1995), *Wellspring of Knowledge: Building and Sustaining the Sources of Innovation* (Cambridge, Mass.: Harvard Business School Press).

LEVINE, H. (1983), 'On the Nature and Location of Entrepreneurial Activity in Centrally Planned Economies: The Soviet Case', in J. Ronen (ed.), *Entrepreneurship* (Lexington, Ky.: D. C. Heath and Co.).

LEWIS, J. W. and XU, L. (1988), *China Builds the Bomb* (Stanford: Stanford University Press).

LO, D. (1994), 'Market and Institutional Regulation in Chinese Industrialization', Ph.D. thesis, School of Business and Economic Studies, University of Leeds.

——(1995), 'Relevance and Irrelevance of Ownership in Economic Reform', *Hong Kong Journal of Social Sciences* (special issue, July).

——(1997), *Market and Institutional Regulation in Chinese Industrialization, 1978–94* (London: St Martins Press).

LUNDVALL, B. (1988), 'Innovation as an Interactive Process: From User–Producer Interaction to the National System of Innovation', in G. Dosi, *et al.* (eds.), *Technical Change and Economic Theory* (London: Pinter).

MASS, W., and MIYAJIMA, H. (14 Dec. 1992), 'Technology Transfer and the First Japanese "Economic Miracle": the Roots of Toyota', Paper presented to the Business History Seminar, Harvard Business School.

——and ROBERTSON, A. (1996), 'From Textiles to Automobiles: Mechanical and Organizational Innovation in the Toyoda Enterprises, 1985–1933', *Business and Economic History*, 25/2: 1–38.

MURREL, P. (1991), 'Can Neoclassical Economics Underpin the Reform of Centrally Planned Economies?', *Journal of Economic Perspectives*, 5/1: 59–76.

NAUGHTON, B. (ed.) (1997), *The China Circle, Economics and Technology in the PRC, Taiwan, and Hong Kong* (Washington, DC: Brookings Institution Press).

NELSON, R., and WINTER, S. (1982), *An Evolutionary Theory of Economic Change* (Cambridge, Mass.: Harvard University Press).

NEW CENTURY GROUP (1997*a*), 'On the Way Up—Chinese PC Companies Gaining Market Share', Market report.

——(1997*b*), 'Manufacturing PCs in China: Profits or Pitfall? For Whom?', Market report.

——(1997*c*), 'China Great Wall Computer Group', Market report.

NOMURA SECURITY (1997), 'China's Computer Industry: The World's Fastest Growing Market for Personal Computers', Industrial report.

O'SULLIVAN, M. (1996), 'Innovation, Industrial Development and Corporate Governance', Ph.D. thesis, Economics Department, Harvard University.

POLYA, G. (1968), *Mathematics and Plausible Reasoning*, vol. ii: *Pattern of Plausible Inference* (Princeton: Princeton University Press).

RAGIN, C. R., and BECKER, H. S. (eds.) (1992), *What is a Case? Exploring the Foundations of Social Inquiry* (Cambridge: Cambridge University Press).

REDDING, S. G., and TAM, S. (1993), 'The Impact of Colonialism on the Formation of an Entrepreneurial Society in Hong Kong', in S. Birley and I. C. McMillan (eds.), *Entrepreneurship Research: Global Perspectives* (Amsterdam: North-Holland).

ROSENBERG, N. (1994), *Exploring the Black Box: Technology, Economics, and History* (Cambridge: Cambridge University Press).

ROSENBLOOM, R. S. and SPENCER, W. J. (eds.) (1996), *Engines of Innovation: US Industrial Research at the End of an Era* (Boston: Harvard Business School Press).

SACHS, J. (1994), *Poland's Jump to the Market Economy* (Cambridge, Mass.: MIT Press).

SAICH, T. (1989*a*), 'Reform of China's Science and Technology Organizational System', in Simon and Goldman (1989).

——(1989*b*), *China's Science Policy in the 1980s* (Manchester: Manchester University Press).

SAXENIAN, A. (1994), *Regional Advantage: Culture and Competition in Silicon Valley and Route 128* (Cambridge, Mass.: Harvard University Press).

SCHUMPETER, J. (1934), *The Theory of Economic Development* (Cambridge, Mass.: Harvard University Press).

——(1950), *Capitalism, Socialism, and Democracy* (New York: Harper).

SIMON, D. F. (1996), 'From Cold to Hot—China's Struggle to Protect and Develop a World Class Electronics Industry', *China Business Review* (Nov.–Dec.), 8–16.

——and GOLDMAN, M. (1989), *Science and Technology in Post-Mao China* (Cambridge, Mass.: Harvard University Press).

——and REHN, D. (1988), *Technological Innovation in China: The Case of Shanghai's Electronics Industry* (Cambridge: Ballinger).

SOETE, L. (1985), 'International Diffusion of Technology, Industrial Development and Technological Leapfrogging', *World Development*, 13: 409–22.

STEINFELD, E. S. (1996), 'Property Rights and Performance in the Chinese State-Owned Enterprise', Ph.D. thesis, Department of Government, Harvard University.

——(1998), *Forging Reform in China: The Fate of State-Owned Industry* (Cambridge: Cambridge University Press).

STIGLITZ, J. (1994), *Whither Socialism?* (Cambridge, Mass.: MIT Press).

SUTTMEIER, R. P. (1988), 'Laying Corporate Foundations for China's High-Tech Future', *The China Business Review* (July–Aug.), 22–6.

VOGEL, E. (1979), *Japan as Number One: Lessons for America* (New York: Harper & Row).

——(1989), *One Step Ahead in China: Guangdong Under Economic Reform* (Cambridge, Mass.: Harvard University Press).

——(1991), *The Four Little Dragons: The Spread of Industrialization in East Asia* (Cambridge, Mass.: Harvard University Press).

WADE, R. (1990), *Governing the Market* (Princeton: Princeton University Press).

WESTPHAL, L. E., KIM, L., and DAHLMAN, C. J. (1985), 'Reflections on the Republic of Korea's Acquisition of Technological Capability', in N. Rosenberg and C. Frischtak (eds.), *International Transfer of Technology: Concepts, Measures, and Comparisons* (New York: Praeger).

WOERKOM-CHONG, W. L. (1986), 'The "New Technological Revolution", China's Modernization and World Economy: Some Chinese Discussion Themes', *China Information*, 1/2: 33–44.

WORLD BANK (1993), *The East Asia Miracle* (Oxford: Oxford University Press).

WORTZEL, L. H., and WORTZEL, H. V. (1981), 'Export Marketing Strategies for NIC and LDC-based Firms', *Columbia Journal of World Business* (Spring), 51–60.

XU, Y., and ZHAN, D. (1990), *Changcheng de jueqi (The Rise of the Great Wall Computer Co.)* (Beijing: Guoji Wehua Chuban Gongshi).

YU, W. (1988), *Xiwang de Huohua (Flame of Hope)* (Beijing: People's University Press).

Index